The Political Economy of East Asia

Post-Crisis Debates

Iyanatul Islam and Anis Chowdhury

OXFORD

UNIVERSITY PRESS

OXFORD

UNIVERSITY PRESS

253 Normanby Road, South Melbourne, Victoria, Australia

Oxford University Press is a department of the University of Oxford. It furthers the University's objective of excellence in research, scholarship, and education by publishing worldwide in

Oxford New York

Athens Auckland Bangkok Bogotá Buenos Aires Calcutta Cape Town Chennai
Dar es Salaam Delhi Florence Hong Kong Istanbul Karachi Kuala Lumpur Madrid
Melbourne Mexico City Mumbai Nairobi Paris Port Moresby São Paulo Shanghai
Singapore Taipei Tokyo Toronto Warsaw

with associated companies in Berlin Ibadan

OXFORD is a trade mark of Oxford University Press
in the UK and in certain other countries

National Library of Australia
Cataloguing-in-Publication data:

Chowdhury, Anis,1954–.
   The political economy of East Asia: post-crisis debates.
   Bibliography.
   Includes index.
   ISBN 0 19 554090 5.

   1. East Asia — Economic conditions — 20th century. 2. East
Asia — Politics and government — 20th century. 3. East
Aisa — Economic policy. 4. East Asia — Politics and
government — 21st century. I. Islam, Iyanatul, 1953–.
   II. Title
   330.95

Edited by Adrienne de Kretser
Indexed by Russell Brooks
Cover designed by David Constable
Typeset by McMillan Design Pty Ltd, Melbourne
Printed through Bookpac Production Services, Singapore

Contents

Tables

Figures

Boxes

Abbreviations

ADB	Asian Development Bank
AMC	Asset Management Corporation
ASEAN	Association of Southeast Asian Nations
ASEAN-4	Indonesia, Malaysia, Thailand, and Philippines
CCP	Chinese Communist Party
EEFSU	Eastern Europe and Former Soviet Union
EOI	export-oriented industrialisation
EPF	employee provident fund
FDI	foreign direct investment
FRA	Financial Restructuring Agency (Thailand)
GDP	gross domestic product
GNP	gross national product
HCI	heavy and chemical industries
HPAEs	high-performing Asian economies
ICOR	incremental capital-output ratio
ILO	International Labour Organization
IMF	International Monetary Fund
ISI	import-substituting industrialisation
KCTU	Korean Confederation of Trade Unions
KEF	Korean Employers Federation
MMO	money market operations
NAFTA	North American Free Trade Area
NBFI	non-bank financial institution
NEP	New Economic Policy (Malaysia)
NIEs	newly industrialised economies
NTB	non-trade barrier
OECD	Organization for Economic Cooperation and Development
PLMO	Property Loan Management Organisation (Thailand)
PPP	purchasing power parity
PRC	People's Republic of China
QIO	quasi-internal organisation
SAL	structured adjustment lending
SOEs	state-owned enterprises
WTO	World Trade Organization

Preface

This book aims to analyse and synthesise critical debates in East Asian political economy. It distinguishes between the pre-crisis literature that was preoccupied with extolling the virtues of the 'East Asian miracle' and the more circumspect, angst-ridden genre that germinated after financial crisis engulfed the region in mid 1997. In making such a distinction, the study argues that the evolution of East Asian political economy is at a critical juncture. The continued relevance of political economy for understanding the opportunities and challenges facing the region depends on the ability of practitioners to grapple with some fundamental issues. How sustainable is the recovery that is underway in the region? Does the reform agenda for preparing East Asia for the twenty-first century entail fundamental changes in national governance, or should the focus primarily be on the realm of global governance?

The book eschews a detailed country-by-country account in favour of a thematic approach, based on the premise that, both as a pedagogical device and as an analytical tool, the developments in East Asia are best interpreted from the perspective of specific themes. These include the relationship between democratic governance and innovation-driven development; the challenge of enacting prudential regulations for harnessing the potential benefits of a competitive financial system; the debate about the relationship between labour rights and economic performance; the politics of globalisation; the perennial debate on the relationship between growth and equity; and the possibility of forging a consensus among stakeholders in the development community on a new social and institutional model for East Asia.

The book is written as a political economy tract from the perspective of economists. We have made a determined attempt to cross the disciplinary divide and have incorporated some well-known contributions from political scientists and regional specialists, but this may not be enough to respond to the expectation of non-economists. The limits of the study are thus acknowledged. Nevertheless, we remain firmly committed to the belief that the productive interface between economics and politics can form the basis for a new research paradigm within which the evolution of the East Asian region can be fruitfully studied.

As an intellectual enterprise, any book project builds on the generosity and cooperation of many people. This study had a rather long gestation period and its completion would not have been possible without the exemplary patience and cooperation of Jill Henry, the publisher. We also benefited from the insightful comments of a number of referees who reviewed the project when it was merely a proposal, and later from two anonymous readers who patiently read the first draft and suggested a number of substantive improvements. Of course, the standard caveat applies: we are solely responsible for any errors and omissions. We would also like to acknowledge the generous support of our institutions, namely, the Department of Economics and Finance at the University of Western Sydney (Anis Chowdhury) and the School of International Business at Griffith University (Iyanatul Islam). The latter was attached to the Jakarta-based UN Support Facility for Indonesian Recovery when the manuscript was completed, and the project received active encouragement and support from Satish Mishra, Chief Economist of the Facility. We must add that despite the pressures that the writing of this book placed on our families, they were generous with affection and patience. This book is dedicated to them.

Chapter 1

The Evolution of East Asian Political Economy: An Analytical History

INTRODUCTION

The study of East Asia is at a critical juncture. Only recently, the ebullient voices of cheerleaders proclaiming the 'East Asian miracle' resonated across the world. A small group of economies stretching across Southeast and Northeast Asia—Hong Kong, Singapore, South Korea, Taiwan, Indonesia, Malaysia, and Thailand—have often been cited as rare exemplars of rapid and shared growth. The People's Republic of China (PRC) was added to this elite list of economies as a fine example of the transition to a market economy.

However, events since mid 1997 have taken the shine off the miracle and stories of East Asian success have been overshadowed by a profound sense of anxiety over the future of the region. The currency crisis that started in mid July 1997 in Thailand soon engulfed most of the region. It pushed the successful economies of Indonesia, South Korea, and Thailand under the tutelage of the IMF and led them into a full-blown recession. Even mighty Japan, often regarded as the model that the East Asian economies emulated, appears to be faced with an uncertain future of rather slow growth. The consensus is that there will be a sluggish recovery in the region over several years. Admittedly, some of the crisis-affected economies have rebounded in impressive fashion, but whether the rapid growth era of the past can be replicated and sustained remains an open question. Some have muttered about the 'decline of the Asian century' (Lingle 1998). Only Taiwan and the PRC seem relatively immune from such grim developments, at least for now.

Any study of East Asia must take account of this striking transformation from boom to gloom. Why were these economies heralded so widely as success stories? Why are they now so widely criticised? To what extent is such criticism justified? Is the future of the region really bleak? In trying to come to terms with these disturbing questions, one is confronted with the task of analysing the history of the role of ideas and ideology in the evolution of the East Asian political economy. This introductory chapter is intended to accomplish that difficult but intellectually exciting task.

Several themes guide this chapter. It begins with the 1950s and 1960s—an era that can be described (somewhat disparagingly) as the golden age of the 'dirigiste' doctrine. That doctrine regarded the state as the engine of growth within the context of inward-oriented industrialisation. It found a natural ally in 'dependency' theory, which regarded the unfettered operation of a free world economy as an agent of oppression that perpetuated the dependence of poor nations at the periphery on rich nations at the core.

Both the dirigiste doctrine and its more radical variant came under the intellectual onslaught of neo-classical economics. Using the tools of conventional economics, practitioners were able to argue that the analytical foundations of the dirigiste doctrine—or the profound pessimism of dependency theory—were suspect, and that their basic premise was not supported by the available evidence. The ascendancy of four East Asian newly industrialised economies (NIEs)—Hong Kong, Singapore, South Korea, and Taiwan—played a central role in the neo-classical resurgence. The key argument was that East Asia prospered because of good policies that represented the virtuous combination of free trade and free markets (Little 1979, 1981, 1982).

A distinctive group of political scientists and regional specialists also began to question the tenets of dependency theory when documenting the rise of the 'four dragons'. Thus, one of the best-known studies of East Asian success characterised it as a case of 'pathways from the periphery' (Haggard 1990). However, criticising dependency theory did not mean embracing neo-classical resurgence and rejecting the notion that the state was an engine of growth. One could argue that the political economy literature on East Asian ascendancy—as shaped by political scientists and regional specialists—was essentially a re-invention of dirigisme under the guise of the 'developmental state' hypothesis. The essence of that argument was that, under certain circumstances, it was possible for a poor nation at the periphery—as were Taiwan and Korea in the 1950s and 1960s—to overcome the burden of dependence on rich nations at the core. The literature documented extensive state intervention in East Asian economies (with the notable exception of Hong Kong) and explained why it proved so effective. The attempt simultaneously became a critique of the neo-classical interpretation of East Asian success.

It is a testimony to the success of the developmental state hypothesis that practitioners sympathetic to the neo-classical tradition found it necessary to construct a 'neo-classical synthesis' in explaining East Asian success. Such a synthesis drew on the notion that the state could be an engine of growth, and combined it with the market-oriented ethos of conventional economics. A much-cited example is World Bank (1993a). One could argue that a sequel to the emerging paradigm of the neo-classical synthesis was provided by the Asian Development Bank (ADB) (1997).

Events since mid 1997 have led to the demise of the developmental state hypothesis and disrupted the neo-classical synthesis, as both focused on explaining economic success. The current literature aims to explain the East Asian crisis and its implications. The stage is thus set for the emergence of the new political economy of East Asia.

BOX 1.1: DIRIGISME, THE NEO-CLASSICAL RESURGENCE, AND EAST ASIA

In the 1950s and 1960s, many countries in the developing world embraced a development strategy whose key components formed the substance of the so-called dirigiste doctrine. This is sometimes construed as a disparaging label, but it is used here as an abbreviated way to define the notion of state-led development. Such a strategy entails various inter-related elements, including:

- import-substituting industrialisation (ISI) sustained by the use of tariff and non-tariff barriers (NTBs) that protect domestic industries from international competition

- extensive state intervention in financial and labour markets, typically entailing nationalisation of banks, selective credit allocation, political patronage of trade unions, minimum wage legislation and strict hiring and firing rules

- significant reliance on state-owned enterprises (SOEs), particularly in key areas such as banking, transport, telecommunications and power generation

- a predilection for detailed planning and regulation.

Why were the first-generation politicians and practitioners attracted to state-led development that entailed detailed planning and regulation and a focus on domestic markets? We must take into account the power of economic ideas and how such ideas are assimilated in the political process. As Krueger (1993: 353), acknowledges: 'There is ample reason to believe that, in many developing countries, the initial choice of an import-substitution development strategy was made by well-intentioned individuals behaving as benevolent social guardians'.

The intellectual underpinnings of dirigisme can be traced to the work of a number of first-generation development economists, such as Rosentein-Rodan, Nurkse, Singer, Prebisch and Myrdal (see Arndt 1987: ch. 3). Bhagwati (1984) has reinterpreted this strand of scholarship as encompassing the twin notions of export pessimism and market failure. The export prospects of the primary products of developing economies were considered limited, and international trade was seen as a mechanism of international inequality enriching the rich nations and impoverishing the poor—a view that developed into dependency theory (Furtado 1973; Sunkel 1969). The typical developing economy was characterised by endemic market failure, expressed specifically as the failure of private producers to internalise external economies (Rosentein-Rodan 1943).

Mainstream economics was belittled as a 'special case' reared in the cultural, social, and political context of Western market economies (Seers 1962). These concerns evolved to a stage where they entailed a focus on state-led 'big-push' industrialisation that relied primarily on domestic markets.

In this intellectual milieu, first-generation policy-makers in the developing world put dirigisme into practice. The notion of autarkic industrial development was particularly influential in India through the role of Mahalonobis, 'physicist turned planner' (Arndt 1987: 76). India was one of the first—if not the first—country in the developing world to produce a detailed development plan (of 671 pages), in 1952 (Turner & Hulme 1997: 136).

NEO-CLASSICAL CRITIQUE OF DIRIGISME: FIRST-GENERATION LITERATURE

It is often suggested that the tide against dirigisme turned with Little, Scitovsky and Scott's (1970) comprehensive evaluation of ISI in seven developing economies. It is possible, however, to detect dissenting voices well before the publication of that report (Rodrik 1992). For example, Raul Prebisch, regarded as one of the prime intellectual architects of ISI, apparently raised concerns about the viability of ISI in his later writings (Arndt 1987: 78–81). Despite such caveats, it would be fair to say that the Little, Scitovsky and Scott report provided the primary intellectual ammunition against ISI.

Another important contribution to the critique of ISI was an ADB-sponsored study of industrialisation in Southeast Asia (ADB 1971; Myint 1972). Drawing attention to the high costs of pursuing ISI in Southeast Asia, it warned that 'industrial growth is in danger of slowing down … because the relatively easy import-substituting possibilities have been exhausted' and counselled the adoption of an 'outward-looking industrialisation strategy' (ADB 1971: 232).

The emerging critique of ISI at the beginning of the 1970s was given a major boost by subsequent contributions (see, for example, Bhagwati 1978). We must also note the seminal contributions by McKinnon (1973) and Shaw (1973) on the deleterious effects of interventions in financial markets, that broadened the attack on dirigisme. Those studies argued that policy measures such as selective credit allocation and general controls on interest rates led to financial repression, which had real sector effects: both the volume and efficiency of saving and investment were adversely affected. The result was a drag on growth.

The issue of interventions in labour markets, and the way they formed part of a comprehensive critique of dirigisme, appeared to receive less attention in the early 1970s. In the 1980s, Fields (1984) drew attention to the thesis that variations in labour market interventions could partly explain variations in growth performance in the seven economies studied. More specifically, competitive or flexible labour markets were seen as a central element in facilitating rapid economic growth.

The neo-classical critique of the dirigiste doctrine was reinforced by the belated discovery of hypergrowth in a handful of countries in East Asia—Hong Kong, Singapore, Korea, and Taiwan (Chen 1979). The discovery was belated because, as Hicks (1989: 39) notes, the four East Asian economies were growing at phenomenal rates for two decades before they came to the attention of mainstream economists. More importantly, as Hicks (1989: 36–7) emphasises, the pioneers of development economics, such as Rosenstein-Rodan, Chenery and others, did not expect them to perform as well as they did. The success stories of the developing world were expected to be in South Asia and Latin America.

Little (1979, 1981, 1982) was one of the first to provide an intellectual framework for the discovery. It transpired that these economies—the so-called Gang of Four—had a brief engagement with ISI, then moved towards export-oriented industrialisation (EOI) through a series of policy reforms initiated in the early 1960s. The conventional wisdom is that the industrial revolution in parts of East Asia can be linked to this decisive policy shift, which entailed a conspicuous deviation from prevailing orthodoxy.

Perhaps the following observations by Little (1982: 141) are the most cogent way to illustrate the conventional neo-classical interpretation of East Asian success:

> Starting in the years around 1960, these countries (i.e. Korea, Taiwan and Singapore) made policy changes that by the middle 1960s combined selective protection for certain import competing sectors with a virtual free trade regime for exporters—by which we mean that exporters could obtain inputs ... at world market prices, while the effective exchange rate for exporters was close to that which would have ruled under free trade. Overall effective protection for industry was zero for Korea and, of course, Hong Kong, and low for Taiwan and Singapore. The consequential growth of exports was phenomenal, far exceeding what anyone could have predicted or did predict.

Elsewhere Little (1981: 45) emphasises the lessons of rapid growth in East Asia. He concludes that:

> The major lesson is that labour-intensive export-oriented policies, which amounted to almost free trade conditions for exporters, were the prime cause of an extremely rapid and labour-intensive industrialisation which revolutionised in a decade the lives of more than fifty million people, including the poorest among them ... nothing else can account for it.

In the 'nothing else' category, Little (1981: 45) lumps together capital markets, tax systems, planning, foreign aid, foreign investment (with the exception of Singapore), and luck. Everything could be attributed to 'good policies and the people'.

A flurry of publications in the early to mid 1980s vindicated Little's account of East Asian success. They include Balassa (1981), Krueger (1983), Galenson (1985), and Corbo, Krueger and Ossa (1985). Their standard refrain is the superiority of EOI over ISI and the fact that the East Asian NIEs are rare exemplars of the successful implementation of EOI.

EMERGENCE OF THE WASHINGTON CONSENSUS

The emerging orthodoxy of the neo-classical interpretation of East Asia received a boost from the burgeoning influence of what Williamson (1990, 1994) has called the 'Washington consensus'. This described the shared ideas of the US Treasury and the Washington-based, Bretton Woods institutions of the IMF and World Bank on appropriate universal economic policies. Thus free markets, free trade, free capital mobility, and limited government represented the virtues pertinent to both poor and rich nations in delivering economic prosperity: they were relevant in the past, are applicable today and will remain valid in the future. Of course, the ascendancy of conservative governments in the USA (the presidency of Ronald Reagan) and Europe (the Tory government led by Margaret Thatcher in the United Kingdom) played an important role in establishing the Washington consensus.

We must remember that the calm of the world economy in the 1960s was broken by the volatility of the 1970s and 1980s. There were sharp movements in oil prices (1973, 1979, 1986) and in other key commodity prices, two deep recessions in the OECD countries (1975, 1982), and, of course, the debt crises that engulfed the developing economies in 1982–83. Such developments meant that macroeconomic management of external shocks became the preoccupation, helping to undermine the long-term structural issues inherent in the dirigiste doctrine.

In this context the Washington consensus began, although neither the IMF nor the World Bank played a decisive role in moulding the anti-ISI tracts of the early 1970s. The National Bureau of Economic Research sponsored the Little, Scitovsky and Scott (1970) study, and the ADB (1971) funded the seminal study on Southeast Asian industrialisation. The World Bank stepped into the scene at a later stage and sponsored a series of studies led by Krueger (1983) on the relationship between trade policy and economic growth. A distillation of the ideas and findings in those studies was reflected in the 1987 World Development Report (World Bank 1987).

More importantly, the World Bank put neo-classical orthodoxy into action through its 'structural adjustment lending' (SAL) programs, a variation of the long-standing IMF principle of 'conditionality'. Access to IMF financial assistance for countries suffering from macroeconomic imbalances was contingent on fulfilling certain policy measures.

SAL applied this idea to medium-term structural issues, based on the notion of dismantling the dirigiste doctrine. Access to World Bank financial assistance for developing member countries depended on them undertaking trade policy and related reforms. Hence, SAL formalised the division of labour between the IMF and the World Bank (the former with its mandate of short-term macroeconomic stabilisation issues, the latter with its charter of long- to medium-term structural issues). It represented the Washington consensus in action.

It is important to emphasise that the notion of 'best practice' economic management at the core of the Washington consensus often sought inspiration from East Asian success (see, for example, World Bank 1987). The East Asian NIEs were usually considered benchmarks for judging the performance of developing economies in other parts of the world, such as the debt-ridden economies of Latin America.

It seemed that the neo-classical resurgence of the 1970s finally triumphed, after decades of questioning the wisdom of the dirigiste doctrine. The state was no longer the engine of growth because it led economies into the trap of unsustainable, inward-oriented industrialisation. 'Good policies' embodied the creation of free trade conditions that paved the way for labour-intensive, export-oriented industrialisation and produced the virtuous outcome of rapid and equitable growth. The East Asian NIEs exemplified such rapid and equitable growth because they followed the prescriptions of good policies. The Washington consensus of the 1980s, developed in an era of US political conservatism and unprecedented volatility in the world economy, simply reinforced the conventional wisdom. Finally, the collapse of the Soviet Union and the East European bloc by the end of the 1980s signified the formal termination of ideological hostility to market economies.

BOX 1.2: EVOLUTION OF POLITICAL SYSTEMS AND THE NATURE OF STATE IN EAST AND SOUTHEAST ASIA

The East and Southeast Asian countries gained independence after World War II (the Philippines in 1946, South Korea in 1948, Indonesia in 1949, Malaysia in 1957, and Singapore in 1963) and immediately embarked upon the stupendous task of constitution-making. A variety of systems emerged, ranging from authoritarian regimes to Western liberal democracies. The experiment with Western-style liberal democracy did not last long. By the 1950s the military had become a decisive force in the political systems of South Korea, Thailand, Burma, and Indonesia. Moreover, political institutions such as an effective parliament, free and fair periodic elections, and an independent judiciary did not develop, and thus could not determine and control the authority of the executive. In establishing 'guided democracy', President Sukarno blamed the instability of the period of parliamentary democracy in Indonesia (1950–57) on the importation of incompatible Western liberal ideas. Indonesia virtually became a one-party military regime during the thirty-year reign of Soeharto, until he was toppled by a mass uprising in 1998. The Philippines too fell under military rule of President Marcos who was removed by the people's power revolution of 1986. Thailand, South Korea, and Taiwan experienced authoritarian regimes connected to the military elite, prior to their move towards democratisation in the late 1980s and early 1990s. Although both Malaysia and Singapore have a nominally Westminster-style democracy, they are ruled by one dominant party. The system rather accommodates essential factors of both authoritarianism and democracy, and sometimes is classified as semi-democratic.

The states in East and Southeast Asia that are generally characterised as strong enjoy relative autonomy from pressure groups. How did this autonomy develop? It is possible to trace the existence of such states in France and Germany under the rule of Napoleon and Bismarck, where the bourgeois class was weak and set against other classes, resulting in the emergence of an authoritarian state with a high degree of autonomy. According to Alavi (1972), in most post-colonial societies no single dominant class exists. Instead there are three contending classes—the domestic bourgeoisie, the metropolitan (old colonial powers) bourgeoisie, and the landed elite. Thus there is a need for a broker or a mediator to form a leadership which works for the benefit of the three classes. The military–bureaucratic elite often performs this role. In return, the three contending classes surrender their political participation and allow the military–bureaucratic oligarchy to become independent of them. They let the authoritarian rule continue as long as the regime maintains economic liberalism from which all three parties are likely to benefit. One may also point to the geopolitics of the Vietnam War and communist insurgencies which played a role in the emergence of strong autonomous states in East and Southeast Asia (see Kang 1995).

EMERGENCE OF THE DEVELOPMENTAL STATE IN EAST ASIA: DIRIGISME REINVENTED

Neither the anti-ISI neo-classical resurgence of the 1970s nor the Washington consensus of the 1980s went unchallenged. Killick (1984) was one of the first to offer a robust critique of IMF conditionality. He followed it with a more general critique of neo-classical orthodoxy and felt that it was a 'reaction too far' (Killick 1989). Mosley, Harrigan and Toye (1991) reinforced the voices of dissent against the Washington consensus by offering an unflattering evaluation of the effectiveness of the World Bank's SAL programs in developing countries. They concluded that using financial leverage to induce policy reforms rarely worked because sovereign nations could find ingenious ways of undermining compliance with the conditions in a typical SAL package.

Developmental state in East Asia: Perspectives of regional specialists and political scientists

Perhaps the strongest attacks on neo-classical orthodoxy in development policy came from a group of political scientists and regional specialists who questioned the empirical validity of the free trade story of East Asian success. Johnson (1982, 1985, 1987) is normally credited with being the pioneer of the anti-neo-classical tracts on East Asia, but Hofheinz and Calder (1982) cover similar terrain. Critiques of the neo-classical orthodoxy on East Asia culminated in the work of Amsden (1989), Wade (1988, 1990), and Haggard (1988, 1990).

What were the contributions of this literature and how does it suggest a new phase in the evolution of East Asian political economy? Two features stand out. First, Johnson and other scholars draw attention to the association between rapid economic growth and pervasive state intervention in Korea, Taiwan, and Singapore. Only Hong Kong appears to approximate the neo-classical ideal. Little and others do not ignore the role of state intervention (referring to 'selective import protection'), but it is insufficiently emphasised. Second, the complex interaction between culture, politics, and history receives scant attention from neo-classical writers. Critics focus on these issues, laying the foundation of the 'developmental state' hypothesis (Onis 1991).[1]

The observation of the close relationship between rapid economic growth and pervasive state intervention in Korea and Taiwan strikes Johnson (1985) as the replication of a relationship in his notable study of Japanese economic development (Johnson 1982), promtping him to question the theory of 'free enterprise economists' who always maintain that 'governmental intervention in the economy is inevitably inefficient and distorting' (Johnson 1985: 64). More generally, Johnson makes the point that neo-classical economists either ignored or down-played the role of the state in East Asian economic development because it represented an awkward fact that could not be easily explained.

If rapid growth in East Asia is indeed associated with pervasive government interventions, it raises the intriguing possibility that the state could, under certain circumstances, be an engine of growth. When such a possibility exists, we encounter the case of the developmental state. The critics of the neo-classical story of East Asian success thus engaged in an imaginative reinvention of dirigisme that, as will be discussed later, was embraced by several economists.

The notion of the state as an engine of growth in developing economies entailed an intellectual battle against Little and others, and against the basic tenet of dependency theory. In a classic dependency framework that relies on a core–periphery distinction, the developed core extracts economic surplus from the underdeveloped periphery through channels such as trade, aid, and foreign investment. The manner in which the surplus extraction occurs can be complex (Amin 1974, 1976). The point is that the state in peripheral nations cannot be an agent of development simply because it is a 'subservient comprador (member) of an international coalition of owning classes' (Arndt 1987, paraphrasing Frank 1967).

Dependency theory has undergone a number of revisions, most notably in the form of 'new wave' dependency theory drawing on the Latin American experience. Examples include Cardoso and Falleto (1979), Evans (1979), Gereffie (1982), Bennet and Sharpe (1983), and Newfarmer (1985). The revisions allow for greater autonomy of domestic political actors from the domination of international capital, but it would be fair to say that the second-generation models still support the 'basic theoretical proposition of dependency theory—stunted or incomplete development in the Third World' (Rodan, Hewison & Robison 1998: 5).

Confronted with evidence of sustained state-led growth in East Asia, despite its dependence on international markets, many commentators felt that it was a 'challenge to dependency theory' (Amsden 1979)—even the reformulated versions. As Hawes and Liu (1993: 630) note: 'Dependency analysis, even in their ... revised formulation ... had not predicted and could not explain this record of economic growth and industrial diversification'. Rodan, Hewison and Robison come to the same conclusion: 'the emergence of countries like South Korea, Taiwan, Hong Kong and Singapore as important industrial exporters in the 1970s ... delivered a mortal blow to the claims of dependency theorists' (1998: 5). The attempts of political scientists and regional specialists to explain the emergence of the East Asian NIEs thus stemmed from the need to cope with the manifest inadequacies of dependency theory, but the endeavour also led to a robust critique of neo-classical orthodoxy.

How does the developmental state model explain economic growth in East Asia? It rightly draws attention to the fact that, while the neo-classical story of East Asian success focuses on outcomes (the successful adoption of EOI), it does not explain the process through which this policy implementation takes place. After all, if the costs of dirigisme are so well-documented and well-known, why has it not been systematically dismantled in developing economies? We need an explicit political economy theory of policy reform.

Haggard (1988: 262–5), focusing on South Korea and Taiwan, develops three sets of arguments about the political economy of export-led growth. First, he draws attention to political systems that enabled the policy-making process to be 'relatively insulated from direct political pressures and compromises'. This was possible because of an authoritarian political system in which legislatures were historically weak, and the channels of political access and representation were tightly controlled. It also meant that the political elites, driven by the need to legitimise their durability through enhanced economic performance, allowed technocrats to have considerable discretion in economic policy-making. The delegation of responsibility was certainly helped by the fact that South Korea and Taiwan could rely on meritocratic bureaucracies for policy implementation.

Second, key social groups involving the rural sector, labour, and protection-seeking domestic business that are traditionally opposed to market-oriented reforms were organisationally weak or co-opted into a corporatist framework in which the government exercised significant authority. The weakness of the rural sector stemmed from historical circumstances. Land reform under the auspices of the USA in South Korea and Taiwan attenuated the development of an anti-industrial rural elite. At the same time, it secured a support base for the regimes and pre-empted the possibility of the rural-based revolutionary movements seen in other parts of East Asia.

Labour movements were also historically weak in South Korea, Singapore, and Taiwan. A combination of co-option and repression of the union movement reinforced the weakness. Thus, the East Asian NIEs embarked on a phase of export-led development under a set of conditions in which the organised political Left that typically drew on labour and peasant movements was virtually non-existent. As left-wing political parties share a consistent ideological animosity towards the private sector, foreign investment, and market-oriented policies in general, the absence or insignificance of such politics facilitated the adoption of export-oriented industrialisation in East Asia.

East Asian governments also managed to exercise political control over domestic business. Despite their business-friendly demeanour, governments in South Korea, Taiwan, and Singapore ensured that the political influence of the business community was limited. This was done through a range of discretionary instruments (taxes, subsidies, and credit allocation), financing of peak business associations, and general control of channels of access to decision-making.

The third element in Haggard's institutional account of East Asian success pertains to international political conditions in which East Asian industrialisation evolved. The defeat of Japan in World War II left the USA as the dominant power in the region. Both South Korea and Taiwan felt the geopolitical benefit of abutting communist Asia, thus attracting expanded political and economic commitments from the USA. The massive inflow of US aid and the ideological influences of US aid advisers in the 1950s and early 1960s facilitated outward-oriented industrialisation in the East Asian NIEs (see Jacoby 1966).

In later writings, Haggard (1994: 269–72) largely retains the essence of his institutional account of East Asian success, but highlights the important role of the government's independence from the business sector. This is epitomised in his summary of the developmental state hypothesis (as he prefers to call it, the institutionalist or statist approach):

> Growth hinges on effective government policy, usually taken to include some mix of stable macroeconomic policies and a growth-promoting industrial policy. Such effectiveness is dependent on bureaucratic capacity, on the existence and control of relevant policy instruments and a certain degree of institutional insulation from social groups, including the private sector. Though governments in the [NIEs] have been broadly pro-business, political

institutions have minimised capture by narrow private interests. Where they have existed, industry associations have not so much represented business interests to the government as communicated government concerns to the private sector (Haggard 1994: 273).

Other prominent advocates of the developmental state hypothesis, such as Wade (1988, 1990), largely share the Haggard theory. Thus, Wade (1988: 157–61) draws attention to the centralised decision-making structure of East Asian governments (by which he means South Korea and Taiwan). It is staffed by the 'best managerial talent available in the system' and 'insulated from all but the strongest pressure groups'. He highlights the 'feebleness of the legislature' and the absence of a 'powerful, or left-wing labour movement'.

Wade highlights how the 'insulation' from pressure groups is institutionalised in corporatist arrangements in East Asia: 'the state creates … a small number of interest groups, giving them a monopoly of representation of occupational interests in return for which it claims the right to monitor them in order to discourage the expression of narrow, conflictual demands' (1990: 27).

It must be emphasised that Wade's primary focus in explaining East Asian success is on demonstrating how the state used a plethora of distinctive policy instruments (financial policy instruments, trade policy instruments, direct foreign investment controls, use of conglomerates and state enterprises, moral suasion or 'administrative guidance') to guide resources to priority industries (shipbuilding, steel, computer peripherals, consumer electronics). He contends that East Asian governments were guided by the conviction that the private sector would underinvest in such priority industries—a phenomenon that earlier discussion highlighted as market failure. Hence, East Asian success derived from the fact that government intervention could overcome market failure. At the same time, bureaucratic inefficiency, waste, and corruption did not undermine the challenging task of 'governing the market' because of the institutional prerequisites embedded in the East Asian state.

Another good example of the developmental state hypothesis is Amsden (1989, 1991), who focuses on South Korea. She posits a model of 'late industrialisation' where policy-makers face a Gerschenkronian compulsion (Gershenkron 1962) to force the pace of industrialisation by manipulating the structure of relative prices, in particular through the allocation of subsidised credit to targeted firms and industries.

South Korea represented a special case of late industrialisation because of the state's unusual capacity to impose discipline on subsidy recipients. The explanation of such unusual state capacity relies on the institutional features—political authoritarianism, bureaucratic competence, insulation from fractious social groups—identified by Haggard and Wade.

Developmental state in East Asia: Perspective of economists and their intellectual affinity with non-economists

The intellectual impact of the work of Haggard, Wade and others began to be recognised by economists, and some added further contributions. A good illustration is the work of Lee and Naya (1988) and Lee (1992). They accept the unusual capacity of the East Asian state to implement growth-promoting policies, but argue that the answer lies in a greater understanding of the nature of government–business relations—a point that is also acknowledged in Bardhan (1990).

Drawing on the theory of corporate governance as reflected in Williamson (1975, 1985), Lee and Naya argue that the East Asian state can be characterised as an efficient 'quasi-internal organisation' (QIO). Williamson makes the point that transactions costs (the costs of negotiating, implementing, and negotiating contracts) were ignored in standard neo-classical analysis. Transactions costs stem from a confluence of bounded rationality and opportunistic behaviour. The former pertains to the notion that individual economic agents have limited capacity to comprehend and foresee all possible contingencies; the latter to the notion that parties to a contract tend to exploit asymmetric information to their advantage.

As Williamson argues, market failure is common in the pervasive presence of transactions costs. Firms emerge as a means of minimising transactions costs, but they are also prone to organisational failure as bureaucratic inertia and opportunistic behaviour by managers and workers sap entrepreneurial vitality. Williamson uses this insight to show how the design of corporate governance could mitigate both market failure and organisational failure. This led to the theory of the multidivisional (M-form) firm.

In an M-form firm, there is a clear separation of functions between a head office and quasi-autonomous operating divisions. The former is entrusted with the strategic mandate of looking after corporate goals, while the divisions are engaged in routine operational activities. The head office monitors the divisions via a range of easily observable performance indicators. It acts as an internal capital market in the sense that funds are allocated to competing divisions on the basis of high-yield use. This critical internal capital market function is supplemented by a range of control and incentive mechanisms, such as internal audits to identify low performance, and salary supplementation and promotions to reward high performers. The outcome, according to Williamson, is that the M-form firm has a better record (as measured by profit) than do alternative forms of corporate governance.

Lee and Naya's conceptualisation of the East Asian state as a QIO relies heavily on analogy to the M-form firm. Centralised policy-makers represent the head office, and the business groups interacting with the government perform a role equivalent to the operating divisions.

How do the policy-makers maintain control over the corporate sector and ensure adherence to state-articulated goals? We can find some equivalence between policy instruments and the *modus operandi* of the head office in the M-form firm. The state acts as a vast internal capital market by allocating subsidised credit to targeted business groups to fulfil the goals of industrialisation. Discipline is imposed on subsidy recipients by applying performance standards that can be related in a directly observable manner to central development goals. Given the commitment of East Asian policy-makers to economic growth via export growth, the use of export targets closely tied to subsidised credit allocations appears to be a logical choice—a point acknowledged by Amsden and others.

Whether relying on Williamson's theory of the firm or sticking to the straightforward accounts of Haggard and others, we can detect a common theme that 'East Asia Inc.' was characterised by an unequal partnership between government and business. Other interpretations of the nature of government–business relations in East Asia suggest a more complex form of interaction. In Okimoto's (1989) notion of the 'network state', developed in relation to Japan, the ruling elite (consisting of key members of the ruling party, technocrats, and managers of large firms) share a common background. This provides the basis for informal but binding ties between key representatives of the private sector and government. Such informal ties are reinforced by a variety of institutional arrangements, such as 'discussion councils' that act as a forum for government and business to exchange views on the future course of the economy and society. The atmosphere of trust and cooperation that is engendered by such repeated interaction among key societal actors enables East Asian policy-makers to reduce the transactions costs of policy-making.

Weiss (1996) arrives at a similar interpretation of the network state by developing the concept of 'embedded autonomy' (see also Evans 1989), which captures the existence of policy networks linking government and industry. Focusing on Japan, South Korea, and Taiwan, Weiss (1996: 185) observes that 'in all three countries, various state agencies have established an elaborate set of linkages to the private sector. These linkages ... provide a vital mechanism for acquiring adequate information and for coordinating agreement with the private sector'.

We can also reinterpret the theory of the East Asian state as a QIO in terms of Olson's principle of encompassing organisations (Olson 1982, 1986). In an Olsonian framework, the rent-seeking proclivities of narrowly based 'distributional coalitions' represent the key threat to sustainable economic growth. Such a threat can be attenuated if encompassing organisations emerge. Narrowly based groups have an incentive to engage in 'zero-sum activities': one group's gain is another group's loss. Encompassing organisations, on the other hand, do not have a similar incentive to engage in zero-sum activities. Given their weight in the economy, the larger the societal output the greater the gain for an encompassing organisation. In terms of Olson's model, the East Asian QIO represents a growth-promoting encompassing organisation.

We noted earlier that some economists embraced the pioneering models of the developmental state and gave them a distinctive theoretical twist. Other economists, such as Rodrik (1996a, 1996b), revisit the developmental state hypothesis and arrive at conclusions that appear to highlight the enduring relevance of the work of political scientists and regional specialists on East Asia. Rodrik recognises that East Asian growth is characterised by a good deal of state intervention in the economy. His theories draw on growth-promoting 'initial conditions' *à la* Haggard and the ability of governments to overcome market failure *à la* Wade.

The initial conditions relate to human capital endowments (an issue that receives insufficient attention from Wade and others) and the incidental benefits of land reform (extensively discussed by Haggard). Rodrik (1996a) develops a formal model in which initial endowment of skills affects subsequent growth, an example of an analytical tradition that stems from new growth theory. He highlights three groups of countries. The first consists of rich countries that are well-endowed with physical and human capital and specialise in skill-intensive, high-tech goods. At the other extreme are poor countries that lack both skills and capital and specialise in standardised, labour-intensive goods. There is also an intermediate category of middle-income countries that are poorly endowed with physical capital but have a well-educated labour force. That category is vulnerable to the risk of multiple equilibria: the economy may get stuck in a low-wage, low-tech equilibrium although it is possible to attain a high-tech, high-wage equilibrium. This particular kind of market failure occurs because of a 'coordination problem inherent in many industial activities. Production and investment decisions in the upstream and downstream parts of indusry will often be interdependent. When these decisions are made in a decentralised fashion, skill-intensive industrialisation may fail to hold in countries which otherwise possess the requisite human resources' (Rodrik 1996a: 2). The coordination problem emerges because of the existence of economies of scale and the imperfect tradability of some goods, services, or technologies associated with skill-intensive industrialisation.

Rodrik uses this framework to argue that government intervention can shift the economy from the low-tech to the high-tech equilibrium. The intervention can take many forms: administrative guidance to coordinate private-sector investment decisions, an investment subsidy, or a minimum wage policy. In each case, the effect is to make the high-tech equilibrium an attractive option to the private sector.

In applying this model to East Asia, Rodrik (1996a: 19–20) draws attention to the fact that the East Asian economies had a favourable initial condition in a critical area. Their human capital endowments exceeded what could have been predicted by per capita income levels as shown by the divergence between actual and predicted values of enrolment ratios and literacy rates in 1960. This skill intensity had two important, related ramifications:

- it allowed those economies to draw on a plentiful pool of educated citizens, some of whom became very able bureaucrats and provided administrative and policy-making leadership (note the resemblance to the institutionalist perspective on East Asian growth as discussed above)

- in terms of the multiple equilibria model, it meant that the East Asian economies conformed to the characteristics of an economy in which governments had two possible scenarios—a low-tech, low-wage equilibrium or a high-tech, high-wage equilibrium. The superior human capital endowments of the East Asian economies yielded the necessary condition for governments to play an active role in 'coordinating, subsidising and guiding private investment decisions ... implemented through ... the allocation of credit, through tax and other incentives, administrative guidance and ... public enterprises' (Rodrik 1996a: 19–20). This steered the economies to the preferred high-tech, high-wage equilibrium. This conclusion by a mainstream economist will delight the pioneers of the developmental state hypothesis.

As part of the discussion of growth-promoting initial conditions, Rodrik (1996b) highlights the incidental benefits of land reform in South Korea and Taiwan. It left those economies with an egalitarian distribution of wealth that attenuated the threat of 'distributive politics'. Alesina and Rodrik (1994) coined that term for a phenomenon where actual and perceived inequality can fuel demands for redistributive measures that are growth-retarding. They assemble international evidence to show that countries with initially low levels of inequality (the East Asian case as recorded in 1960) grew faster than countries with initially high levels of inequality.

Another example of economists embracing the developmental state hypothesis is Stern et al. (1995), who reinterpret a controversial episode in Korean economic history. The 1973–79 period is generally acknowledged as the heyday of activist Korean industry policy, when the government embarked on its heavy and chemical industries (HCI) drive. Neo-classical economists generally regard the period as evidence that aggressive state intervention hindered, rather than helped, Korea's progress (e.g. World Bank 1987). Stern et al. conclude, however, that the HCI drive may have accelerated Korea's industrialisation. The acceleration of heavy industrial exports (such as steel and automobiles) after 1985 would not have been possible without the investment in the HCI program during the 1970s.[2]

This discussion on the intellectual affinity between economists and non-economists on the efficacy of East Asian-style dirigisme highlights the fact that it became an orthodoxy and seriously challenged the neo-classical account of East Asian success. It is in this intellectual context that we must place the ambitious attempt by the World Bank to reconcile the first-generation neo-classical story with the developmental state hypothesis. The discussion now turns to the construction of the neo-classical synthesis of the East Asian miracle.

EAST ASIAN DEVELOPMENTAL STATE AND THE NEO-CLASSICAL SYNTHESIS

The 1993 World Bank study on seven East Asian economies (Hong Kong, Singapore, South Korea, Taiwan, Indonesia, Malaysia, and Thailand) is generally seen as an attempt to soften its adherence to the Washington Consensus of the 1980s. It was no longer possible to ignore the pervasive degree of state intervention in East Asia, despite the case of Hong Kong which did approximate the 'free trade cum free markets' story reasonably well. It was necessary to explain why dirigisme failed elsewhere but seemed to work so well in East Asia. In addition, as Awanohara (1993: 79) has noted, the World Bank was responding to Japanese pressure to develop a version of the East Asian model of economic development that explicitly incorporated the central role of the state. This led to the World Bank's functional approach to understanding the interaction between public policy and economic growth.

The World Bank's functional approach

Figure 1.1 captures the essentials of the 1993 World Bank study and enables us to demonstrate why we can regard the study as a neo-classical synthesis. As Figure 1.1 shows, the policy choices undertaken by East Asian governments had two components: those affecting economic fundamentals and those belonging to the realm of selective intervention. Economic fundamentals pertain to:

- macroeconomic management, especially fiscal prudence

- high human capital endowments

- effective and secure financial systems

- moderate price distortions in foreign exchange, labour, and goods markets

- openness to foreign technology

- agricultural development policies.

Figure 1.1: A Functional Approach to Growth

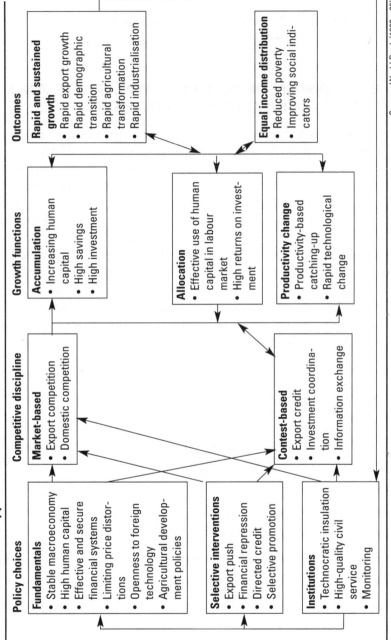

Source: World Bank (1993a: 88)

Policies that fall within the purview of selective intervention include:
- measures to facilitate exports (export push)

- financial repression entailing controls on interest rates

- selective credit allocation

- a range of measures to selectively promote certain industries (activist industry policy).

The policy choices and their sustained implementation were contingent on a set of institutional arrangements that entailed:
- wealth-sharing programs to include non-economic elites in growth

- economic technocrats insulated from narrow political pressures (technocratic insulation and high-quality civil service)

- mechanisms for sharing information with, and to win the support of, business elites.

The policy choices also evolved in a context of competitive discipline that affected the behaviour of firms. The competitive discipline was both market-based (stemming from international and domestic competition) and contest-based, a distinctive East Asian innovation. An example of a contest-based competitive discipline is the allocation of credit to firms, dependent on the firm reaching prescribed standards of export performance.

The interaction of policy choices with competitive discipline yielded growth functions that economists can usually measure: high saving, high investment, rapid skill accumulation, effective utilisation of capital and labour, and improved factor productivity driven by adaptation of technology and innovation. The outcome was rapid, sustained, and equitable growth in East Asia.

The World Bank study sought to include three distinctive features of the East Asian developmental state into its framework: selective intervention, contest-based competitive discipline, and the institutional framework that underpinned policy choices. Chapter 4 of the study expanded the theme of the institutional framework. Its reliance on concepts such as technocratic insulation and its examination of the interaction between government and business recognises the insights of the advocates of the developmental state hypothesis. At the same time, its emphasis on economic fundamentals and competitive discipline affirms the intellectual primacy of neo-classical economics.

It must be noted that the World Bank study regards some aspects of the rubric of selective intervention in East Asia as empirically more credible than other aspects. For example, it is rather circumspect in accepting that the promotion of targeted industries worked in East Asia. It highlights the risks inherent in activist industry policy and notes that its effectiveness depended on the unusual policy implementation capacities of East Asian governments—an institutional trait that may not be replicable elsewhere. The study is, however, willing to accept that export push or export facilitation measures generally produced the desired outcomes.

Distinctiveness of East Asian economic growth: Perspective of the ADB

We can regard a study on economic growth in Asia by the ADB (1997: chs 1, 2) as a sequel to the neo-classical synthesis embedded in the 1993 World Bank study. It notes: 'The lesson of history and international comparisons are that countries' growth rates depend ... primarily on ... the performance of their institutions and policies' (ADB 1997: 8). A distinctive feature of the ADB study is that it provides an econometric investigation of the determinants of cross-country growth in which East Asia is treated as the critical comparator. Thus, other regions' growth records (South Asia, sub-Saharan Africa, Latin America) are measured and explained in relation to the extent to which they fall below the East Asian benchmark.

Chapter 2 of the ADB study (which draws on Radelet, Sachs & Lee 1996) aims to illuminate the debates on the sources of economic growth. It distinguishes between classical growth theory, neo-classical growth theory, and endogenous growth theory. As the study notes, 'the three approaches offer different explanations for East Asia's rapid growth during the past thirty years, and yield different predictions about the future' (ADB 1997: 65). The distinctive features of the different growth theories are summarised in Table 1.1.

The ADB study then sets up a statistical model where differences in economic growth across countries are determined by the following variables:

• trade policy (as a measure of openness or the lack of it)

• government saving (as a measure of fiscal prudence or the lack of it)

Table 1.1: Growth Theory and East Asia

Type of growth theory	Key sources of growth and implications for future evolution of East Asia
Classical theory (e.g. Adam Smith)	Outward orientation maintained through trade policy, relatively strong protection of property rights and effective enforcement of contracts. East Asia's geography, with its fine natural ports and easy access to major markets, is a bonus. Growth in East Asia can be sustained as long as these preconditions are sustained
Neo-classical growth theory (e.g. Robert Solow)	Rapid capital accumulation reflected in high saving and high investment. While the gap between East Asia and poor nations will diminish (the 'catch-up' factor), the rate of East Asian economic growth will slow because of diminishing returns to new investment as the ratio of capital to labour rises
Endogenous growth theory, also known as 'new' growth theory (e.g. Paul Romer)	New ideas and new products represent the engine of long-term growth. The superior institutions and human capital of East Asia have led to productivity-driven growth. Given that investments in knowledge are subject to constant, or even increasing, returns to scale, the prediction is that East Asia may eventually overtake richer countries

Source: Adapted from ADB (1997: 63–5)

- quality of government institutions (based on survey data that captures the perceptions of the business community)

- structural factors entailing demographic, geographic, and natural resource endowments

- initial conditions pertaining to initial level of per capita income (as measured in 1965) and initial human capital endowments (as measured by schooling in 1965).

Based on the cross-country statistical analysis of the 1965–90 period, the study concludes that:

> The evidence best supports a synthesis of the classical and neo-classical approaches, augmented by demographic considerations. East Asia has benefited from rapid capital accumulation ... and (outward-orientation) ... supported by good policies and institutions and a rapid demographic transition ... The predictions of endogenous growth theory do not apply (ADB 1997: 67).

The study (1997: 80) draws attention to the significance of different variables in explaining why East Asian growth was much higher than other parts of the world. South Asian, sub-Saharan Africa, and Latin American growth rates (as measured in terms of per capita GDP) were 3–4 per cent lower than East Asian benchmarks over the 1965–90 period. At least 60 per cent of this difference in growth rates can be statistically explained by differences in policy and institutional variables between East Asia and other developing regions.

Although the ADB study is not explicitly a test of the developmental state hypothesis, the above finding is consistent with the hypothesis. It is not, however, entirely consistent with the 1993 World Bank study, which can be reinterpreted as an attempt to encompass classical, neo-classical, and endogenous growth theory, given that accumulation, allocation, and productivity are considered primary sources of East Asian growth and that policy and institutional variables are highlighted (see Figure 1.1 and related discussion above). The ADB study's rejection of the empirical validity of endogenous growth theory in explaining the East Asian experience is thus a partial endorsement of the World Bank's functional approach.

The ADB study backs up its statistical exercise with an institutional account of East Asian success. The observations suggest a cautious endorsement of the developmental state hypothesis.

Consider first the role of selective intervention in the industrial revolution of East Asia. Like the World Bank study, the 1997 ADB study distinguishes between export facilitation measures and activist industry policy. The former measures are enthusiastically endorsed, but considerable reservations are expressed about the efficacy of the latter. Although success stories of activist policies are acknowledged, the ADB study notes some offsetting cases of failures and is reluctant to accept that such policies in Korea, Taiwan, and Singapore produced net benefits.

In terms of policy lessons, the ADB study makes the following points. First, activist industry policy should be limited to removing biases against exports and making exporters competitive. Second, while governments may hasten the pace of comparative advantage, too much haste may engender costs that may outweigh the initial benefits of policy activism. Third, activist industry policy of the type employed in 'Korea and [Taiwan] could only succeed in countries with an effective and disciplined civil service' (ADB 1997: 103). Fourth, the first-generation East Asian NIEs could implement activist industry policy because they were only small players in world markets, to be noticed by others. Today, the rules of the game that govern international trade have changed, with the World Trade Organisation (WTO) and the Uruguay Round of GATT talks limiting the ability of developing countries to use protectionist measures to promote targeted industries.

In trying to explain why the quality of East Asian governance was high relative to other developing regions, the ADB study ends up with an account that is a ringing endorsement of the developmental state hypothesis. It draws attention to:

- stable political leadership

- an unusually high premium on rapid economic growth, because the political leaders saw it as critical to the survival of their regimes

- well-trained economic technicians in charge of policy management, backed by a generally competent civil service

- close government–business interactions that helped build broad consensus on key policy initiatives.

Both the World Bank and the ADB readily acknowledge that conventional economic variables as well as more complex institutional forces shaped rapid growth in East Asia. The studies can thus accommodate the developmental state hypothesis. However, they display considerable ambivalence about the efficacy of activist industry policy in shaping East Asian growth, although they accept the effectiveness of export facilitation measures. In emphasising the primacy of policy fundamentals (including trade policy) in understanding East Asian development, both the World Bank and the ADB affirm the insights of the first-generation neo-classical theory into East Asian success. They differ, however, in the importance placed on the relevance of endogenous growth theory to East Asia: the ADB rejects it, but the World

Bank considers it an essential component of its analytical framework. Despite this, the World Bank and ADB are united in advocating the neo-classical synthesis as a means of understanding the East Asian miracle.

EAST ASIAN DEVELOPMENTAL STATE: REGIONAL VARIANTS

Although the 1993 World Bank study on the 'East Asian miracle' and the 1997 ADB report on 'emerging Asia' discuss a diverse group of economies, they tend to arrive at generalisations. Some commentators have wondered whether such generalisations are possible. It may be more fruitful to emphasise regional variants of the developmental state. Perkins (1994), for example, highlights the need to deal with at least three models of East Asian development: the two fully urbanised economies of Hong Kong and Singapore; the three interventionist states of Japan, Taiwan, and South Korea; and the resource-rich countries of Southeast Asia. The PRC is excluded from the World Bank study. The ADB, although including it, questions whether it fits the typical East Asian case.

There is now a vibrant political economy literature that seeks to highlight both the differences and the shared features of the first-tier NIEs and their Southeast Asian counterparts of Indonesia, Malaysia, and Thailand (e.g. Jones 1997). The politics of the PRC's transition to a market economy has also spawned a distinctive literature (e.g. Watson 1994). It is therefore necessary to go beyond the generalisations of the neo-classical synthesis and examine more carefully the extent to which the developmental state hypothesis can withstand regional variations.

Developmental state and Southeast Asia

How relevant is the institutional framework derived from the experience of the core East Asian economies to explaining the economic transformations of Southeast Asia? The World Bank (1993a: ch. 4) tries to argue that the framework applies to both the East Asian NIEs and Southeast Asia. The 1997 ADB study (ch. 2) also blurs the distinction between the two groups, in its brief comments on the role of growth-promoting institutional factors.

Hill (1997), an economist well-known for his expertise on Southeast Asia, seems to concur with the framework offered by the 1993 World Bank study and its ADB sequel. He regards macroeconomic orthodoxy, openness, and equity as the core factors driving Southeast Asia's (including Singapore, which he analytically categorises with Taiwan and South Korea as East Asian NIEs) economic growth (Hill 1997: 103–4). He argues that such growth-promoting factors stem from a conjunction of 'political leaders committed to economic growth' supported by 'able technocrats ... who have to some extent been insulated from political pressure groups' (1997: 108). Such insulation reflects the fact that 'the political bureaucratic elites and the commercial elites have been rather distinct'.

Hill (1997: 138–9) dismisses the relevance of activist industry policy in understanding the rapid growth in Southeast Asia. Such an interpretation, combined with the above depiction of the political economy of policy-making in Southeast Asia, pitches it very close to the neo-classical synthesis of the World Bank and ADB studies. It also pits it against dissidents—such as Jomo (1997)—who regard the Southeast Asian economies of Indonesia, Malaysia, and Thailand as 'misunderstood miracles'. They appear to be much more sympathetic to the cause of activist industry policy.

Hill's (1997) interpretation of Southeast Asian political economy also contrasts with the work of some political scientists. They have maintained, for some time, that the relatively straightforward relationship between political structures and rapid, internationally oriented economic growth in Korea and other countries cannot be easily extrapolated to interpret the experiences of Southeast Asian economic development. As Mackie (1988: 291) notes, the 'differences ... turn out to be more significant than the similarities'. What are these differences?

To start with, scholars agree that the economies of Southeast Asia lack the bureaucratic competence and technocratic insulation of the core East Asian NIEs. MacIntyre (1994: 7) emphasises the 'pervasive importance of patrimonial and clientalistic links between government figures and business people'. This means that perceptions of corruption are significantly higher in Southeast Asia than in the core group.

The multi-ethnic nature of many Southeast Asian societies also undermines attempts to develop a model of governance that has regional applicability—a point emphasised by Chowdhury and Islam (1996: 491–2) with specific reference to Malaysia. The essence of the argument is that technocratic insulation is difficult to uphold in a polity such as Malaysia that is ethnically diverse and has apparently been captured by a demographically dominant ethnic group (Malays). The mechanisms for building a reputable civil service entail merit-based and competitive recruitment procedures and a compensation package that is closely aligned with the private sector. The World Bank acknowledges that none of these mechanisms is well-established in Malaysia: 'civil service exam results are subject to affirmative action guidelines meant to increase the number of Malays in government. Because this reduces the pool of eligible applicants, it probably hinders the development of the bureaucracy' (World Bank 1993a: 175).

The same problem occurs in government–business relations in Malaysia—the political imperative of affirmative action has meant that it has not always worked as well as it allegedly has in, say, Korea. The World Bank recognises this when it notes that 'From 1972 to 1985 ... relations between government and big business tended to be contentious, in part because of the requirement that all enterprises have at least 30 per cent Malay participation' (World Bank 1993a: 185).

The economies of Southeast Asia are well-endowed with natural resources compared to the first-tier NIEs. It has been argued that resource-rich economies tend to rely on export income from primary commodities to finance inefficient domestic manufacturing industries (Ranis 1981). Such an argument may help to explain why the move towards trade liberalisation occurred later in Southeast Asia than in the core economies.

One would expect that a combination of limited bureaucratic competence, inadequate technocratic insulation, political clientalism, and dependence on primary commodities would limit the growth potential of Southeast Asia but, with the exception of the Philippines, this is manifestly not the case. How do we explain this apparent paradox?

A possible explanation lies in the crisis imperative engendered by the external economic shocks in 1982–86—falling oil prices followed by sharp downturns in other commodity prices.[3] Indonesia, Malaysia, and Thailand responded fairly rapidly to restore macroeconomic imbalances (Warr 1992; Horton, Kandur & Mazumdar 1994) and created incentives for export-oriented, foreign capital-dependent industrialisation. These domestic policy initiatives were supported by the World Bank and IMF and coincided happily with the burst of Japan and NIE-led foreign direct investment (FDI) that followed the exchange rate realignments between the US dollar and the yen in the mid 1980s.

What political forces led to such responses to the external shocks of the mid 1980s? One line of argument is that, despite a tradition of clientalism, the 1980s saw the emergence of assertive business associations that played an important part in the economic reform agenda of the mid 1980s. This development is evident in Thailand, and can also be detected in Indonesia. The business associations were able to form alliances with reform-minded technocrats in the economic ministries and prevail in domestic policy debates (see, e.g., Laothamatas 1988, 1992; Doner 1991a, 1991b, 1992). MacIntyre (1990, 1992, 1993) has also supported that interpretation, although he is now doubtful about the sustainability of such a political configuration (MacIntyre 1994: 16–17).

Developmental state and the PRC

The political economy of the PRC is, in many respects, more complex than that of Southeast Asia or the first-tier NIEs. A simple transplant of the notion of technocratic insulation—derived from the experience of the East Asian NIEs—is not useful. In the PRC, the politics of policy-making is compounded by the constant tension between socialist ideology and the transition to a market-oriented economy.

The transition to a market-oriented economy, and the PRC's progressive integration with its regional neighbours and the world has spawned a significant literature (see, e.g., the admirably lucid survey by Watson 1994). The contemporary PRC is one of the most buoyant economies in the world and an emerging giant in the Asia–Pacific region. Judged from the perspective of a wide range of welfare indicators (dietary standards, incidence of poverty, consumption of durables etc.), one must acknowledge that the PRC represents an admirable case where the benefits of growth have percolated down to broad layers of society (Nolan 1996/97).

It should be noted that not all scholars uncritically embrace the story of the PRC's economic miracle. Krugman (1994), for example, has observed that much depends on the reference point. In relation to the calamities of the Great Leap Forward under Mao, the changes do appear to be a miracle. Lal (1995), in a perceptive comparative study of the PRC and India, has argued that in areas such as trade liberalisation and productivity growth, the performance of the PRC is not significantly different from that of India. He concedes, however, that the PRC's growth rate is about twice India's largely because of its rather high rate of investment.

Despite some reservations about the nature and pace of economic growth in the PRC, the weight of scholarly opinion favours the view that the PRC is successfully engaged in transition to a market economy. What are the political forces behind this? The reform process has been:

> characterised by experiments, pragmatic adjustments, and debates over what to do next ... This strongly pragmatic focus has contributed to the relative success of China's reforms and must be seen as a strategic choice by the reformist forces. It has enabled old orthodoxies to be set aside or reconstructed and created the space for innovative experiments ... It has also accommodated the changing balance of political forces in China (Watson 1994: 49).

Underpinning this pragmatism is the successful alliance between the technocrats and party political leaders, but it is an alliance that encompasses different levels and layers of the bureaucracy, academia, and the media (Watson 1994: 50). In this institutional setting, considerable debate and consensus-building occurs before broad policy directions are set—a point emphasised in the perceptive study by Shirk (1992). In this respect, the notion of technocratic insulation is rather more complex than suggested by the literature on the NIEs.

The complex nature of the PRC's political economy and its impact on the transition to a market economy is highlighted by Liew (1998). Drawing on the work of Young (1998), Liew (1998: 36) notes that the growth of the private sector in the post-Mao period:

> owes much to the ingenuity of entrepreneurs in securing political support from local officials who can see the advantages of having a vibrant private sector in their localities. Many private businesses are disguised as collectives or as state-owned enterprises with the connivance of local officials so as to bypass official restrictions and/or to gain preferential government treatment.

The PRC's experiment with market-oriented reforms and its efforts at globalisation within a framework of socialist ideology has spawned considerable discussion and speculation about its sustainability. Can the growth of the private sector continue to rely on informal relations between local business and local officials? What are the risks that a repeat of events such as the 1989 tragedy of Tiananmen Square will lead to sharp divisions between the need to maintain the status quo and the need to align the political system with a rapidly evolving market-oriented system? For the time being, it appears that the separation between the political system—driven by socialist ideology and the one-party state—and the economic system will be maintained. The underlying logic for such separation is that continuity, stability, and strong political leadership are prerequisites for sustained rapid growth.

The political economy of public policy in the PRC has also highlighted the perennial debate on the costs and benefits of 'gradualism' compared to the 'big bang' approach in economic reform. Should a country make a decisive, one-step move towards a market economy, as advocated and attempted in Eastern Europe and the Former Soviet Union (EEFSU), or should it proceed incrementally, as in the case of the PRC?

The PRC's gradualist strategy has been described as 'muddling through' (McMillan & Noughton 1992). Noughton (1995: 22) provides a more nuanced account and distinguishes between the 'ex post coherence' of its reform policies and the lack of a coherent, ex ante vision of 'ownership structure or a fully renovated financial system'. One could argue that gradualism has its costs. It has been partly responsible for the 'stop–go' cycles of recent PRC economic growth: periods of rapid growth offset by bouts of macroeconomic austerity. It has also sustained the coexistence of profit-driven, relatively efficient market sectors and subsidised, relatively inefficient plan or state sectors. Byrd (1991) has highlighted the point that such coexistence spawns rent-seeking opportunities and engenders microeconomic distortions.

Perhaps the most ardent critics of the PRC's gradualist strategy are Sachs and Woo (1994, 1995, 1996). They dismiss its approach to a market economy by suggesting that it has no relevance to the transition of the EEFSU, as the size of the subsidised state sector is much higher in the EEFSU than in the PRC. Boosting the size of the private sector in the EEFSU requires 'shock therapy' entailing large-scale changes in relative prices that will induce significant re-allocation of resources between the state and non-state sectors.

Benziger (1998) offers a robust rebuttal of the work of Sachs and Woo, which he characterises as the 'neo-classical critique of China's gradualism'. His point is that the 'proof of the pudding is in the eating'. The PRC's gradualist strategy, despite its incompleteness and seeming incoherence, has yielded substantial economic and social benefits, inspiring Fischer (1994: 131) to proclaim it 'the greatest increase in economic well-being within a 15-year period in all of history'. In contrast, the former Soviet Union has had a dismal experience. The output of such basic items as shoes and textiles has fallen by about two-thirds (Nolan 1996/97). There has also been serious deterioration in living standards, judged in terms of various welfare indicators such as life expectancy, health care, and dietary standards (Heleniak 1995).

Taking account of the contrasting experiences of the EEFSU and the PRC, Benziger upholds the pragmatism and wisdom of the PRC's strategy of gradualism. A big bang approach applied to the core economies of Eastern Europe will simply 'result in a flood of workers out of the state sector before new jobs are ready for them … China's strategy of a gradual change … is called for, in order to allow the state sector time to melt away' (1998: 38).

Liew (1995) illustrates the political benefits of a strategy of gradualism. He maintains that a subsidised state sector acts as a de facto social welfare system, providing a safety net for those left behind by the growth process. This maintains the momentum for reform: 'winners' gain from the expansion of the market sector while 'losers' are compensated through the protection offered by the state sector.

The future of the reform process in the PRC will remain the subject of debate and speculation, but one can at least predict that sustained growth will itself sow the seeds of further change. Those who gain least from change, such as the workers and managers of SOEs, are becoming less dominant. Evidence suggests that the bulk of industrial production and employment, for both domestic and export markets, was generated outside the state sector (Findlay & Watson 1992; Xio 1991; Wei 1995). Such evidence has motivated Gang, Perkins and Sabin (1996) to argue that the dynamism of the PRC lies with the non-state sector that is driven by domestic competition, low taxation, and international trade. These are the hallmarks of the market economies of East Asia.

DEMISE OF THE DEVELOPMENTAL STATE AND THE NEW POLITICAL ECONOMY OF EAST ASIA

The onset of the financial crisis in East Asia in mid 1997, and its persistent aftermath, has shaken the very foundation of the developmental state hypothesis, whether in the original or the reconstructed version.

Both the pioneering advocates of the developmental state in East Asia and the neo-classical synthesis that followed must undergo a phase of painful rethinking. Admittedly, scholars specialising in Southeast Asia and the PRC developed a distinct tradition of political economy that rejected a Pan-Asian version of the developmental state, but even there the literature has focused on explaining economic success. The intellectual challenge now confronting scholars is to develop a paradigm that allows us to understand the crisis and its ramifications for the future of the region. Efforts are certainly underway and, over time, they will provide shape and substance to the new political economy of East Asia.

Developmental state in pre-crisis East Asia: Voices of dissent

Although no one fully anticipated the severity and scale of the crisis engulfing the region, it would be fair to say that there were voices of dissent well before the mid 1990s. Such dissenting voices can be grouped into two clusters: those who highlight the analytical limitations and the questionable empirical relevance of the developmental state even in the core East Asian NIEs; and those who highlight a range of concerns overlooked during the phase of robust growth.

Among the first group, Islam (1992, 1994) and Chowdhury and Islam (1993: ch. 3) have consistently highlighted an analytical gap that is common to the literature on the developmental state. The political system, at least as interpreted in the literature on East Asia, is not a truly exogenous variable in explaining economic outcomes. This point deserves amplification.

Consider two scenarios: one where all the features of the developmental state—technocratic insulation, bureaucratic competence, close interaction between government and business—exist but the trade regime is 'inward-oriented'; another where such institutional features operate within an 'outward-oriented' trade regime. The trade regime will dominate the outcomes that flow from a system of governance, causing deleterious effects in the first case (inward orientation) and desirable results in the second (outward orientation). The key logic is that once government and business become aware that domestic economic fortunes are tied to successful performance in international markets, they attach a premium to economic efficiency. This logic prevails not because of the political system, but because of the domestic economy's exposure to international competition.

All advocates of the developmental state recognise the centrality of developing an analytical model of East Asian governance in which the trade regime plays a key explanatory role. Consider, for example, the observations by Wade (1988:155–6):

> Korea has strongly encouraged [the infant industries] to start exporting very soon ... thus exposing them directly to international competitive pressures ... Taiwan ... seems to have put less pressure on the infants to export, and relied more on the threat of allowing in imports if the prices of domestic substitutes moved much above international prices. This may be part of the reason why ... Taiwan's public enterprises are more effective than those in many other countries; they supply to downstream firms which do export, from whom comes the pressure to match the costs of overseas competitors.

Amsden's (1989: 16) depiction of the Korean government's performance-contingent assistance to business also highlights the key role played by export competition:

> The sternest discipline imposed by the Korean government on virtually all large ... firms—no matter how politically well connected—related to export targets. There was constant pressure from government bureaucrats to sell more abroad—with obvious implications for efficiency.

Once the concession is made that international competition plays a vital role in understanding the efficacy of East Asian-style governance, the novelty of the developmental state hypothesis wears off. It merely supplements, rather than supplants, the original insights of Little and others that the trade regime is the central variable in understanding the industrial revolution in East Asia.

Adherents of the developmental state often seek inspiration from Japan in substantiating the empirical credibility of their ideas (Johnson 1982, 1985, 1987; Wade 1988, 1990; Matthews & Ravenhill 1994; Weiss 1996). Yet some political scientists specialising in the Japanese economy depict a policy-making process that is significantly at variance with the basic tenets of the developmental state. Okimoto (1989: 23) maintains that 'one of the great myths enshrouding Japanese industrial policy is that it has been error-free and costless. Nothing could be further from the truth'.

We should also draw attention to the seminal study by Samuels (1987) of state intervention in the Japanese energy sector. He could not find a single case, among the seventy studied, where relative state autonomy (the capacity of the state to formulate policies that are not compromised by responding to special interest groups) could be established.[4]

Perhaps the most damning indictment of the empirical relevance of the Japanese developmental state comes from Friedman's (1988) study of prewar and postwar policy interventions in the machine tools industry. Claiming that Japan is a 'misunderstood miracle', Friedman makes the novel point that the Japanese government completely misunderstood the nature of the nation's competitive advantage in the production of machine tools. Innovation-oriented small and medium-sized firms led the industry. The bureaucrats, however, felt that the industry ought to be consolidated into larger units in order to reap economies of scale. Friedman's study shows that the government failed to consolidate the industry, largely because of private-sector resistance. His conclusion conveys the startling implication that if the bureaucrats had been successful in carrying out their program of consolidation, Japan would have been a loser rather than a winner in international competition. Such a conclusion would delight even the most strident neo-classical economist.

Apart from critics of the developmental state, some scholars sympathetic to the cause of East Asian-style dirigisme have been uncertain about their convictions. Lee and Naya, the creators of the concept of the QIO, are apprehensive that East Asian governments that operate as QIOs may be prone to organisational failure as the economic system becomes more complex:

> It is important to point out that ... the quasi-internal organisation is not relatively efficient under all circumstances. As the economy grows and the number of enterprises increases within the organisation, it will run into more ... 'organisational failure'. Moreover, as the economy graduates from producing simple labour-intensive products, choosing the right industries to promote will become more difficult. Consequently, the quasi-internal organisation is more likely to make mistakes of choosing wrong policies than before (Lee & Naya 1988: 147).

The message is clear. The developmental state may be a historically specific phenomenon, relevant in some periods but less relevant in others. As the socioeconomic system becomes more complex, the developmental state—as a prototype hierarchy—may perform poorly.

Another example of an advocate of East Asian-style dirigisme who has wavered in his conviction is Rodrik (1996a). After constructing an elegant economic model in which state intervention can push an economy from a low-tech equlibrium to high-tech equilibrium and applying it to interpret the East Asian experience, Rodrik concedes that:

> A theoretical demonstration does not on its own amount to policy advice ... East Asian efforts to coordinate investment activities have often been criticised for having led to wasteful industries ... Hence, the empirical relevance of these ideas remains to be demonstrated. In the absence of such a demonstration, *government intervention to promote industrial diversification must be judged a risky strategy* (1996a: 20, emphasis added).

Pre-crisis Asia: Emerging social concerns

So far, the discussion has focused on criticisms of the concept of the developmental state without questioning the high quality of East Asian growth. It seems appropriate to move on to a group of scholars who provide a stronger critique of East Asian development by highlighting a range of economic and social concerns that receive little attention in the developmental state literature.

Yoshihara (1988) develops the notion of 'ersatz capitalism' in Southeast Asia, in many ways the precursor to the 'crony capitalism' that forms part of the lexicon of East Asian political economy. Yoshihara (1988: 4) derides the phenomenon of Southeast Asian 'paper entrepreneurs' and expresses concern about their inability to foster indigenous manufacturing and technology.

Others want to delve beneath the East Asian miracle. Deyo (1987, 1989) has consistently argued that the miracle economies were characterised by the suppression of the labour movement—a phenomenon he called a case of 'labour subordination' and 'exclusionary politics'.

Another example of the dissenting voices on the nature of East Asian economic growth is the work of Bello and Rosenfeld (1992), who called the East Asian NIEs 'dragons in distress'. They draw attention to the social costs of rapid growth, such as the loss of cultural identity among the Malays of Singapore, lack of participation in decision-making, exploitation of migrant workers, and environmental degradation.

Perhaps the most provocative and telling critique of East Asian economic development comes from a high-profile economist. Krugman (1994) gained a great deal of notoriety when he articulated the 'myth of Asia's miracle'. He draws attention to the possibility of a slowing of economic growth in the region. Applying conventional neo-classical growth theory and selective evidence, Krugman develops the proposition that growth in East Asia is primarily input-driven rather than productivity-driven, and hence subject to the limits of diminishing returns.

None of these dissenting scholars on East Asia actually predicted the crisis. However, they did draw attention to emerging social concerns which received scant attention in the literature on the developmental state. Their contributions should be treated as forerunners to the literature on the East Asian crisis and as key planks in the new political economy of East Asia.

The 1997 crisis and beyond

Any attempt to construct the new political economy of East Asia needs to focus on the following interrelated questions.

1 What caused the 1997 crisis?
2 What are the long-term economic, social, and political influences that will affect East Asia's pathway to recovery and the resumption of 'miraculous' growth?
3 What kinds of economic and institutional reforms are required to respond to those issues?

The rest of the book discusses these questions in some detail. The key message is that, unless these emerging social concerns are resolved, recreating the East Asian miracle will be a hopeless task.

CONCLUSION

This chapter has taken a long journey through a diverse terrain of competing ideas and ideology on East Asian political economy. Its emphasis is that we should distinguish between the 'old' political economy that was preoccupied with understanding the sources of rapid East Asian growth, and the 'new' political economy that seeks to comprehend the currency crisis and the post-crisis scenarios for the region. However, it is impossible to construct the new political economy of East Asia without appreciating the issues that dominate the pre-crisis literature. Hence, the chapter presented an analytical history of the evolution of East Asian political economy.

The industrial revolution in East Asia that has been underway since the 1960s played a central part in the demise of dirigisme as an intellectual force. When neo-classical economists eventually 'discovered' East Asia, approximately two decades after the onset of hypergrowth in the region, they were quick to identify the causes of the growth as export orientation, competitive domestic markets, and limited government intervention.

Throughout the 1980s, a group of political scientists and regional specialists drew attention to the pervasive presence of state intervention in East Asia, particularly in Taiwan and South Korea, which resembled the economic strategy of Japan in the 1950s and 1960s. The association between state intervention and rapid growth in East Asia appeared to vindicate their conviction that it negated the basic tenets of dependency theory (which denied the possibility that states in peripheral nations could foster self-sustained growth) as well as the neo-classical interpretation of market-driven growth.

The analysis of East Asian ascendancy thus shifted towards understanding the institutional framework of economic growth. Authoritarian politics, technocratic insulation, bureaucratic competence, and close interaction between government and business were identified as growth-promoting traits and became part of the rubric of the developmental state in East Asia. The World Bank—often regarded as the bastion of neo-classical economics—accepted this framework with some modifications, and the ADB affirmed the key tenets of the World Bank study, albeit with reservations. Thus was born the neo-classical synthesis of the East Asian miracle. Rapid and egalitarian growth, in this paradigm, stemmed from conducive initial conditions, macroeconomic stability, export-driven industrialisation marked by interventionist measures, and institutional features associated with the developmental state.

A key issue in East Asian political economy is the extent to which the concept of the developmental state can withstand regional variations. Some scholars of Southeast Asian political economy maintain that technocratic insulation and bureaucratic competence appear to be only weakly present in Southeast Asia. Rapid growth in the region was partly driven by reform measures implemented in response to external shocks. Assertive pro-reform business associations also played a role in Thailand and, to some extent, Indonesia.

A straightforward application of the developmental state also appears problematic in the case of the PRC. There is a constant tension between socialist ideology and the transition to a market economy. Although this may have affected the ex ante coherence of policy-making, a tradition of consensus-building has led to a gradualist approach in the transition to a market economy. There are well-known costs of gradualism as a political and economic strategy, but it seems to have worked far better than the big bang approach in the EEFSU.

Since the onset of the currency crisis in East Asia, the orthodoxy on East Asian political economy has been in disarray. The developmental state hypothesis—in both its original and reconstructed forms—was preoccupied with explaining economic success. The challenge now is to understand the crisis and its aftermath. This has set the basis for constructing the new political economy of East Asia.

The new political economy of East Asia did not stem only from the events of 1997. A strand of the pre-crisis literature questioned the analytical coherence and empirical credibility of the developmental state hypothesis. Some scholars argued that East Asian-style governance worked only when combined with an export-oriented strategy, speculating that it would be ineffective when combined with an inward-oriented industrialisation strategy. Economists who supported the cause of East Asian-style dirigisme accepted this caveat and conceded that the strategy was fraught with risks.

The pre-crisis literature on East Asia was also notable for its concern with a range of emerging social and economic issues that had received scant attention from the advocates of the developmental state. Such issues included ersatz capitalism, suppression of the labour movement, environmental degradation, and the sustainability of input-driven growth. The East Asian crisis has provided a window of opportunity to re-engage in a discourse on such issues.

How will East Asian political economy evolve as a region? The fact that the 'Asian way' of managing national economies appears to have been discredited does not necessarily mean a return to the neo-classical orthodoxy of free markets and limited government. There is an emerging view that the time is ripe for fostering a 'post-Washington Consensus' in development policy—a theme that is taken up in chapter 7 of this book. This view seems to focus on second-generation institutional reforms that emphasise ways in which both markets and states may be made to work more effectively. It highlights the desirability of capital controls in dealing with the instability associated with short-term capital flows. It also urges the need to renew the trust in Keynesian-style demand management policies in coping with recessions engendered by financial crises. Concepts such as accountability, transparency, and the politics of inclusion have become part of the lexicon of the political economy of the region. The aim is to provide a unified vision of the various policy initiatives being debated in East Asia. Whether the post-Washington Consensus will be implemented, and whether it will set the basis for a resumption of miraculous growth in the region, remains to be seen.

Chapter 2

Crisis, Democratic Governance, and Prosperity

INTRODUCTION

The rapid expansion of the East Asian tigers—many by an average of more than 8% a year over the past three decades—has provoked fear in the West and pride back home. Never before in the world history has any region sustained such rapid growth for so long (Economist 1997).

> The emergence of Asia ... on the world economic scene has been a remarkable story ... Asia is in the midst of an economic and social transformation unrivalled in history. In virtually every dimension, life in Asia is changing at a pace never seen before in any part of the world during a comparable period of time (ADB 1997: xi, 1).

These quotes encapsulate the spectacular success of four East Asian economies—Hong Kong, South Korea, Singapore, and Taiwan—since the mid 1960s, followed later by three economies of the Association of Southeast Asian Nations (ASEAN)—Indonesia, Malaysia, Thailand, and to some extent the Philippines—since the mid 1970s. Until the recent crisis, these economies, grouped together as high-performing Asian economies (HPAEs), grew for nearly three decades at an average annual rate of 7–9 per cent, which was earlier thought unachievable.[1] As a result, in less than three decades the four East Asian economies were transformed from poverty-stricken underdeveloped economies to newly industrialised economies (NIEs). From being one of the poorest countries in the world in the early 1960s, South Korea has become the newest member of the club of rich countries, the Organization for Economic Cooperation and Development (OECD). The per capita gross national product (GNP) of Hong Kong and Singapore in 1995 exceeded that of their former colonial master, the United Kingdom. In terms of purchasing power parity (PPP) estimates, Hong Kong's per capita GNP has almost reached the level of the USA and Singapore's per capita GNP is around 85 per cent that of the USA. Several terms have been used to describe this unprecedented success story, of which the best-known is Woronoff's (1986) 'miracle economies'. Sarel (1997: 1) has rightly remarked, 'The spectacular growth of many economies in East Asia ... has amazed the economics profession ... [who] ... refer to the phenomenon as "miraculous"'. The latecomers—the ASEAN four—are dubbed as next-tier NIEs. The successive transformation of these Asian economies has been described as a 'flying geese' formation, with Japan as the leader followed by four East Asian NIEs, followed by four ASEAN economies and then by China (the PRC).

Table 2.1: Convergence and Growth Rates of Real GDP

Economy	Real GDP growth rates (%)			GDP per capita relative to USA	
	1971–80	1981–90	1991–95	1965	1995
Hong Kong	9.3	7.2	5.6	0.30	0.98
Indonesia	7.7	5.5	7.6	0.05	0.13
Korea	9.0	8.8	7.2	0.09	0.49
Malaysia	7.8	5.2	8.7	0.14	0.37
Philippines	6.0	1.0	2.3	0.11	0.09
Singapore	7.9	6.3	8.7	0.15	0.85
Taiwan	9.3	8.5	6.5	0.14	0.56
Thailand	7.9	7.9	8.4	0.10	0.26
Middle-income countries	6.2	2.9	0.1	NA	NA
South Asia	3.7	5.1	4.6	0.08	0.09
Latin America	6.1	1.6	3.2	NA	NA

Sources: Growth rates: *World Development Report* (various issues), *Key Indicators of Developing Asian and Pacific Countries* (various issues). Convergence: ADB (1997: Table 2.11)

The broad economic indicators presented in Tables 2.1–2.3 show the extent of East and Southeast Asian economies' growth and structural transformation. The middle-income countries and two other regions (South Asia and Latin America) are used as comparators. The performance of HPAEs has been far superior to that of any of the groups. The Asian economies (Japan, NIEs, ASEAN-4, and the PRC)

Table 2.2: Structural Change (% share of sectors in GDP)

Economy	Agriculture			Industry			Services		
	1970	1980	1997	1970	1980	1997	1970	1980	1997
Hong Kong	NA	0.9	0.2	NA	32.0	15.5	NA	67.2	84.4
Indonesia	35.0	24.4	14.3	28.0	41.3	43.2	37.0	34.3	42.0
Korea	29.8	14.2	6.1	23.8	37.8	43.7	46.4	48.1	50.2
Malaysia	NA	22.9	11.7	NA	35.8	47.6	NA	41.3	40.8
Philippines	28.2	23.5	20.5	33.7	40.5	35.9	38.1	36.0	43.6
Singapore	2.2	1.1	0.1	36.4	38.8	34.3	61.4	60.0	65.5
Taiwan	NA	7.9	2.9	NA	46.0	35.3	NA	46.1	61.8
Thailand	30.2	20.2	10.8	25.7	30.1	42.2	44.1	49.7	47.0
Middle-income countries	NA	NA	11.0	NA	NA	35.0	NA	NA	52.0
South Asia	38.4	36.2	24.8	23.5	23.4	27.5	44.1	40.5	47.8
Latin America	NA	10.0	10.0	NA	37.0	33.0	NA	38.0	55.0

Sources: *World Development Report* (various issues), *Key Indicators of Developing Asian and Pacific Countries* (various issues)

Table 2.3: Share of Manufacturing Value Added in GDP (%)

Economy	1965	1980	1995
Hong Kong	24	24	9
Indonesia	8	13	24
Korea	18	29	27
Malaysia	9	21	33
Philippines	20	26	29
Singapore	15	29	27
Taiwan	17	36	32
Thailand	14	22	29
Middle-income countries	20	NA	18
South Asia	15	15	17
Latin America	23	25	21

Sources: *World Development Report* (various issues), *Key Indicators of Developing Asian and Pacific Countries* (various issues)

now account for about 21 per cent of measured global production and around 22 per cent of world merchandise trade (Corbett & Vines 1998). They have become dominant trading partners of both European Union countries and the North American Free Trade Area (NAFTA), accounting for 21 and 42 per cent respectively. The East Asian NIEs rank among the top twenty and the ASEAN-4 rank among the top thirty exporters and importers in the world. It is not surprising that the world economy faced the prospect of significant slowing as a result of the Asian crisis, justifying the phrase 'when Asia sneezes, the world economy catches cold'.[2]

What was also remarkable about this spectacular economic transformation was its quality. Except for a few episodes, the phenomenal growth was achieved with reasonable price and balance of payments stability. Furthermore, as shown in Table 2.4, the rapid growth in income was accompanied by impressive advances in social development. While poverty, infant mortality, and adult illiteracy all declined significantly, life expectancy at birth and the overall quality of life (measured by the human development index) rose considerably. These impressive achievements led Hughes (1989) to label the East and Southeast Asian economies 'leaders in social development'. Like their rapid economic growth, the sustained decline in inequality also defied the conventional wisdom, codified in the Kuznets' inverted-U hypothesis that inequality first rises then declines with economic growth. The World Bank (1993a) has dubbed the phenomenon of rapid economic expansion with sharp declines in poverty and inequality as 'shared growth'.

Despite their achievements, these economies did suffer episodic distress (Chowdhury & Islam 1993). For example, Thailand experienced serious balance of payments problems in the late 1970s and early 1980s which required doses of International Monetary Fund (IMF)/World Bank structural adjustment programs. However, in the euphoria of rapid growth the episodes did not receive much attention. In an atmosphere of heightened optimism, HPAEs did not find it difficult to attract foreign capital to solve their problems. HPAEs were hailed for their ability to overcome their difficulties reasonably quickly. For example, the IMF termed Thailand's adjustment in the 1980s 'an excellent example of growth with adjustment' (Robinson et al. 1991: 1). No one imagined that the successful economies of Asia could have ever come down to earth with such rapidity as that experienced since mid 1997. The faith in Asia's ability to generate sustained economic growth is reflected in the Asian Development Bank's (ADB) projections into 2025 (see Table 2.5). The sharply downward-revised estimates show the depth of these economies' sudden fall from grace. Optimists, of course, could see in them not the depth of the fall but the heights to which the economies had risen. They may also point to these economies' remarkable resilience by highlighting their reasonably quick

Table 2.4: Social Development Indicators

Economy	Infant mortality[1] 1965	1995	Adult illiteracy[2] 1960	1995	Life expectancy[3] 1960	1995	Inequality (Gini coefficient)	Poverty[4] 1995	Human development Index 1994	Rank 1994
Hong Kong	38	5	29	8	63	79	0.41 (1991)	NA	0.668	22
Indonesia	132	51	53	16	40	64	0.34 (1994)	14.5	0.914	99
Korea	65	10	29	4	63	72	0.40 (1988)	NA	0.890	32
Malaysia	69	12	77	17	52	71	0.48 (1989)	17.0	0.832	60
Philippines	85	39	28	5	49	66	0.43 (1994)	27.5	0.672	98
Singapore	35	4	25 (1974)	9	63	76	0.49 (1989)	NA	0.900	26
Taiwan	31	4	36	10	64	72	0.31 (1990)	NA	NA	NA
Thailand	92	35	32	6	49	69	0.46 (1992)	0.1	0.833	59
Middle-income countries	97	39	61	18	49	68	NA	NA	0.576[5]	
South Asia	153	75	72	51	44	61	NA	NA	0.911[6]	
Latin America	165	92	34	13	51	69	NA	NA	0.764[7]	

Sources: *World Development Report* (various issues), *Key Indicators of Developing Asian and Pacific Countries* (various issues)

Notes: [1] per 1000 live births; [2] at birth; [3] %; [4] % of people living on less than $US1 a day (PPP); [5] all developing countries, [6] industrial countries, [7] world recovery, which defied all predictions. In fact, the recovery pattern can be characterised as a sharp-end V rather than a flat-bottom U.

Table 2.5: Projected Growth: Pre-crisis (1995–2025), post-crisis (1998, 1999)

Economy	Projected per capita GDP growth			Projected GDP growth	
	1995–2025	1998	1999	1998	1999
Hong Kong	2.8	0.5	1.5	3.0 (–5.0)	3.5 (0)
Indonesia	5.0	–1.4	–0.5	–3.0 (–15.0)	
Korea	3.5	–1.9	2.1	–1.0 (–7.0)	3.1(–1.0)
Malaysia	3.9	1.1	2.1	3.5 (–6.4)	4.5
Philippines	5.3	–0.4	1.2	2.4 (–0.6)	4.0
Singapore	2.5	0.4	3.2	3.0 (0)	4.5 (0.2)
Taiwan	3.1	5.0	5.4	5.0 (4.0)	6.2 (3.9)
Thailand	3.8	–4.7	–0.5	–3.0 (–8.0)	1.0

Sources: ADB (1997, 1998)

Note: Figures in parenthesis show the estimates of IMF (1998)

Just as in the past, although their ability to recover quickly may impress all, there is always a danger of complacency in maintaining the status quo. The ability to 'quick-fix' the episodic difficulties must not mask structural and institutional problems whose resolution is essential for the long-term sustainability of shared growth. As mentioned in chapter 1, a few observers have pointed out various weaknesses in the structure of the 'miracle' economies of Asia. Although none predicted such a sharp and sudden decline in the economies, they raised the prospect of a slow-down. Chowdhury and Islam (1993) in particular allude to the idea that the ability of the current institutional and political arrangements to deliver high growth may have come to an end. They emphasise the need for these developmental states to move to a more open and democratic society in order to sustain high growth. For example, in summarising their findings Chowdhury and Islam (1993: 251–5) make the following observations:

> What is germane to the guts of the analysis is that the central challenge facing the NIEs is the transition to innovation-driven development ... The East Asian NIEs have been remarkably successful in achieving factor-driven development ... What is crucial to the thrust of this discussion is that the internal

institutional framework has to adapt to facilitate the development sequencing from the factor-driven to the innovation-driven phase. Much has been made of the virtues of the 'strong state' in East Asia ... This has provided policy-makers with the capacity to pursue coherent economic policies ... but this framework is inappropriate in achieving innovation-driven development ... Emphasis has to shift from mass production to flexible production, from hierarchical control to decentralised governance, both at the level of the state and at the level of the firm ... In sum, the transition to innovation-driven economic progress entails a virtual reconstruction of the ideology of development. In carrying out such a reconstruction, the policy-makers in East Asia face twin pressures from the democratic reform movement and conservative hard-liners ... It remains to be seen how the much acclaimed East Asian policy-makers will juggle with these twin pressures in their bid to achieve advanced country status by the year 2000.

Walton (1997: 6) is more succinct:

East Asia has, in many respects, entered new territory in the pursuit of development. Past successes have sometimes led to problems being brushed under the carpet, and new issues are emerging ... But sustaining this momentum into the twenty-first century will require tackling the structural and institutional challenges ... The region's past success provides cause for optimism, but the transition to the next century will undoubtedly include interesting times.

While much has been said about the HPAEs' success and their strong fundamentals in terms of high savings and investment rates, disciplined and highly trained labour, and a well-developed physical infrastructure, this chapter will highlight some underlying weaknesses which led to the crisis. In particular, it will trace these weaknesses to the inability to make the transition to a more open and democratic society, which is essential for innovation-driven growth. The chapter will also reflect on some long-term issues which may have bearings on economic progress, the solutions for which must be found within a democratic framework. We begin with a brief overview of the causes of the East Asian crisis.

CAUSES OF EAST ASIAN CRISIS: AN OVERVIEW

The literature on the East Asian crisis is now voluminous as well as contentious. At the risk of oversimplifying, we can identify two approaches to the issue. One looks at exogenous factors, such as the volatility of private capital flows and the behaviour of foreign investors affecting such volatility. Here, the culprits are foreign investors and East Asia is the innocent victim of contagion and herd behaviour afflicting short-term capital flows. Private short-term capital surged into the East Asian region on a wave of irrational exuberance. Foreign investors then deserted the region in a stampede, provoked by exaggerated fears of deteriorating economic fundamentals. Such volatility wreaks havoc on individual economies.

Immediately prior to the crisis was the fall in the external demand for the region's key export commodities, such as electronics. Again, this was an external shock that was beyond the control of policymakers.

Compounding the malaise in the region is the problem of Japan. Weakened by mediocre growth throughout the 1990s and stymied by a looming domestic recession, Japan has failed to act as a locomotive. The 'Japan effect' is another example of an exogenous variable affecting the rest of East Asia.

Sachs (1997) and Radelet and Sachs (1998) are prominent examples of mainstream economists who subscribe to the exogenous theory of the Asian crisis and believe that the policy fundamentals that characterised success in the past are intact. Politicians within the region are certainly sympathetic to the theory, most notably Prime Minister Mahathir of Malaysia. He has made strident remarks about a Jewish conspiracy against Muslim Malaysia and, more generally, has expressed fears about the recolonisation of the region by Western capitalists.

Commentators representing international agencies—such as Stanley Fischer of the IMF (Fischer 1998b) and Joseph Stiglitz of the World Bank (Stiglitz 1997b)—certainly ascribe some importance to the exogenous theory of the crisis, but concede that domestic policy mistakes and institutional imperfections played a significant role in bringing about the crisis. Thus, the regional trauma originated from both exogenous and endogenous factors. In its report on the East Asian crisis, the World Bank (1998b) extends this explanation. The ADB (1998), in its annual survey of the region, concurs, as does the IMF (1998).

When focusing on domestic policy mistakes, the impression is given that the much-vaunted macroeconomic management capabilities of East Asian policy-makers apparently lapsed on the eve of the crisis. Many made important technical errors in exchange rate and monetary policies. In retrospect, they pursued what Frankel (1995) has called the 'impossible trinity'—simultaneous attempts to maintain stable exchange rates, financial openness, and independence in executing monetary policy.[3] This inconsistent policy mix eventually led to an appreciation of the real exchange rate, a widening of the current account deficit and external indebtedness with a preponderance of short-term maturities.

The crisis in the region also reflects a deeper problem of governance. It stems from a mix of political patronage, financial sector frailties, weak corporate governance, and lax bankruptcy laws. When this mix evolves in a context of capital account liberalisation, it can fuse a currency crisis and a financial crisis into a fatal phenomenon. Variations of this theme are now widely subscribed to—see, for example, Krugman (1998d, 1999c).

What used to be regarded as a virtuous case of close government–business interaction in East Asia (such as South Korea) is now regarded as crony capitalism or the politics of patronage. One example is the way financial institutions are cajoled or forced to extend loans to politically well-connected borrowers or to projects deemed to serve the national interest. In such a context, moral hazard can be a major problem: both lenders and borrowers feel that their actions are covered by implicit government guarantees. This provokes overindulgent behaviour. Lenders invest excessively in risky projects, and borrowers make seemingly imprudent borrowings. The consequences are rapid accumulation of private-sector indebtedness and asset price bubbles.

In a context of politics of patronage, prudent regulation and supervision of the financial sector becomes difficult and bankruptcy laws become lax. Thus, overindulgent behaviour by the private sector becomes institutionalised and sows the seeds of a financial crisis.

The weaknesses in the corporate governance structure of East Asian firms also contributed to the financial crisis. Such a structure may be characterised as an 'insider system' (Mayer 1996), where ownership and control are vested in families. 'This is', as the ADB (1998: 32) observes, 'equally true of the large Korean *chaebols* as of the companies owned by Chinese families in Indonesia and the Philippines'. The coupling of ownership and control can lead to a preference for borrowing from banks rather than the stock market because it enables firms to avoid shareholder intrusion into business affairs. The preference for bank borrowing is reinforced by implicit government guarantees.

Throughout the 1990s, the capital account was liberalised in many East Asian economies (Radelet & Sachs 1999). Private short-term capital flows to East Asia surged. Such flows were driven partly by perceived economic fundamentals of East Asia based on past performance, partly by the false sense of security that stemmed from the implicit government guarantees, and partly from the expectation that foreign investors would be bailed out either by their governments or by the IMF. The counterpart of such capital flows was the acquisition of large-scale, short-term liabilities denominated in foreign currency by the corporate sector and financial institutions in East Asia.

When the robustness of economic growth in East Asia began to be questioned in the wake of the 1996 export slow-down, investor confidence—both domestic and foreign—turned sour. The ensuing speculative attack led to depreciating currencies. As the crisis developed and capital flight persisted, the combination of depreciating currencies and falling asset prices resulted in large-scale insolvency among the corporate sector and financial institutions. Currency crises thus became full-fledged financial crises. When governments responded to these traumatic developments with sharp rises in interest rates, fiscal contractions, and credit restraints, often with the urging of the IMF, full-blown recessions ensued. Millions have been pushed back into poverty, threatening to wipe out the historically unprecedented gains of the previous three decades.

This is, in brief, the complex story of the East Asian crisis. Obviously, the generality of the explanation ignores country-specific details. The fact that some economies have been affected a lot more than others implies that the domestic forces behind the crisis were more prevalent in some countries than in others. Unfortunately, for reasons that are not yet fully understood, currency crises and financial turbulence tend to occur in regional waves. Such contagious behaviour can thus end up punishing both weak and strong economies.

The full story of the East Asian crisis is yet to be told but, from a policy perspective, a great deal hinges on one's convictions. If the crisis is believed to be the product of exogenous factors, then its solution lies in international assistance to the affected economies and reform of the global financial system. If the crisis is believed to be primarily the product of domestic policy errors and embedded institutional imperfections, a sustainable solution involves large-scale institutional reform. The current thinking seems to suggest a broad-based approach that emphasises both global and country-specific solutions to the crisis. East Asian policy-makers and the global financial community are occupied with solving the crisis, but the resumption of rapid growth in East Asia also requires assessment of the range of emerging social concerns identified in the pre-crisis literature (human rights, environmental degradation, the need for productivity-driven growth etc.).

BOX 2.1: THE SINGAPORE DILEMMA

Singapore has nominally a Westminster-type parliamentary democracy, but the government is not very keen on allowing opposition. The Singapore government maintains tight control of the political process for the sake of stability, which is crucial for the economic progress of the island nation. In February 1998, the government passed a Bill outlawing political films and allowing authorities to fine or imprison the producers, importers, and distributors of such films. It defines a political film as one that is made by a political party, directed toward a political end, or includes partisan or biased views on issues of public controversy.

However, the lack of freedom of speech (self-censorship) is at odds with the government's desire to proceed to an innovation-driven phase of economic development. This dilemma has been wonderfully captured by Dr Lee Yuan: 'Notoriously conservative Singapore needs to embrace creativity and risk if it's to insure its future'. She fears that without the spark of innovation, the city-state will be unable to shift from traditional manufacturing to knowledge-based businesses.

Democracy allows for an environment conducive to scientific advancement. Free enquiry, healthy scepticism, and scrutiny of facts are the basic requirements of science. Yet she is ambivalent about the image of a truly open, questioning society: 'once you go down that road, there's no return'. She worries about anarchy and lawlessness. The examples of neighbouring Indonesia and Malaysia are too frightening.

This sentiment was shared by Prime Minister Goh in an interview with the *Far Eastern Economic Review*, in which he said that he was not trying to change an entire system that has brought stability and dramatic growth for thirty-three years, 'But in the new world when you have to compete against others in terms of ideas ... you just can't be looking towards a paternalistic government all the time. So, this is the kind of dilemma which we are in: How paternalistic should we be, and how much room can we give to the people?'

Singapore is trying to create a thinking society, starting with schools loosening their very strict syllabus or emphasising case studies, leaving more time for students to do project works. The government is aware of the irony: Is it possible to teach creativity? The government is prepared to give it a try.

Sources: *Far Eastern Economic Review*, 16 July, 17 December, 24 December 1998

INVESTMENT-DRIVEN GROWTH: PERSPIRATION VS INSPIRATION

What has been alluded to by Chowdhury and Islam (1993) in terms of the challenge of transition from a factor-driven phase to an innovation-driven phase has been captured by famous debate dubbed 'perspiration vs inspiration', sparked by Krugman (1994). The extraordinarily rapid growth of East Asia in a context of rich endowments of human capital creates the presumption that such growth must be productivity-driven. Unfortunately, the available evidence is rather different—at least according to some observers.

Tables 2.6 and 2.7 present various estimates of the contribution of technological progress to the growth of output per worker by using the conventional growth accounting approach (for alternative estimates see Hsieh 1999; Dowling & Summers 1998; Crafts 1998). Despite some variations, the overall picture is that the contribution of total factor productivity (TFP) to growth in East and Southeast Asian economies has not been very significant. These estimates are broadly consistent

Table 2.6: Total Factor Productivity Growth in East Asia

Economy	Young (1966–90)	World Bank (high-income sample) 1960–89	Bosworth & Collins (1960–94)	Sarel (1979–96)
Hong Kong	2.3	2.4	NA	3.8 (1975–90)
Indonesia	NA	−0.8	0.8	0.9
Korea	1.7	0.2	1.5	3.1 (1975–90)
Malaysia	NA	−1.3	0.9	2.0
Philippines	NA	NA	−0.4	−0.9
Singapore	0.2	−3.0	1.5	2.5; 1.9 (1975–90)
Taiwan	2.1	1.3	2.0	3.5 (1975–90)
Thailand		0.5	1.8	2.0
OECD	1.0	NA	1.1[1]	NA
South Asia		NA	0.8	NA
Latin America	1.3	−1.0	0.2	NA

Sources: Young (1995), World Bank (1993a), Bosworth & Collins (1996), Sarel (1996, 1997)

Notes: OECD average (seven countries) and Latin American average (seven countries); [1] industrial countries *minus* USA

Table 2.7: Total Productivity Results: Kim & Lau (average annual growth rates %)

Economy/approach Meta-production function	Contributions of sources of growth			
	Output	Capital	Labour	Technical progress
Hong Kong	7.8	3.7	1.3	2.7
Korea	8.6	5.8	1.6	1.2
Singapore	8.9	4.9	2.0	2.0
Taiwan	8.7	6.3	1.1	1.3
Average of five industrial countries[1]	3.8	1.4	0.1	2.4
Conventional TFP approach	**Output**	**Capital**	**Labour**	**Technical progress**
Hong Kong	7.8	4.3	1.4	2.1
Korea	8.6	7.9	1.2	−0.5
Singapore	8.9	6.9	1.6	0.4
Taiwan	8.7	6.8	1.1	0.8
Average of five industrial countries[1]	3.8	2.3	0.2	1.3

Note: [1] The five industrial countries are France, West Germany, Japan, the United Kingdom and USA with the view that the contribution of capital growth has been significantly greater than TFP contribution. For some countries, the finding is more striking, as depicted by negative contributions of TFP.

What implications follow from the estimates presented in the above tables? There are critics who would be concerned about the volatility of the estimates and would raise concerns about their reliability. Indeed, Young (1995: 666) reports six studies of TFP (including his own) in the Korean economy, with estimates ranging from 1.3 per cent to 4.1 per cent. Although he makes a serious effort to resolve the discrepancies, critics are unlikely to be placated. Hence, what has really happened to TFP in East Asia will be the source of contention for some time (for comprehensive surveys see Crafts 1998; Chen 1997; Ito 1997).

Another reaction to the TFP estimates is to adopt a comparative approach and argue that, although the record is not extraordinarily good, it is still better than elsewhere (see World Bank 1993a). According to those (e.g. Radelet & Sachs 1997) who believe that TFP growth has made a greater contribution, deceleration in economic growth is inevitable as a result of technological catch-up, but it is still possible to sustain relatively high rates of growth at lower rates of factor accumulation.

Young (1995), however, argues that one must confront the implications of the 'statistical realities of the East Asian growth experience'. Moderate TFP growth in conjunction with virtually unprecedented rapid growth in GDP in East Asia must mean that most of it is due to factor accumulation and one-shot structural change. As Young (1995: 674–6) observes:

> The remarkable postwar rise in East Asian living standards is primarily the result of one-shot increases in output brought about by the rise in participation rates, investment to GDP ratios, and educational standards and the intersectoral transfer of labour to other sectors ... with higher value added per worker.

Kim and Lau (1994: 266) react to their findings with considerable concern:

> It is troubling to find that despite their high rates of growth and rapid capital accumulation, the East Asian [NIEs] have actually experienced a significant decline in their productive efficiency relative to the United States. As their capital stock continues to grow,

the capital elasticity will continue to decline, and the increases in the capital input alone will not be sufficient for the East Asian [NIEs] to maintain their current rate of economic growth. It will be necessary for the East Asian [NIEs] to devote greater resources to research and development and to innovation in order to attain a positive growth in productive efficiency ... It may also be necessary for the East Asian [NIEs] to upgrade further the quality of their investment in human capital and in the software necessary to realise the full productive potential of technology.

In sum, the Krugman hypothesis can by no means be dismissed, although it is difficult to support it conclusively. By engaging in a provocative discourse on the need to shift to productivity-driven growth as the only effective insurance against an economic slow-down, Krugman has certainly asked the right questions. Countries seeking to learn from East Asia cannot ignore the Krugman hypothesis.

BOX 2.2: DEVELOPMENT AND DEMOCRACY

Both Karl Marx and Max Weber recognised the historical development in the West where the bourgeois class played the most significant role in democratisation. The bourgeois class considers that an authoritarian system where trades and industries are significantly monopolised by royalty or the state is inimical to its development; democracy is the alternative where it can achieve economic power. Thus, capitalist development leads to democratisation of the polity.

Authors such as Lipset (1959), Cutright (1963), and Bollen (1983) have demonstrated a high degree of correlation between economic development and democratisation. Two arguments are given to support the hypothesis that economic development causes democracy. First, through better education and awareness economic development allows people a substantial role in politics and public affairs. Second, economic development turns a relatively passive and homogenous society into a more mobile and stratified society where various groups compete for the state's favour. This necessitates a system which is more transparent and accountable (see Hewison, Robison & Rodan 1993). Once the initial, and necessarily painful, step towards self-sustained growth is accomplished, progressive affluence will generate demands for political liberalisation and the system will eventually respond to those demands—a proposition that forms part of modernisation theory.

Harris (1988) extends the economic development–democracy nexus to highlight the particular nature of capitalist development. He maintains that when a Third World capitalist economy moves to export-oriented industrialisation, a new kind of bourgeoisie emerges. Having to compete in the global market, they press for a more liberal and privatised economy. Thus, the authoritarian state which initially propels the economy along the path of accelerated development and creates the new bourgeoisie class, becomes the enemy of its own creation.

Certain authors, such as Crouch and Morley (1993) and Pye (1990), emphasise the level of development—rather than just economic development or growth—that is crucial for democratisation. According to them, the higher the level of development, the more advanced is the democratic polity. Thus, there is a spectrum of countries where poorer countries are authoritarian, middle-income countries are semi-democracies and more industrialised countries are democratic.

This analysis fits reasonably well with the countries of East and Southeast Asia. The drive for democratisation in the region could well be interpreted as the result of economic affluence and economic liberalisation. As Laothamas (1997: 7) observes, 'It is probably not a mere coincidence that the economic structural adjustment reforms that entail the privatisation and globalisation of the economy in East and Southeast Asia in the early 1980s were closely followed by the democratisation wave of the late 1980s'. However, drawing on Fukuyama (1992), Laothamas (1997: 17) emphasises that coincidence and causality are not the same. Democratisation is a political-ideological process and for democracy to exist there must be a vibrant civil society and a 'desire for universal and equal recognition' (Fukuyama 1992).

EFFICIENCY OF INVESTMENT

An alternative approach to the productivity debate is advocated by Kasa (1997), who draws on the pioneering work of Diamond (1965) and subsequent analytical refinements by Abel et al. (1989). He focuses on a notion of dynamic efficiency at the national level: if gross investment consistently exceeds gross capital income 'then the financial sector is draining resources from the economy. This is inefficient, since the whole point of investment is to augment future consumption possibilities' (Kasa 1997: 3). An economy that is dynamically inefficient is unlikely to be characterised by high productivity growth. Applying this method to Singapore using 1975–95 data allows him to suggest—or at least does not allow him to rule out the possibility— that Singapore is overinvesting and is dynamically inefficient, unlike the G-7 countries (including Japan), which, by this criterion, are dynamically efficient. The IMF reports a similar finding for Korea: between the mid 1970s and mid 1990s, the share of total capital income in GDP fell substantially (from 55 per cent to less than 40 per cent) whereas the share of total investment in GDP rose from 25 per cent to about 40 per cent (IMF 1998).

Further evidence of excessive capital accumulation or overinvestment can also be found in declining profitability or returns on capital. For example, according to Radelet and Sachs (1997) the rate of return on capital in Korea declined from around 22 per cent in the mid 1980s to 19 per cent in the mid 1990s. They also report falling rates of return in Hong Kong and Taiwan from around 21 per cent to 15 per cent. In Singapore, the rate of return on foreign direct investment (FDI) fell from 27 per cent in the late 1980s to 19 per cent in the mid 1990s.

Another indication of investment inefficiency is the increased proportion of investment in non-traded or protected sectors such as real estate or petrochemicals, which generated low returns, or in sectors such as semiconductors, steel, ships, and automobiles which had high or excess capacity. For example, in Thailand the value added in construction and real estate sector grew during 1992–96, resulting in an office space vacancy rate of 15 per cent by the end of 1996. The same phenomenon was observable in another two crisis countries— Malaysia and Indonesia. Korea, on the other hand, made excessive investment in the steel, ships, semiconductors, and automobile sectors (Corsetti, Pesenti & Roubini 1998).

Figure 2.1: Efficiency of Investment in Selected Economies (share of capital income and total investment in GDP, %)

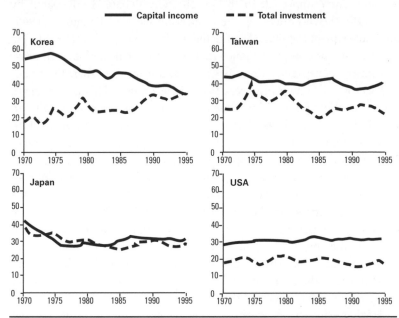

Note: Given differences in the way the income of the self-employed is treated, cross-country comparisons of capital income should be interpreted with care

Sources: Korean National Statistical Office; Taiwan Directorate-General of Budget, Accounting, and Statistics; World Economic Outlook database, OECD database; IMF staff estimates. Taken from IMF (1998)

The rate of non-performing loans before the crisis was above 15 per cent in Thailand, Indonesia, and Malaysia (Corsetti, Pesenti & Roubini 1998). As Table 2.8 shows, the profitability in major Korean chaebols declined in 1996. According to Corsetti, Pesenti and Roubini (1998), in 1996, twenty of the largest Korean conglomerates had a rate of return below the cost of capital, and by mid 1997 eight of the thirty largest Korean conglomerates were virtually bankrupt.

Table 2.8: Profitability of Korean Chaebols (%)

Chaebols	1992–95	1996
Hanbo	3.0	1.7
Sammi	2.9	3.2
Jinro	2.7	1.9
Kia	18.9	8.7
Dainong	6.8	5.5

Source: Lee (1997) cited in Corsetti , Pesenti & Roubini (1998)

From a macroeconomic perspective, a standard indicator of investment efficiency is incremental capital-output ratio (ICOR), which provides an estimate of the additional investment required for producing an extra unit of output (GDP). A rising ICOR may be interpreted as indicating a declining output response to investment, and hence a falling efficiency of investment.[4] Table 2.9 and Figure 2.2 present estimates of ICOR in selected Asian economies.

Table 2.9: Incremental Capital Output Ratio

	1987–92	1993–96	1987–89	1990–92	1993–95
East Asia					
Hong Kong	3.7	6.1	NA	NA	NA
Korea	3.8	4.9	3.5	5.1	5.1
Singapore	3.6	4	NA	NA	NA
Taiwan	2.4	3.9	NA	NA	NA
ASEAN-4					
Indonesia	4	3.8	4.0	3.9	4.4
Malaysia	3.7	4.8	3.6	4.4	5.0
Philippines	6	5.5	3.3	22.8	6.0
Thailand	3.4	5.1	2.9	4.6	5.2
China		3.1	2.9		

Sources: Corsetti, Pesenti & Roubini (1998); Radelet & Sachs (1998). Taken from IMF (1998)

As can be seen, in almost all the crisis countries ICORs increased, indicating that the efficiency of investment in these economies generally declined during the 1990s. However, this should be interpreted cautiously as ICORs do not allow for lags between investment and changes in output, hence capital upgrading may also result in a temporary rise in ICORs. But it is unlikely that it was happening. For example, given the similarity in their economic and trade structure, there is no reason to believe that Thailand was upgrading its technology and Indonesia was not. Likewise, the difference in the behaviour of ICORs in the very similar economies of Singapore and Hong Kong cannot be explained by their different rates of capital upgrading.

BOX 2.3: DEMOCRACY, 'ASIAN VALUES', AND ECONOMIC DEVELOPMENT

The discussion in Box 2.2 implied that economic development must precede democratisation. More than three decades ago Bhagwati (1966: 204) argued that developing nations faced a 'cruel choice between rapid (self-sustained) expansion and

**Figure 2.2: Incremental Capital Output Ratios
(five-year moving average): Selected Economies**

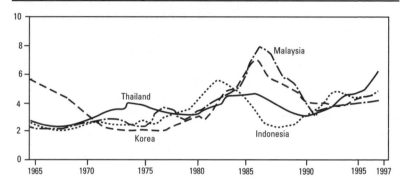

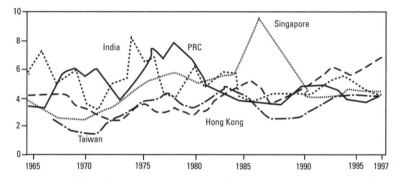

Source: IMF (1998)

democratic processes'. This appears sensible when economic
growth is driven primarily by capital accumulation. The political implication of this line of thinking is that authoritarian
regimes would be better able than democracies to raise investment and saving rates to levels that would promote and
sustain economic growth. Why?

> authoritarian regimes would be able to extract a greater
> surplus from their populations through taxation and
> 'takings' ... than democracies. The latter, after all, ha[ve]
> to persuade voters to pay the needed taxes and make
> other necessary sacrifices' (Bhagwati 1995: 53).

The 'Asian values' argument is part of the new version of the 'cruel choice' hypothesis. It would be fair to say that the Asian values hypothesis has attracted considerable attention and, superficially at least, seems to have credibility. Two factors in particular have played a role in its current status. First, the spectacular economic transformation of the region occurred under authoritarian (or at best semi-democratic) regimes. Second, there is the perceived decline of the liberal democratic West—most notably the USA—as a centre of economic power, but more importantly as a bearer of moral standards. To some sections of East Asian society, rampant crime, breakdown of the family, and racial tensions are seen as typically US problems that have tarnished the USA as a worthy exemplar.

US scholars have added substance to adverse perceptions about liberal democratic regimes. There is the well-known view of Olson (1982) that mature democracies have built-in mechanisms for stagnation through the institutionalisation of distributional coalitions. A more recent variant of this argument is the hypothesis of demosclerosis, that is alleged to be the 'silent killer' of good governance in the USA (Rauch 1994).

The new version of the cruel choice arguments also has a cultural dimension. The emphasis is now on discipline and the need to maintain social cohesion as key ingredients of economic development (Hewison, Robison & Rodan 1993). As Lee Kuan Yew puts it: 'what a country needs ... is discipline more than democracy. The exuberance of democracy leads to indiscipline and disorderly conduct which are inimical to development' (*Economist*, 27 August 1994: 15–17; see also Zakaria 1994). Discipline in turn is the product of core 'Asian values'—a generic term that is used here in preference to 'Confucian' values because its ideological appeal cuts across both Confucian (such as the PRC and Singapore) and non-Confucian societies (such as Malaysia). Note that the Lee Kuan Yew thesis does not even seem to condone the sequential 'development first, democracy later' approach. Instead, it seems to suggest paternalistic authoritarianism (buttressed by nominally democratic institutions, such as free elections) as a durable political system.

Fukuyama (1995a: 12) maintains that Lee Kuan Yew is not alone in that view. Such overt anti-democratic sentiment has also been expounded by Malaysian intellectuals and officials, in particular by Mahathir: 'many people in Asian societies have come to share [such] beliefs' (Fukuyama 1995b: 20). This prompts him to warn that 'Asian paternalistic authoritarianism' is the 'most serious new competitor to liberal democracy' (Fukuyama 1995a: 11).

Lee Kuan Yew and Dr Mahathir's views have been contested by other political leaders in the region. Burma's democracy leader Ms Ang San Suu Kyi and democratically elected President Kim Dae Jung are among the Asian leaders who have argued that human rights and freedom are universal values, and Malaysia's deposed Deputy Prime Minister Anwar Ibrahim claims that 'no Asian tradition can be cited to support the proposition that in Asia the individual must melt into a faceless community' (*Economist* 1998: 24). The Forum of Democratic Leaders in the Asia–Pacific Region, located in Seoul, commits itself to refuting the 'false judgement that the Asia–Pacific region is devoid of historical legacy and cultural heritage suitable for democracy' (Documents on Democracy 1995: 186).

There is an emerging rift in ideas and opinions about the relationship between Asian values and democracy in the region—a rift that follows the ideological divide between new democracies and their non-democratic or quasi-democratic counterparts. Moreover, the Asian values hypothesis has considerable limitations.

First, the weight of theory and evidence suggests that core Asian values are neither necessary nor sufficient for rapid growth (Chowdhury & Islam 1993: ch. 2). The lack of progress in imperial China and Korea—quintessential Confucian regimes—bear witness to this.

Second, Fukuyama (1995b) has made the point that Confucianism is compatible with democratic traditions, once we move away from its emphasis on discipline and social cohesion. The Confucian emphasis on self-improvement through education, non-discriminatory, and meritocratic examination systems encourages social mobility and spawns a middle class that provides a durable basis for democratic transitions. However, once core Asian/Confucian values are diluted to this level of generality, they lose their distinctiveness and become part of universal human values.

Third, it may well be that the Asian values hypothesis is essentially an argument that tries to justify the current political order in parts of East Asia and, like all state-sanctioned ideology, is not really intended to be a carefully constructed, intellectually rigorous proposition. Indeed Fukuyama (1995b: 28) makes the controversial claim that a Lee Kuan Yew-type hypothesis is simply a weapon of political control because, paradoxically, Sinitic societies exhibit a culturally ingrained distrust of state authority and low level of 'spontaneous citizenship'.

See Haggard (1999) for a review of literature on the link between regime type and economic growth, and Lee (1998) for a critique of Asian values.

INFRASTRUCTURE BOTTLENECKS

As Figure 2.3 shows, the share of public investment in GDP in East and Southeast Asian economies has declined dramatically since the mid 1980s. This is consistent with a worldwide trend since financial sector liberalisation led to the rise of the international capital market. Governments are now under constant pressure from the financial market to balance their budgets (discussed further in chapter 3). Historically, governments in HPAEs invested heavily in infrastructure and human capital, which increased the productivity of private investment and international competitiveness as explained by the new growth theory (Barro 1997; Lucas 1988; Mankiw 1995; Romer

Figure 2.3: Public Investment/GDP (%) (average, East and Southeast Asia)

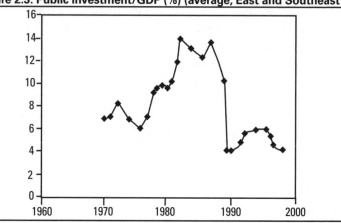

Sources: *Key Indicators of Developing Asian and Pacific Countries* (various issues)

1990). As pointed out by Walton (1997), the decline in public capital expenditure was not matched by increased private investment. Even with nearly $US9 billion of foreign capital inflows into East Asia during 1995–96, private capital amounted to only 10 per cent of total infrastructure spending (Walton 1997). This had serious consequences when the importance of maintaining the competitive edge of telecommunications, transport, power, and other infrastructure services continued to increase.

It is estimated that East Asia will need new infrastructure amounting to $US1.2–1.5 trillion by 2010 if it is to grow at the projected rates of 6–8 per cent. The most acute need is in the power and electricity sector—total investment of about $US550 billion is required for the necessary upgrading of power generation, transmission, and distribution (Malhotra 1997).

BOX 2.4: RISKS TO DEMOCRACY IN EAST AND SOUTHEAST ASIA

More representative and accountable political systems seem to be gradually emerging in Southeast and Northeast Asia, but the transition to democracy is an intractable process. As Huntington (1996: 6) has pointed out, 'the difficulties that new democracies face include problems inherited from their authoritarian predecessors, as well as others peculiar to democracy and democratising societies ... the process of democratisation itself can also create or exacerbate other problems with which new democracies must then grapple'. Thus, doubts remain about whether the transition to democracy in various countries of East and Southeast Asia is widespread and durable (Alagappa 1995).

Two factors that may derail the democratisation process are the growing racial tension and the rise in separatist movements in the region. Ironically, although the financial crisis triggered the democratisation process (and in some countries has accelerated it), it also removed the lid on racial tensions and the autonomy (independence) aspirations of minorities. Although these racial tensions may not amount to Huntington's 'clash of civilisation', the military and the ruling elite can easily use the argument of stability and national integrity to maintain or regain power. We must also recognise the fact that institutions that protect civil society are either non-existent or very weak in the nascent democracies.

First, we will consider Taiwan and South Korea, widely regarded as in a phase of democratic consolidation. The biggest challenge for Taiwan is that democratically elected governments may adopt a more aggressive stance against the PRC. This may heighten tensions, generate demands for stronger national security, and provide the basis for a renewed military role in Taiwanese politics. The prospect of the opposition leader, Chen Shu-bian, winning the 2000 election raised the cross-strait tension. However, since his election as the first non-KMT president, he has taken a much more conciliatory stance, which is a very promising sign for maturing democracy in Taiwan.

In addition to corruption, horse-trading among political parties is still very much part of the political process in South Korea, and there is a concentration of power in the executive. As in the case of Taiwan, national security considerations due to the perceived threat of a North Korean invasion loom large. Despite discussions about reunification, relations with North Korea remain tense, posing the risk that the situation could be manipulated by the military to reassert its role in South

Korean politics. The risk may, however, diminish after the summit between the leaders of North and South Korea.

Democracy returned to Thailand after a bloody mass uprising in 1992. However, political parties in Thailand are fractured along regional lines, have weak organisational structures, and are so numerous that they generate a need for potentially unstable coalition governments. Three governments fell in two years after the economic crisis in 1997. Although the Thai military remains a central force in Thai politics and casts a shadow on the durability of civilian governance, there are some encouraging signs since the appointment of General Surayud as army chief in 1998. General Surayud has initiated major reforms in the army. He has declared politics off-limits to army personnel and set an example by giving up his Senate seat.

The same cannot be said of Indonesia, which got its first democratically elected president in 1999 after thirty years of military rule. The army is still represented in the cabinet and remains a force to be reckoned with. The separation of East Timor and the growing demands for independence by resource-rich Aceh and Irian Jaya are constant causes of concern. The military can easily utilise the concern for national integrity to re-enter politics. The Civil Defence Minister, Dr Juwono Sudarsono, has alluded to the threat of a military takeover: 'If civilian leaders aren't able to develop a healthy and independent political life then we will return to a military rule sooner or later just like we find in Pakistan and some African countries' (*Sydney Morning Herald*, 24 November 1999: 12).

In the case of the Philippines, little substantive progress has been made since the restoration of democracy in 1986. Politics is controlled by old political clans and dominated by pork-barrelling and patronage. The shadow of Marcos still looms large. The legal system is weakened by widespread corruption and inaccessible to most citizens. Furthermore, the independence of East Timor has added fuel to the separatist movement of Moro nationalists. The regime can use the threat of constant communist insurgency and regional separatist movements to curtail civil rights. The Philippines also has geopolitical problems arising from the PRC, Malaysia, and Vietnam's claims to oil-rich islands in the South China Sea.

Singapore and Malaysia are the only cases of long-standing and well-functioning democracies in the Asia–Pacific region in a formal sense. They have free elections and the rule of law is well-established relative to regional standards. Political scientists, however, are inclined to treat them as semi-democracies. A dominant party has been in power for a long time; the opposition is weak, and the personalities of particular leaders—Mahathir in Malaysia and Lee Kuan Yew in Singapore—are writ large on the body politic. Although Lee Kuan Yew has formally stepped down from prime ministership his legacy of tight political control remains intact, particularly in the way dissidents are treated. The sacking of Deputy Prime Minister Anwar Ibrahim highlights the way politics is conducted in Malaysia, and Mahathir's leadership style. Also, political and regional instability in Indonesia is constantly cited by the ruling party as a case against political liberalisation in Singapore and Malaysia.

The PRC is a fascinating case for observers of the democratisation process in the Asia–Pacific region. Limited political liberalisation was undertaken in combination with market-oriented reforms by the Chinese Communist Party (CCP) in 1979. A salient feature of this political transformation was the self-liberalisation of the PRC's mass media in the 1980s. In allowing such limited changes, the CCP chose what Pei (1994) has called the 'evolutionary authoritarian route', in which a market-based economy is allowed to consolidate before full democratisation sets in. However, as the notorious June 1989 Tiananmen Square incident demonstrated, the government is prepared to use force to suppress mass-based pro-democracy movements. At this juncture, the PRC runs the risk of being stuck at the 'politically disreputable half-way point of market authoritarianism' (Prybala 1995: 165). The CCP is the greatest obstacle to the emergence of a democratic system. It is antagonistic towards any organised opposition and its separation from the government, which are essential ingredients of a viable democratic system. A judiciary independent of the executive government is a long way from reality, and hence is vulnerable to interference by party officials due to the symbiotic relationship between the CCP and the government (see *Far Eastern Economic Review*, 9 December 1999).

In sum, Huntington's (1991) 'third wave' may not prove decisive enough to overwhelm non-democratic regimes in the region. As evident in the case of Malaysia and Singapore, opposing camps may try to use forces unleashed by successful development for their political interest. 'The question of whether development will pave the way to democracy is still open' (Laothamas 1997:15).

LONG-TERM ISSUES

The discussion so far has focused on some aspects of structural weakness which began to develop in the mid 1980s, and contributed to the decline in productivity prior to the onset of the crisis. Various social and economic issues are also likely to impede HPAEs' capability to sustain rapid growth in the long run. Environmental degradation, worsening inequality, labour relations, and demographic change are likely to be particularly challenging.

Protection and management of the environment

It is generally agreed that the East Asian region has a poor record in a range of environmental indicators (see Table 2.10). As the ADB (1997: 200) proclaims: 'For far too long, Asian policy-makers ignored the environmental impact of rapid growth. Concern about pollution or degradation was simply not a priority'. Fifteen of the seventeen indicators pertaining to air and water pollution, access to safe water and sanitation, deforestation and land degradation, and energy consumption in East Asia show either 'very severe' or 'severe' environmental problems (ADB 1997: Table 4.1, 203). Most Southeast Asian countries rely heavily on the export of their natural resources to import capital goods to support rapid growth. This has resulted in a rapid clearance of land. For example, in Malaysia, the area of land under cultivation increased from 15 per cent to 23 per cent between 1980 and 1994. In the same period, the area of land under cultivation in Thailand rose from 36 per cent to 41 per cent. Their forestry policies have failed to implement sustainable harvesting. In Indonesia, for example, the annual sustainable harvest is estimated as 22 million m³, but annual production exceeds 40 million m³. As a result of overdependence on natural resources, HPAEs have lost more of their forest area in the last few decades than any other region (World Bank 1998b: 102).

Table 2.10: Environmental Indicators

Countries	Carbon dioxide emissions per capita (tonnes)		Energy use (oil equivalent) Average annual growth rate		Annual deforestation (% change)
	1980	1992	1980–90	1990–94	1980–90
Indonesia	0.6	1.0	7.4	9.3	1.1
Hong Kong	3.3	5.0	7.0	7.7	−0.5
Korea	3.3	6.6	8.5	10.2	0.1
Malaysia	2.0	3.8	9.4	11.2	2.1
Philippines	0.7	0.8	2.6	8.3	3.4
Singapore	13.2	17.7	7.2	10.5	2.3
Taiwan	NA	NA	NA	NA	NA
Thailand	1.9	1.7	9.5	10.0	3.5
Middle-income countries	2.9	4.8	NA	NA	0.5
South Asia	0.4	0.7	7.0	5.1	0.8
Latin America	2.4	2.3	2.5	2.7	0.7

Source: *World Development Report* (various issues)

The economic and social costs of environmental degradation are enormous. World Bank estimates suggest that the annual cost of air pollution is as high as $US3.1 billion in Bangkok, $US1.6 billion in Kuala Lumpur, and $US800 million in Jakarta. The estimates would be as much as 40 per cent higher if they included costs due to congestion (Brandon 1994: 22). As a proportion of GDP, economic costs stemming from environmental damage appear to be as high as 8.5 per cent in the PRC (Smil 1996) and 1–2 per cent in Indonesia, the Philippines, and Thailand (World Bank 1992, 1993c).

What factors have led to this evidence of environmental degradation? To some extent, it is a byproduct of factor-driven rapid economic growth and consequent urbanisation. One of the drawbacks of investment-driven or capital-intensive industrialisation is that it is inevitably energy-intensive, notorious for emission-related pollution. However, to a considerable extent the evidence reflects more deep-seated problems: the lack of political will and governance to tackle environmental problems; and widespread market failures compounded by inefficient policies, such as sub-optimal pricing of infrastructure services. Hammer and Shetty (1995: 11) point to the inadequate nature of property rights in parts of East Asia as a major source of failure in environmental management. They observe:

> In China, unsustainable forestry practices for obtaining fuelwood and building materials can be directly linked to the lack of clear property rights. In Indonesia and Malaysia, encroachment by illegal loggers and conflicts over the use of public lands are also a product of unclear or unenforced property rights.

The countries of East Asia are slowly beginning to recognise the need for much greater vigilance in managing and maintaining environmental standards. This awareness is due primarily to two factors. First, an assertive domestic middle class is increasingly demanding reduced air, water, and noise pollution. Second, industrialised countries are imposing stiffer environmental standards on trade. For example, there is a move to label all imported timber products whether or not they are from sustainably harvested forests. Thus, the long-term viability of export-oriented HPAEs depends on improving their environmental standards.

The re-emergence of inequality

A common view, reaffirmed by Fields (1995: 103), is that the East Asian economies are characterised by moderate degrees of inequality and that trends have generally been egalitarian. New evidence suggests a less optimistic interpretation:

> The available data indicate that the distribution of income in ... [East Asia] has shown a tendency to become more unequal in recent years. This is in contrast to their earlier periods of

development where income inequality declined as the economies grew (Medhi 1994: 70).

Other observers have also highlighted cases of growing inequality in East Asia.[5] Focusing on the PRC and Thailand, Walton (1997: 5) notes that they bear the dubious distinction of registering one of the highest increases in inequality in the developing world in recent decades. These findings have been corroborated by the World Bank (1998b), which shows that inequality has risen in the PRC, Hong Kong, Thailand, and the Philippines. The World Bank (1998b) has attributed the rise in inequality to two factors: a rise in returns to higher education, which has driven a wedge between the earnings of skilled and unskilled workers; and a concentration of economic activities in certain areas, which has contributed to regional income disparity.

High inequality undermines poverty alleviation. Despite substantial reductions of poverty in HPAEs, the World Bank (1998b: 77) study shows that people remain vulnerable. For example, a 25 per cent increase in the poverty line more than doubles the head-count index from eleven to twenty-five. It also reports a high incidence of poverty in pockets of regions. For instance, in 1990, the poverty incidence in Indonesia ranged from 1.3 per cent in Jakarta to 46 per cent in West Nusa Tenggara. Likewise, the northeast of Thailand has that country's highest incidence of poverty and highest concentration of poor people.

The re-emergence of inequality (see Table 2.11) is a cause of concern, particularly in ethnically diverse societies such as Indonesia and Malaysia. If the inequality is thought to be due to one group's grasp of economic power, this may trigger social tension and race riots, as occurred in 1965 and during the recent economic crisis in Indonesia, and in 1969 in Malaysia. It could sow the seeds of demand for redistributive measures, which retard growth through policy distortions. Such a phenomenon is characterised as 'distributive politics'. The World Bank (1997: 3) has given the 'new' view of the growth-retarding effects of inequality a broader interpretation. As it observes:

> Growing inequality is of concern: an increase in inequality is not only likely to slow down the rate of poverty reduction ... it is also damaging in its own right, given the value that East Asian societies place on social cohesion, relative income inequality, and parity of opportunities. Finally, inequality may hamper future growth through either imperfect capital markets leading to credit

constraints and lower productivity or efficiency; or through increased voter support for inefficient redistributive policies.

Thus, the re-emergence of inequality can negatively affect HPAEs in at least three ways: making people more vulnerable to poverty, impeding economic growth, and contributing to social tension.

Labour relations

There is wide agreement that most HPAEs maintained relatively unfettered labour markets during their early stage of economic transformation at the expense of workers' rights. For example, until the late 1980s labour conditions in Malaysia, Korea, the Philippines, Taiwan, and Thailand were determined unilaterally by employers with or without the assistance of government (World Bank 1998c). However, observers disagree on the virtues of labour subordination. For example, neo-classical economists believe that the cost of infringement of labour rights has been more than compensated by the rapid growth in real wages and full employment. On the other hand, critics regard the failure to uphold basic rights as a glaring weakness of the pre-crisis period. In any case, progressive affluence in the region has made workers more assertive of their rights. For example, Korea and Taiwan witnessed waves of industrial unrest in the late 1980s and the role and power of their unions have increased substantially. Malaysia agreed to allow unionisation in the export-oriented, FDI-dependent electronics sector in 1988. Thailand and Indonesia have been forced to raise minimum wage a number of times since the mid 1980s.

Adding to the pressure is the International Labour Organization's (ILO) persistent efforts to improve labour standards in the region. The ILO is pressing for a new social contract for East Asia, which will include full respect for basic labour rights (ILO 1998b). There are also attempts to bring labour standards under the purview of the World Trade Organization (WTO). Industrialised countries express major concerns about the prevalence of child labour in countries like the Philippines, Thailand, and other countries of Southeast Asia, and the discrimination against women in work conditions and pay.

Thus, failure to improve labour standards and industrial relations will be very costly for HPAEs. It may lead to growing industrial unrest, and it is highly likely that industrial countries will use labour standards as a protectionist device against exports from HPAEs.

Table 2.11: Trends in Income Inequality (Gini ratio; year)

Indonesia	Hong Kong	Korea	Malaysia	Philippines	Singapore	Taiwan	Thailand
0.34; 1976	0.49; 1966	0.34; 1964	0.50; 1968	0.49; 1961	0.50; 1966	0.36; 1964	0.41; 1965
0.34; 1980	0.44; 1971	0.33; 1970	0.53; 1976	0.49; 1965	0.46; 1973	0.30; 1970	0.43; 1968
0.32; 1987	0.37; 1980	0.39; 1976	0.49; 1979	0.48; 1971	0.41; 1980	0.31; 1980	0.45; 1975
0.32; 1990	0.42; 1986	0.39; 1980	0.46; 1988	0.45; 1986	0.46; 1986	0.32; 1985	0.50; 1986
0.34; 1994	0.45; 1991	0.40; 1988	0.47; 1995	0.45; 1989	0.49; 1989	0.31; 1990	0.50; 1990

Sources: Medhi (1994: Table 1); Shari (1998)

Demographic change

The high-performing economies of East and Southeast Asia have gone through the demographic transition from both high fertility and mortality rates (the burden phase) to low fertility and mortality rates (the gift phase). Between 1965 and 1990, the working-age population in East Asia grew 2.39 per cent per year, nearly twice the rate of annual population growth (1.58 per cent) and substantially higher than the annual rate of growth of dependent population (0.25 per cent). Although less dramatic, the working-age population grew at a faster rate than the entire population in Southeast Asia. According to Bloom and Williamson (1998), this demographic transition can explain 1.37–1.87 percentage points of growth in GDP per capita in East Asia, or between a third and half of the miracle in Northeast and Southeast Asia.

However, it is predicted that the East Asian economies will soon enter the final phase of demographic transition—a decline in working-age population and a rise in the older dependent population. For example, according to UN (1991) projections, the ratio of working-age population to non-working-age population will peak in East Asia in 2010. ADB (1997) estimates show that by 2025 more than 10 per cent of population in Singapore, Hong Kong, China, and Taiwan will be aged sixty-five or more. This transition holds at least two important implications. First, as the share of working-age population declines, the economic growth rate will fall unless the participation rate rises or there is technological upgrading. According to Bloom and Williamson (1998), this will probably shave 0.14–0.44 percentage points from the growth rate of GDP per capita. The loss is estimated to be higher for countries such as Hong Kong (2.0–2.4 percentage points), Singapore (2.5–3.0 percentage points), and Korea (1.9–2.2 percentage points).

Second, ensuring financial security and providing aged care will become a major challenge. Currently most HPAEs do not have universal pension or social security systems and, traditionally, the elderly are looked after by families. But as the societies lose their traditional values due to economic transformation, there will be a growing need for the state to provide care and income support to the elderly. The budget deficit is likely to rise as the share of tax revenue declines and demand for public provision of aged care and pensions rises (Heller 1998). Some countries may have to depend increasingly on migrant labour, which might create social tension.

CONCLUSION

Although no one could predict the arrival and depth of the economic crisis in HPAEs, the crisis has spawned a large and contentious literature. Some see East Asia as the innocent victim of the volatility of private capital flows and the slowing in export demand. Japan's failure to act as a locomotive in the region compounded the malaise. Stimulating the Japanese economy and reforming the global financial system thus dominate the thinking about ways of dealing with the region's problems.

Many see the current crisis as the product of domestic policy failures and embedded institutional imperfections. Significant errors were made in exchange rate management and the implementation of monetary policy. A combination of the politics of patronage, financial sector frailties, lax bankruptcy laws, and weak corporate governance in a context of capital account liberalisation fused a currency crisis and a financial crisis into a ruinous phenomenon. As not all countries in the region were equally affected, some of the forces were perhaps more relevant in some economies than in others.

The East Asian crisis has focused attention on rectifying errors in macroeconomic policy and achieving broad-based reform in the financial sector. Recreating the East Asian miracle requires a vision about the future that has to look beyond the crisis and cope with a range of long-term issues and challenges. These involve the need to foster and sustain productivity-driven growth, manage environmental degradation, cope with the problem of growing inequality, and develop a tradition of democratic governance.

The epoch of development is characterised by self-destruction—that is, every system reaches its limit of usefulness. When the system falls behind the level of development, it crumbles—after considerable tensions. In East and Southeast Asia, although the system of semi-democracy or a strong state has been virtuous it can longer aid further development.

It is necessary to accept that East Asian political systems have been authoritarian, until the movement towards democratisation (most notably Taiwan and Korea since 1987). In trying to attain technocratic insulation, human rights have been attenuated and the labour movement has been politically excluded. Admittedly, rapid growth in such economies provided durable political legitimacy even without democratic institutions. It is also true that wealth-sharing programs in a context of rapid growth (such as affordable public housing in Singapore, and using oil wealth to alleviate rural poverty in Indonesia) have made the process of social and economic change more 'inclusive'.

Sah (1991) makes the point that, in the presence of human falli-bility, societal performance in an authoritarian political system becomes unusually sensitive to the particular abilities of benevolent dictators. Romer (1993: 88) makes a very similar point: 'strong, authoritarian government ... require a configuration of bureaucratic competence and ruthless dedication to national economic success that is relatively rare and may be impossible to sustain'. Olson (1982: 52) argues in the same vein, observing that political systems characterised by insufficient 'diversity of advocacy, opinion and policy and fewer checks on erroneous policies and ideas ... may perform unusually badly in some periods and unusually effectively in others'.

There is another critical issue that affects the tenuous link between authoritarian regimes and economic performance—the proposition that authoritarian regimes, at least of the East Asian variety, may be less effective in fostering innovation-driven growth. This revisits the Krugman hypothesis on the nature of East Asian growth, from a different perspective.

Once East Asian-style governance is seen to deliver spectacular results, it may end up creating a durable culture of compliance. Why question a system that has created such remarkable outcomes within a lifetime? The political leadership, inspired by its success and the legiti-macy that such success confers, may construct an ideology that rewards compliance and consensus. Such an interpretation is not too far-fetched, as shown in the consistent attempts by Mahathir of Malaysia and Lee Kuan Yew of Singapore to construct core Asian values (see Box 2.3 on the limits of the Asian values argument). Nevertheless, the Asian values argument can perhaps be justified in so far as it is used to seek common ground in a region which includes different cultures and religions, and has a history of mutual hostility. But it becomes highly suspect when a regime uses the argument as an excuse for autocratic practices and the denial of basic rights and liberties.

Thus, by adhering to the unsubstantiated view that there are distinctive Asian values that promote economic growth, political leaders may expose their polities to the risk that ideas and human ingenuity—the wellsprings of innovation-driven growth—are insuffi-ciently recognised and rewarded. Ideas and human ingenuity are not simply market-driven outcomes. They require a conducive institutional context characterised by a robust civil society, free-flowing information, debate, and dissent. The costs and risks inherent in sustaining a culture of compliance may not be evident to the current leadership or even to the society in general because input-driven growth may take a long time to lead to diminishing returns.

It is in this context that we must analyse these governments' thirst for foreign capital when there was no shortage of domestic savings. To begin with, authoritarian regimes can maintain their legitimacy only through their success in generating rapid economic growth: their claim to legitimacy becomes tenuous as the economy confronts diminishing returns. Their inability to make a transition to an innovation-driven stage of development to counteract the diminishing returns eventually causes them to crumble. The East and Southeast Asian authoritarian regimes found a reprieve in the surge of foreign capital inflows during the early 1990s. The access to foreign capital helped them in two ways. First, it enabled them to push prestige projects which could be used to justify the government's continuance on nationalistic grounds. Second, to the extent that the capital flows were private and the regime had lax control, it kept businesses happy. The general population also remained happy, as the economy continued to grow despite increasing inefficiency. Thus, the regimes which were once hailed for their relative autonomy from interest groups and for their growth-promoting relationship with business, degenerated into crony capitalism.

A vicious circle developed on the economic front. To maintain the capital flows, governments had to follow inconsistent policies. They had to maintain a stable or semi-fixed nominal exchange rate to encourage capital inflows, but this led to an appreciation of real effective exchange rate to the detriment of their export growth and current account developments. Also, to keep the financial sector pleased, governments had to either reduce the budget deficit or maintain a surplus budget, which was achieved predominantly by cutting infrastructure investment. This had adverse impacts on the productivity of, and hence returns to, private investment. In other words, the infrastructure bottlenecks added to the problem of diminishing returns as more and more investment was required with the rise in the ICOR. Thus, the demand for foreign capital continued to rise.

As the profitability of investment in the real sector declined, funds moved to financial and speculative investment. The investment in the

financial sector was also encouraged by the governments' low inflation rate policy, as it removed uncertainty about real returns.
However, the policies of nominal exchange rate targeting and low
inflation came under increasing pressure from capital flows although,
paradoxically, these policies were designed to attract capital inflows.
The countries found it increasingly difficult to sterilise the developments in capital account. They had to let the money supply increase
(and hence accept higher inflation), or let the exchange rate appreciate. In either case, they could not avoid the adverse impact on the
current account. The more they tried to hold out, the more vulnerable
they became to speculative attack and capital flight (discussed further
in chapter 3).

Ironically, foreign capital inflows were largely responsible for
delaying the democratisation of East and Southeast Asian countries
and for prolonging investment-driven growth. Furthermore, to the
extent that foreign capital inflows hindered the development of a
robust civil society, they contributed to the authoritarian regimes'
restraint of social movements that heighten public awareness of issues
such as environmental degradation, the plight of those left behind by
fast-paced growth, and gender discrimination. This in turn reduced
the state's ability to develop effective mechanisms for dealing with the
emerging social problems.

It is possible to hold a more positive view about the 1990s surge in
international capital flows to East and Southeast Asia. By creating the
financial crisis it has brought such issues to light and given impetus to
democratic reform. The financial crisis has brought the simmering
social and economic tensions to a boil, as shown in Indonesia and
Malaysia. It is abundantly clear that the sustainability of the 'Asian
century' depends on the ability of Asian countries to move successfully
to a more accountable, responsive, and transparent form of governance. Such governance requires durable democratic traditions.

Chapter 3

Capital Flows and Macroeconomic Management

INTRODUCTION

July 1997 marked a watershed in Asian economic history. Until the financial and economic crisis, the high-performing Asian economies (HPAEs) had remarkable macroeconomic stability characterised by moderate or low inflation and manageable internal and external debt (budget and balance of payment deficits). They were also able to adjust to external economic shocks reasonably quickly (see Chowdhury & Islam 1993: chs 10, 11; Chowdhury 1996 for detailed analyses of macroeconomic policies of HPAEs). The following quotes from a celebrated study (World Bank 1993a) of HPAEs capture the essence of HPAEs' macroeconomic management:

> Macroeconomic management was unusually good and macroeconomic performance unusually stable ... *Policies to increase the integrity of the banking system*, and to make it more accessible to non-traditional savers, raised the levels of financial savings (1993a: 5, emphasis added).

More than most developing economies, the HPAEs were characterised by *responsible* macroeconomic management. In particular, they generally limited fiscal deficits to levels that could be prudently financed without increasing inflationary pressures and responded quickly when fiscal pressures were perceived to be building up. During the past thirty years, annual inflation averaged approximately 9 per cent in these economies, compared with 18 per cent in other low- and middle-income economies.

Because inflation was both moderate and predictable, real interest rates were far more stable than in other low- and middle-income economies ... The HPAEs also adjusted their macroeconomic policies to terms of trade shocks more quickly and effectively than other low- and middle-income economies (1993a: 12, emphasis added).

Low inflation and manageable debt ... facilitated *realistic exchange rates and the avoidance of the appreciation* that elsewhere undermined export performance (1993a: 106, emphasis added).

The economies which were widely hailed for their excellent macroeconomic management over three decades, were overnight condemned for their misguided economic policies. This chapter examines the macroeconomic performance and policy settings of HPAEs in the 1990s, prior to the crisis. The following observations are based on the macroeconomic data presented in Tables 3.1–3.3.

Internal balance and fiscal policy

Table 3.1: Internal Balance and Fiscal Policy, 1991–97

A: Hong Kong

Indicators	1991	1992	1993	1994	1995	1996	1997
Real GDP growth (% annual)	5.1	6.3	6.1	5.4	3.9	4.9	5.3
Inflation rate (% annual)	11.6	9.3	8.5	8.1	8.7	6.0	6.5
Unemployment rate (% annual)	1.8	2.0	2.0	1.9	3.2	2.8	NA
Budget surplus (deficit)/GDP (%)	3.2	2.5	2.3	1.3	−0.3	2.2	4.2

B: Indonesia

Indicators	1991	1992	1993	1994	1995	1996	1997
Real GDP growth (% annual)	8.9	7.2	7.3	7.5	8.2	8.0	5.0
Inflation rate (% annual)	9.5	5.0	10.2	9.6	9.0	6.6	11.6
Unemployment rate (% annual)	2.6	2.7	2.8	4.4	7.2	4.9	NA
Budget surplus (deficit)/GDP (%)	NA	−1.2	−0.7	NA	0.8	1.4	2.0

C: Korea

Indicators	1991	1992	1993	1994	1995	1996	1997
Real GDP growth (% annual)	9.1	5.1	5.8	8.6	8.9	7.1	6.0
Inflation rate (% annual)	9.3	6.2	4.8	6.3	4.5	4.9	4.3
Unemployment rate (% annual)	2.3	2.4	2.8	2.4	2.0	1.9	2.6
Budget surplus (deficit)/GDP (%)	−1.6	−2.6	−1.0	1.0	0.2	NA	NA

D: Malaysia

Indicators	1991	1992	1993	1994	1995	1996	1997
Real GDP growth (% annual)	8.6	7.8	8.3	9.2	9.5	8.6	7.0
Inflation rate (% annual)	4.4	4.8	3.5	3.7	5.3	3.5	2.7
Unemployment rate (% annual)	4.3	3.7	3.0	2.9	2.8	2.5	NA
Budget surplus (deficit)/GDP (%)	0.1	−3.5	−2.6	2.5	3.8	4.2	1.6

E: Philippines

Indicators	1991	1992	1993	1994	1995	1996	1997
Real GDP growth (% annual)	−0.6	0.3	2.1	4.4	4.8	5.7	4.3
Inflation rate (% annual)	18.7	8.9	7.6	9.0	8.1	8.4	5.1
Unemployment rate (% annual)	9.0	9.8	9.3	9.5	9.5	NA	NA
Budget surplus (deficit)/GDP (%)	−2.1	−1.2	−1.6	−1.6	−1.4	−0.4	−0.9

F: Singapore

Indicators	1991	1992	1993	1994	1995	1996	1997
Real GDP growth (% annual)	7.3	6.2	10.4	10.5	8.8	7.0	7.2
Inflation rate (% annual)	3.4	2.3	2.3	3.1	1.7	1.4	2.0
Unemployment rate (% annual)	1.9	2.7	2.7	2.6	2.7	NA	NA
Budget surplus (deficit)/GDP (%)	10.3	11.3	14.3	13.7	12.0	8.4	8.3

G: Taiwan

Indicators	1991	1992	1993	1994	1995	1996	1997
Real GDP growth (% annual)	7.6	6.8	6.3	6.5	6.0	5.7	6.7
Inflation rate (% annual)	3.6	4.5	2.9	4.1	3.7	3.1	0.9
Unemployment rate (% annual)	1.5	1.5	1.5	1.6	1.8	2.6	NA
Budget surplus (deficit)/GDP (%)	0.5	0.3	0.6	0.2	0.4	0.2	0.2

H: Thailand

Indicators	1991	1992	1993	1994	1995	1996	1997
Real GDP growth (% annual)	8.6	8.2	8.6	8.9	8.7	5.5	−0.4
Inflation rate (% annual)	5.7	4.1	3.4	5.1	5.8	5.9	5.6
Unemployment rate (% annual)	3.5	3.6	2.6	2.6	1.7	1.5	3.5
Budget surplus (deficit)/GDP (%)	4.2	2.6	2.1	2.0	2.6	1.6	−0.4

Sources: IMF, *International Financial Statistics* (various issues), IMF, *World Economic Outlook* 1997, ADB, Key Indicators of Member Countries; country sources

- Economic growth (real GNP) averaged nearly 8 per cent per annum, except in the Philippines, Hong Kong, and Taiwan, which averaged around 5 per cent. However, it slowed in 1996, and in Thailand the real GDP growth rate fell from over 8 per cent in 1995 to 5.5 per cent in 1996.

- Although inflation rates remained less than 10 per cent, there were some signs of overheating. For example, in Malaysia and Thailand the inflation rate rose from around 3 per cent in 1993 to over 5 per cent in 1996, and the inflation rate remained above 8 per cent in Hong Kong, Indonesia, and the Philippines, although it fell in Indonesia to 6.6 per cent in 1996. Korea and Singapore also experienced some rise in inflation, but were able to contain it at less than 5 per cent.

- There was no significant rise in unemployment.

- There was no significant budget deficit; in fact, some countries had sizeable surpluses.

- Fiscal balance was achieved mainly by reducing expenditure rather than by raising revenue.

Credit growth and monetary policy

Table 3.2: Credit Growth and Monetary Policy, 1991–97

A: Hong Kong

Indicators	1991	1992	1993	1994	1995	1996	1997
M2 growth (% annual)	NA	8.5	14.5	11.7	10.6	12.5	NA
Nominal GNP growth (% annual)	14.8	16.6	15.2	12.6	7.3	9.9	11.3

A: Hong Kong (Cont.)

Indicators	1991	1992	1993	1994	1995	1996	1997
Domestic credit growth (% annual)	NA	9.6	21.0	25.0	8.6	18.0	NA
Growth of credit to private sector	NA	10.2	20.1	19.9	11.0	15.8	NA
Bank credit to private sector/GDP	NA	NA	NA	NA	NA	NA	NA
Deposit rates							
Nominal	NA	NA	NA	NA	NA	NA	8.5
Real	NA	NA	NA	NA	NA	NA	2.0

B: Indonesia

Indicators	1991	1992	1993	1994	1995	1996	1997
M2 growth (% annual)	17.5	19.8	20.2	20.0	27.2	27.2	23.2
Nominal GNP growth (% annual)	18.3	14.7	17.0	16.0	17.7	16.0	13.0
Domestic credit growth (% annual)	18.9	14.1	21.0	22.9	21.7	22.7	NA
Growth of credit to private sector	16.7	11.4	25.5	23.0	22.6	21.4	NA
Bank credit to private sector/GDP	50.3	49.5	48.9	51.9	53.5	55.4	62.0
Deposit rates							
Nominal	23.3	19.6	14.5	12.5	16.7	17.3	20.0
Real	13.8	14.6	4.4	2.9	7.7	10.6	8.4

C: Korea

Indicators	1991	1992	1993	1994	1995	1996	1997
M2 growth (% annual)	21.9	14.9	16.6	18.7	15.6	15.8	14.1
Nominal GNP growth (% annual)	20.6	11.4	11.1	14.5	15.0	10.8	8.0
Domestic credit growth (% annual)	22.4	11.7	12.7	18.4	14.7	19.4	23.3
Growth of credit to private sector	20.1	11.5	13.3	19.5	15.6	19.8	21.5
Bank credit to private sector/GDP	52.8	53.3	54.2	56.8	57.0	61.8	69.8
Deposit rates							
Nominal	10.0	10.0	8.6	8.5	8.8	7.5	10.8
Real	0.7	3.8	3.8	2.2	4.4	2.6	6.5

D: Malaysia

Indicators	1991	1992	1993	1994	1995	1996	1997
M2 growth (% annual)	16.7	29.2	26.6	12.7	20.0	25.3	17.5
Nominal GNP growth (% annual)	11.2	12.5	11.8	12.9	12.9	12.1	10.7
Domestic credit growth (% annual)	18.5	16.6	12.3	14.8	29.5	27.4	29.2
Growth of credit to private sector	20.6	11.2	11.6	15.3	30.5	25.7	26.8
Bank credit to private sector/GDP	77.0	75.2	75.6	76.5	86.8	93.4	NA
Deposit rates							
Nominal	7.2	NA	NA	NA	5.9	7.1	NA
Real	4.6	NA	NA	NA	2.5	3.6	NA

E: Philippines

Indicators	1991	1992	1993	1994	1995	1996	1997
M2 growth (% annual)	17.3	13.6	27.1	24.4	24.2	23.2	26.1
Nominal GNP growth (% annual)	15.9	8.3	9.1	14.8	12.6	15.2	11.6
Domestic credit growth (% annual)	−2.6	17.6	131.2	19.0	31.3	40.3	30.8
Growth of credit to private sector	7.3	25.4	39.6	26.5	45.2	48.7	28.8
Bank credit to private sector/GDP	17.8	20.4	26.4	29.1	37.5	48.4	55.9
Deposit rates							
Nominal	18.8	14.3	9.6	10.5	8.4	9.7	10.2
Real	0.1	5.4	2.0	1.5	0.3	1.3	5.1

F: Singapore

Indicators	1991	1992	1993	1994	1995	1996	1997
M2 growth (% annual)	12.4	8.9	8.5	14.4	8.5	9.8	10.3
Nominal GNP growth (% annual)	11.0	7.5	16.4	15.1	11.6	9.5	9.3
Domestic credit growth (% annual)	13.9	5.5	12.0	12.8	17.4	17.3	19.6
Growth of credit to private sector	12.4	9.8	15.2	15.3	20.3	15.8	12.7
Bank credit to private sector/GDP	83.3	85.1	84.1	84.2	90.8	96.0	NA
Deposit rates							
Nominal	4.6	2.9	2.3	3.0	3.5	3.4	3.5
Real	1.2	0.6	0.0	−0.1	1.8	2.0	1.5

G: Taiwan

Indicators	1991	1992	1993	1994	1995	1996	1997
M2 growth (% annual)	19.4	19.1	15.4	15.1	9.4	9.1	8.0
Nominal GNP growth (% annual)	11.7	11.0	10.1	8.5	8.1	8.5	8.8
Domestic credit growth (% annual)	26.3	28.9	20.6	15.4	11.2	8.9	9.2
Growth of credit to private sector	21.2	28.7	19.3	16.2	10.0	6.0	8.9
Bank credit to private sector/GDP	109.1	126.4	136.8	146.8	148.8	144.1	145.2
Deposit rates							
Nominal	8..3	7.8	7.6	7.3	6.7	6.0	6.0
Real	4.7	3.2	4.7	3.2	2.9	2.9	5.1

H: Thailand

Indicators	1991	1992	1993	1994	1995	1996	1997
M2 growth (% annual)	19.8	15.6	18.4	12.9	17.0	12.6	16.4
Nominal GNP growth (% annual)	13.8	12.9	12.0	14.5	15.4	9.8	5.0
Domestic credit growth (% annual)	NA	18.7	21.2	27.6	23.7	13.8	28.0
Growth of credit to private sector	20.4	20.5	24.0	30.3	23.8	14.6	19.8
Bank credit to private sector/GDP	67.7	72.2	80.0	91.0	97.6	101.9	116.3
Deposit rates							
Nominal	13.7	8.9	8.6	8.5	11.6	10.3	10.5
Real	8.0	4.8	5.2	3.4	5.8	4.4	4.9

Sources: IMF, International Financial Statistics (various issues), IMF, *World Economic Outlook* 1997, ADB, Key Indicators of Member Countries; country sources

Notes: Nominal deposit rate = maximum rate offered by commercial banks on 3–6 month savings deposits

Real deposit rate = nominal rate less inflation

- Money growth (measured by M2) was in line with the growth rates of nominal GDP in Hong Kong, Korea, and Singapore. Taiwan managed to lower the M2 growth rate to rates consistent with its nominal GDP growth rates by 1995.

- In Indonesia, Malaysia, and the Philippines, the growth rates of monetary aggregates were considerably higher than their nominal GDP growth rates.

- Thailand was between the above two groups. Its money growth exceeded nominal GDP growth but less than that in Indonessia or Malaysia.

- The differential growth rates of money and nominal GDP were reflected in the pattern of inflation in these economies—moderate and falling inflation in Korea and Singapore, relatively high inflation in Indonesia and the Philippines, and the inflation rate in Thailand between those two sets of economies.

- Growth of domestic credit was generally higher in all countries, and there was a rising trend in bank credit/GDP ratios. In general, the growth of domestic credit in the Philippines and Thailand was much higher, followed by Indonesia, Malaysia, Korea, Hong Kong, Taiwan, and Singapore. However, Thailand managed to lower it considerably, from around 24 per cent in 1995 to around 14 per cent in 1996.

External balance and the exchange rate

Table 3.3: External Balance and Exchange Rates, 1991–97

A: Hong Kong

Indicators	1991	1992	1993	1994	1995	1996	1997
Nominal exchange rate (local/$US)	7.77	7.74	7.74	7.73	7.74	7.73	7.75
Real effective exchange rate	111.2	118.1	122.5	132.6	135.6	142.4	159.1
Growth of nominal export values	18.5	20.2	13.2	11.8	15.1	4.8	NA
Growth of nominal import values	20.5	21.5	11.7	16.7	18.8	3.1	NA
Current account/GDP	7.1	5.7	7.4	1.6	–3.9	–1.3	–1.5
Foreign reserves/imports (months)	8.2	8.6	10.1	10.0	9.1	10.9	10.7
Debt service/exports							

B: Indonesia

Indicators	1991	1992	1993	1994	1995	1996	1997
Nominal exchange rate (local/$US)	1992	2062	2110	2200	2308	2383	4650
Real effective exchange rate	106.4	110.5	123.3	128.1	136.6	154.7	113.9
Growth of nominal export values	19.9	22.7	15.5	14.8	18.0	15.0	NA
Growth of nominal import values	20.5	14.6	11.4	23.7	29.6	13.0	NA
Current account/GDP	–3.4	–2.2	–1.5	–1.7	–3.3	–3.3	–2.9

B: Indonesia (Cont.)

Indicators	1991	1992	1993	1994	1995	1996	1997
Foreign reserves/imports (months)	5.7	6.6	7.5	6.2	5.0	5.5	NA
Debt service/exports	32.0	33.0	33.6	30.7	30.9	29.5	30.0

C: Korea

Indicators	1991	1992	1993	1994	1995	1996	1997
Nominal exchange rate (local/$US)	760.8	788.4	808.1	788.7	774.7	844.2	1696
Real effective exchange rate	96.6	93.0	92.8	93.2	98.5	98.6	77.2
Growth of nominal export values	13.6	14.3	12.6	17.9	26.3	8.5	27.6
Growth of nominal import values	21.4	8.8	7.1	22.6	27.3	18.2	15.2
Current account/GDP	−3.0	−1.5	0.1	−1.2	−2.0	−4.9	−2.9
Foreign reserves/imports (months)	1.8	2.2	2.5	2.6	2.5	2.3	NA
Debt service/exports	7.1	7.6	9.2	6.8	4.9	4.8	4.7

D: Malaysia

Indicators	1991	1992	1993	1994	1995	1996	1997
Nominal exchange rate (local/$US)	2.7	2.6	2.7	2.6	2.5	2.5	3.9
Real effective exchange rate	95.7	105.8	105.9	103.8	104.5	109.3	89.8
Growth of nominal export values	18.5	5.6	22.6	23.5	20.1	10.1	NA
Growth of nominal import values	27.7	−7.2	33.4	18.6	22.9	4.5	NA
Current account/GDP	−8.8	−3.8	−4.8	−7.8	−10.0	−4.9	−5.8
Foreign reserves/imports (months)	3.3	4.7	6.2	4.5	3.3	NA	NA
Debt service/exports	7.7	6.6	7.8	4.9	6.2	NA	NA

E: Philippines

Indicators	1991	1992	1993	1994	1995	1996	1997
Nominal exchange rate (local/$US)	26.7	25.1	27.7	24.4	26.2	26.3	40.0
Real effective exchange rate	102.8	115.6	107.6	125.1	126.6	133.4	115.6
Growth of nominal export values	24.6	6.6	17.4	23.8	21.0	33.0	23.2

E: Philippines (Cont.)

Indicators	1991	1992	1993	1994	1995	1996	1997
Growth of nominal import values	13.4	13.1	27.6	15.8	23.9	35.0	19.9
Current account/GDP	−2.3	−1.6	−5.5	−4.6	−4.4	−4.7	−4.5
Foreign reserves/imports (months)	2.8	3.1	2.7	2.8	2.3	NA	NA
Debt service/exports	23.0	17.0	17.1	17.4	15.8	12.0	10.4

F: Singapore

Indicators	1991	1992	1993	1994	1995	1996	1997
Nominal exchange rate (local/$US)	1.63	1.64	1.61	1.46	1.41	1.40	1.68
Real effective exchange rate	105.2	106.1	108.1	113.2	114.8	118.6	119.4
Growth of nominal export values	NA	NA	NA	NA	NA	NA	NA
Growth of nominal import values	55.2	−7.6	−0.4	116.0	15.9	−4.6	NA
Current account/GDP	11.2	11.3	7.4	17.1	16.9	15.0	14.0
Foreign reserves/imports (months)	5.8	6.1	6.3	6.3	6.1	6.5	NA
Debt service/exports							

G: Taiwan

Indicators	1991	1992	1993	1994	1995	1996	1997
Nominal exchange rate (local/$US)	25.7	25.4	26.6	26.2	27.3	27.5	32.6
Real effective exchange rate	98.8	104.4	97.7	96.3	94.6	96.8	90.6
Growth of nominal export values	13.2	1.5	12.2	8.2	19.5	8.0	10.7
Growth of nominal import values	14.6	6.9	12.9	8.2	19.9	3.6	13.7
Current account/GDP	6.7	3.8	3.0	2.6	1.9	5.2	4.2
Foreign reserves/imports (months)	17.5	15.3	14.7	14.6	NA	NA	NA
Debt service/exports							

H: Thailand

Indicators	1991	1992	1993	1994	1995	1996	1997
Nominal exchange rate (local/$US)	25.3	25.5	25.5	25.1	25.2	25.6	47.2
Real effective exchange rate	99.8	99.8	101.5	100.4	103.8	109.4	82.7

H: Thailand (Cont.)

Indicators	1991	1992	1993	1994	1995	1996	1997
Growth of nominal export values	21.0	16.1	14.5	17.5	24.2	3.3	25.7
Growth of nominal import values	17.2	8.9	13.6	19.0	28.3	3.2	7.9
Current account/GDP	−7.7	−5.6	−5.0	−5.6	−8.0	−7.9	−3.9
Foreign reserves/imports (months)	5.0	5.2	5.5	5.5	5.3	5.4	NA
Debt service/exports	13.0	13.7	18.5	11.3	11.4	12.2	25.0

Sources: IMF, International Financial Statistics (various issues), IMF, *World Economic Outlook* 1997, ADB,
Key Indicators of Member Countries; country sources
Note: Real effective exchange rate = trade-weighted relative to CPI; 1990 = 100

- Current account balances worsened in all economies, except Singapore. Thailand had the worst situation, with current account deficit averaging around −8 per cent of GDP in 1995 and 1996. Malaysia managed to lower it from −10 per cent of GDP in 1995 to about −5 per cent in 1996 with import controls.

- Growth of export revenue plummeted in all economies in 1996 except in the Philippines. For example, export earnings growth fell from 23 per cent (1995) to 3 per cent (1996) in Thailand, from 20 per cent (1995) to 10 per cent (1996) in Malaysia, and from 26 per cent (1995) to 8 per cent (1996) in Korea.

- There was no pattern of declining official reserves (in months of imports), although there were significant cross-country differences in levels.

- External debt remained stable. However, in Indonesia the debt service ratio (as a percentage of export earnings) reached 30 per cent.

- The nominal exchange rate (local currency/$US) remained stable, except in Indonesia and Korea where it depreciated (increased), and Singapore where it appreciated (decreased). In Taiwan, there was a very slight depreciation.

- The real effective exchange rate (trade-weighted relative CPI) appreciated in all economies, except in Taiwan where it remained stable. However, the real appreciation was small, save in Hong Kong, Indonesia, and the Philippines where the competitiveness declined by more than 10 per cent between 1990 and 1996.

The above key indicators show that the general macroeconomic health of HPAEs was quite robust prior to the onset of financial crisis. However, there were a number of weak spots: the overheating of the economy as reflected in the movements of inflation rates and current account deficits; faster growth of domestic credit and money supply, reflecting private-sector overborrowing (McKinnon & Pill 1998); and declining international competitiveness. This chapter examines these weaknesses and analyses HPAEs' macroeconomic policy—fiscal, monetary, and exchange rate—settings. In particular, it will highlight inconsistencies in the policies and attempt to locate the origin of such inconsistencies in the international and domestic political economy. This involves understanding the impacts of international macroeconomic events on domestic macroeconomic outcomes.

CAPITAL INFLOWS AND DOMESTIC MACROECONOMIC PERFORMANCE

An international macroeconomic phenomenon that had a profound impact on HPAEs was the sudden surge in short-term foreign private capital inflows. The 1980s and 1990s witnessed the opening of the capital account in most developing countries, against a backdrop of declining interest rates in most industrialised countries. The liberalisation of capital accounts thus coincided with an unprecedented increase in the flow of private portfolio capital into the emerging economies. After a brief pause in the mid 1980s due to the Latin American debt crisis, the capital flow resumed. The major recipient region was East and Southeast Asia, accounting for over 40 per cent cumulatively of total flows to developing countries during the first half of the 1990s (Dean 1996; Dooley, Fernandez-Arias & Kletzer 1996; Spiegel 1995). East Asia received an average of about $US8 billion a year during 1986–89, rising to $US63 billion in 1993 and $US98 billion in 1995 (Glick 1998). According to Goldstein (1998), an estimated $US420 billion of private capital flowed into Asian developing countries. The People's Republic of China (PRC) attracted the largest dollar amounts, followed by Malaysia, Thailand, and Indonesia. Malaysia ranked eighth in the developing world, and on a per capita basis Malaysia was one of the largest recipients (with Hungary) of private capital inflows (Dean 1996). Indonesia ranked twelfth. At their peak, capital inflow as a percentage of GDP was above 20 per cent for Malaysia, 13 per cent for Thailand, 10 per cent for the Philippines, and about 5 per cent for Indonesia (Glick 1998). This was well in excess of their current account deficits, implying that the current account developments in HPAEs were driven by developments in their capital account (Grenville 1999).

The overheating of HPAEs can be traced to the surge in capital inflows. As Razin and Rose (1994) point out, increased capital inflows allow enhanced investment opportunities as well as smoothing consumption. The link between capital inflows and overheating is summarised in Box 3.1. The growth of domestic demand in Korea rose sharply during 1994–95, contributing around 9 per cent to GDP growth compared with 4 per cent in 1993. In Malaysia, the contribution of domestic demand growth to GDP growth rose from 3.5 per cent in 1992 to over 9 per cent in 1993, and accelerated to around 13 per cent during 1994–95 (Alba et al. 1998). A similar trend can be seen in Thailand and Indonesia, and to some extent in the Philippines. As noted above, the demand pressure was reflected in a widening of current account deficits and increases in inflation rates. The current account deficit as a percentage of GDP in Malaysia rose from around –4 per cent in 1992 to –10 per cent in 1995, which forced Malaysia to introduce a host of import controls in 1996. The current account deficit increased from –5 per cent in 1993 to –8 per cent in 1995 in Thailand, and from less than –2 per cent in 1993 to over –3 per cent in 1995 in Indonesia. In the Philippines, the current account deficit increased from –1.6 per cent of GDP in 1992 to –4.6 per cent in 1995. Korea, which had a small current account surplus in 1993, had a deficit accounting for nearly –5 per cent of GDP in 1996. Hong Kong's healthy current account surplus turned into a deficit amounting to nearly –4 per cent of GDP in 1995. Consistent with the current account developments, inflation rates also showed signs of overheating. In Thailand, the inflation rate rose from less than 4 per cent in 1993 to nearly 6 per cent in 1996; in Indonesia it jumped from 5 per cent in 1992 to over 10 per cent in 1993 and remained around 9 per cent during 1994–95. Despite some price controls, the inflation rate in Malaysia rose to 5.3 per cent in 1995. In the Philippines and Hong Kong, the inflation rates remained around 8 per cent during 1992–96, and in Korea the inflation rate reached over 6 per cent in 1994.

BOX 3.1: PRIVATE CAPITAL FLOWS AND DOMESTIC MACROECONOMIC CYCLES

In theory, private capital flows can generate as well as exacerbate domestic macroeconomic cycles through the following channels.

- The ability to borrow overseas can have an expansionary bias for the domestic economy. That is, private capital flows validate excess demand pressures by relaxing the liquidity constraint. If the excess demand falls on the tradable sector, it will be manifested in a widening of the current account deficit. If it falls on the non-tradable sector, it will manifest in higher domestic inflation.

- Even when the private capital inflow finances investments, it can lead to problems of domestic absorption and overheating due to the time lag involved in translating investment into productive capacity. Thus, there is likely to be a widening of the current account deficit and/or increased inflationary pressures.

- If the increased private capital inflow finances demand for domestic assets, it will contribute to asset price inflation. The resultant increase in financial wealth can contribute to a consumption boom. This too will have an adverse impact on the current account position and inflation.

Figure 3.1 shows that capital flows were closely related to domestic macroeconomic cycles in Indonesia, Thailand, and Korea between 1990 and 1996. In Malaysia, the co-movement of capital flows and domestic demand pressure was more pronounced after 1994, after a brief breakdown during 1992–93.

Source: Alba et al. (1998).

Figure 3.1: Capital Flows and Excess Demand Pressures, 1990–96

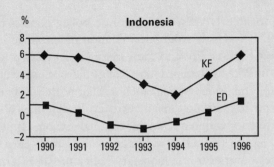

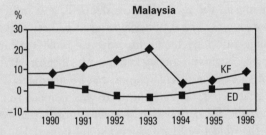

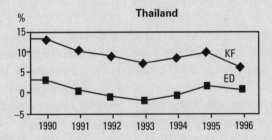

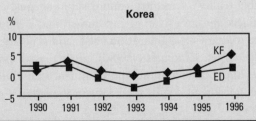

Notes: KF = capital flows (% GDP); ED = excess demand defined as the percentage deviation of actual GDP from potential GDP, estimated using the Hodrick Prescott filter

FISCAL–MONETARY–EXCHANGE RATE POLICIES: IMPOSSIBLE TRINITY

In export-oriented HPAEs, exchange rate policy plays a very important role. The aim is to avoid overvaluation of exchange rates, which would affect exports. Prior to the surge in short-term private capital inflows most HPAEs (except Hong Kong) did not use exchange rates primarily to establish a nominal anchor. That is, they did not peg their exchange rate to a strong foreign currency. Rather, they allowed their currencies to vary within a band, albeit a narrow one. If pegged (as in Thailand), it was pegged to a composite basket of currencies. This allowed the countries to use monetary policy for short-term stabilisation—tightening in the face of excess demand, and loosening during demand slow-downs. Fiscal policy was used to keep inflation in line with exchange rate movements in order to avoid real appreciation. Thus, the macroeconomic policy framework of most HPAEs prior to the influx of short-term foreign capital can be summarised in terms of assignment rules. First, the exchange rate was assigned to competitiveness. Second, the fiscal policy, which was mostly conservative, was assigned to the objective of price level stabilisation. Third, monetary policy played the supporting role, primarily in stabilising domestic demand.

However, a country wishing to remain attractive to foreign private capital inflows must earn the confidence of the international capital market—it must maintain the stability of its currency. The country cannot afford to have swings in its exchange rate, as that introduces uncertainty about the real value of returns on invested funds. The country must either peg its exchange rate, or manage it strongly in order to maintain a steady flow of capital (and thus liquidity) in the economy (Krugman 1998d). However, this poses a problem known as the 'impossible trinity': a country cannot simultaneously maintain an open capital account, an exchange rate target, and a monetary policy that is geared to domestic stabilisation needs and is independent of the exchange rate target. Krugman (1998d) labels these elements respectively as the liquidity condition, the confidence condition, and the adjustment condition, and calls the problem the 'eternal triangle' (see Figure 3.2).

To what extent have HPAEs been successful in achieving the impossible trinity? Have they been able to escape the policy dilemma of the

Figure 3.2: The Eternal Triangle

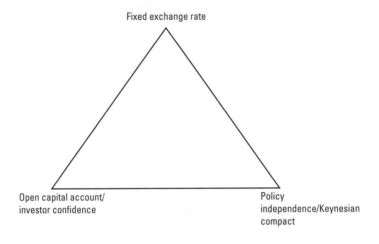

Fixed exchange rate

Open capital account/
investor confidence

Policy
independence/Keynesian
compact

Notes: The following conditions are possible: fixed exchange rate/open capital account; policy independence/fixed exchange rate and capital controls; policy independence/flexible exchange rate and open capital account

eternal triangle? Reisen (1993a, 1993b) believes that Asian economies, particularly Singapore, have been remarkably successful in maintaining an open capital account, an exchange rate target, and an independent monetary policy. According to Reisin, this has been possible due to 'fiscal complicity'—the ability to achieve either budget surplus or only a small budget deficit. On the other hand, Moreno and Spiegel (1997), Glick and Moreno (1995), and Krugman (1998d) find that the Asian economies are not exempt from the impossible trinity: the efforts to violate the impossible trinity contributed to speculative attacks on their currencies.

In order to understand the debate and the empirical facts, we must examine the theoretical relationship between fiscal stance, money supply, and net foreign assets.[1] The total money supply (M) is linked to the stock of domestic credit (DC) and net foreign assets (NFA) as follows:

$$M = DC + NFA \quad (1)$$

where domestic credit (DC) is composed of central bank credit to the government (CG) and commercial bank credit to the public (CP), and the stock of net foreign assets (NFA) is determined by the current account deficit/surplus (CDS) and the capital account surplus/deficit (KSD). Thus, equation (1) can be rewritten as:

$$M = CG + CP + CDS + KSD \quad (2)$$

If a country is running a fixed exchange rate system, its central bank's holding of NFA is determined by its balance of payments position. For example, if the inflow of foreign capital is more than that required to cover the current account deficit (KSD > CDS), there will be pressure on the exchange rate to appreciate. In order to maintain the fixed exchange rate, the central bank buys the foreign exchange at the predetermined rate. As a result, the holding of NFA by the central bank increases which, according to equations (1) and (2), will have an expansionary effect on money supply (M). The monetary effect of changes in NFA can be sterilised by corresponding reverse changes in domestic credit (DC), in particular central bank credit to the government (CG).

However, the ability to sterilise depends on the level of development of the domestic capital market, in particular the depth of the secondary market for government securities. If the capital market is not well-developed, the central bank cannot successfully conduct open market operations (buying and selling of government securities) to achieve offsetting changes in CG in response to changes in NFA. Furthermore, sterilisation through open market operations does not solve the problem of capital inflow—the source of the problem—as the central bank is forced to offer higher interest rates to attract commercial banks and private citizens to buy government bonds. The differential between domestic and foreign yields is known as quasi-fiscal cost, which the central bank must bear as it invests in low-yielding foreign reserves while simultaneously issuing domestic debt at high-enough yields. If the sterilisation is achieved through changing CP by raising the reserve requirement which restricts commercial banks' ability to advance credit, the quasi-fiscal cost is simply transferred to the customers of commercial banks. This happens as the spread between loan and deposit rates widens, due to the fact that central bank reserves do not attract any interest.

There is a limit to sterilisation. For example, if NFA continues to decline due to large and persistent current account deficits unmatched by capital account surpluses or net capital outflow, the central bank will run out of foreign exchange reserves and be forced to allow either the exchange rate to depreciate or the money supply to contract. On the other hand, if the central bank is sterilising a continued inflow of capital above that required by the current account deficit, it will soon run out of domestic assets (CG) to trade. Eventually, it will have to allow either the appreciation of domestic currency or an expansion of the money supply. Thus, if capital is mobile, a country can either peg the exchange rate or control its money supply but not both—the impossible trinity.

There are two important implications of the impossible trinity. First, the country cannot avoid real appreciation of currency and loss of international competitiveness in the face of continued capital inflows. When the peg is abandoned, the real appreciation happens through nominal appreciation of the domestic currency. When sterilisation is abandoned, the real appreciation happens through the rise in the domestic inflation rate as a result of monetary expansion. Second, as soon as the market expects a devaluation in response to persistent and large current account deficits, there will be a speculative attack on the currency. That is, investors will sell domestic currency, to be bought back after the devaluation. The expectation becomes self-fulfilling once the selling spree begins.

However, it is argued that a country can avoid the impossible trinity through fiscal complicity. For example, if the government maintains a budget surplus or a very small deficit, the size of CG in equation (2) will be either shrinking or small, which will have a contractionary effect on the domestic money supply. In such circumstances, the central bank either does not need to sterilise capital inflows or does it intermittently and less vigorously. The use of fiscal policy to overcome the impossibility trinity can also be explained by using the identity linking the fiscal stance to the external balance as:

$$CDS = S - I + FDS \quad (3)$$

where S is private savings, I is private investment, and FDS is fiscal deficit/surplus.

Equation (3) is derived from the national account identity. If the private sector balance (PB = S – I) is stable then, according to equation (3), the current account position is directly determined by the fiscal

Table 3.4: Summary of Capital Inflow Experiences

Country	Capital inflow surges	Non-bank sterilisation	Bank sector sterilisation	Real exchange rate impact	1986–93 average annual change in banking asset ratio (%)
Indonesia	1986–87, 1990–91		Increased regulatory restrictions, decreased public sector assets in commercial banks	Moderate real exchange rate appreciation	5.99
Korea	1991, 1992	Used 'money stabilisations' in open market operations	Increased reserve requirements	Large real exchange rate appreciation	−3.41
Malaysia	1991–93	Used government and pension fund securities in open market operations	Increased reserve requirements, increased regulatory restrictions	Moderate real exchange rate appreciation	6.24
Philippines	1988–93	Increased foreign debt service	Increased reserve requirements	Moderate real exchange rate depreciation	4.26
Singapore	1987, 1990, 1992–93	Used pension funds in open market operations		Moderate real exchange rate appreciation	−0.24

Table 3.4: Summary of Capital Inflow Experiences (cont.)

Country	Capital inflow surges	Non-bank sterilisation	Bank sector sterilisation	Real exchange rate impact	1986–93 average annual change in banking asset ratio (%)
Taiwan	1986–87		Required commercial banks to directly purchase treasury bills and central bank certificates of deposit, decreased public sector assets in commercial banks	Moderate real exchange rate appreciation	–0.14
Thailand	1988–92	Increased foreign debt service, eased restrictions on capital outflows		Moderate real exchange rate depreciation	1.75

Source: Spiegel (1995)

deficit/surplus. If, however, private investment exceeds private savings, which is the case in most HPAEs, its impact on CDS can be offset by corresponding changes in FDS, thus limiting the need for capital inflows.

The official exchange rate regimes in HPAEs range from unilateral pegs to the US dollar (Hong Kong since 1983), to fixed or adjustable pegs to a currency basket (Malaysia, Singapore, Korea until 1990, Indonesia in 1986–97, and Thailand in 1984–97), to managed floats (Taiwan until 1989, Korea since 1990). However, to varying degrees, almost all East and Southeast Asian economies (except Japan) have pegged their currencies to the ·US dollar, as is evident from the very small variation of their US dollar rates (Glick & Moreno 1995). Frankel and Wei (1993) find that during 1979–92 the weight of the US dollar in estimated currency baskets averaged 90 per cent for East Asian economies, compared with a 6 per cent weight for the yen and a 3 per cent weight for the deutschmark. As reflected in the relative stability of their dollar exchange rates, these economies successfully limited adjustment of their currencies against the US dollar until the onset of the crisis. They were thus able to earn the confidence of the international capital market, which was vindicated by the unprecedented rise in capital flows to East and Southeast Asian economies.

As documented by Dean (1996), the East and Southeast Asian economies sought to sterilise capital inflows by using various instruments (see IMF 1995). The most widely used instrument was open market sales by the central banks of their own or government securities for domestic money (Box 3.2). They also raised the statutory reserve requirement for commercial banks in order to curtail banks' ability to advance loans (Box 3.3). Indonesia, Malaysia, Singapore, Taiwan, and Thailand sterilised capital inflows by shifting public sector or pension funds from commercial banks to the central bank (Box 3.4). This too had the effect of reducing commercial banks' ability to create credit. Box 3.5 presents evidence of the fiscal policy response to capital inflows in Malaysia and Thailand. By reducing government expenditure, especially on non-traded goods, fiscal austerity dampens the inflationary pressure of capital inflows and thereby seeks to avoid upward pressure on the real exchange rate. Table 3.4 provides a summary of capital inflow experiences and the responses of HPAEs.

BOX 3.2: STERILISATION THROUGH OPEN MARKET OPERATION

The year next to the country name denotes the first year of the surge in inflows.

Indonesia (1990)

- February 1991: Significant monetary tightening. Sales of Bank Indonesia certificates (SBIs) increase sharply.

- March 1991: State enterprises are instructed to convert Rp10 trillion in bank deposits to SBIs.

- May 1993: Monetary policy begins to ease and sterilisation efforts diminish.

Malaysia (1989)

- 1990: Bank Negara begins to borrow in interbank market.

- 1992: Heavy open market operation begins as Bank Negara steps up sales of treasury bills and borrows heavily in the interbank market.

- 10 February 1993: Bank Negara begins to issue Bank Negara bills (BNBs), which are similar to Malaysian government treasury bills. This move is prompted by the need to have an instrument through which to conduct open market operations, since treasury issuance is dwindling in line with the shrinking government deficit. During the first half of 1993, issuance is RM9300 billion,; during the second half, issuance tapers off to RM4300 billion.

- 16 February 1993: Bank Negara sells the first issues of the Malaysia Saving Bond (MSB) for RM1 billion.

Philippines (1992)

- 1992: Sterilisation efforts intensify through issuance of central bank bills and borrowings under the central bank reverse repurchase facility. In view of the central bank's lack of holding of treasury bills, the government was called to issue government securities and deposit the proceeds with the central bank.

- Mid 1993: Sterilisation efforts diminish and the government shifts its deposits from the central bank to commercial banks. More adjustment comes through allowing the nominal exchange rate to appreciate.

Thailand (1988)

- 1989–91: Heavy sterilisation period. During this period the Bank of Thailand increases its rediscount rate from 8 per cent at the end of 1989 to 12 per cent at the end of 1990.

- Late 1989: The Bank of Thailand reduces commercial banks' access to refinancing facilities, from 100 per cent to 50 per cent of the face value of qualifying notes.

- Mid 1993: Sterilisation efforts cease.

Source: IMF (1995)

BOX 3.3: STERILISATION THROUGH CHANGES IN RESERVE REQUIREMENTS

The year next to the country name denotes the first year of the surge in inflows.

Malaysia (1989)

- 2 May 1989: Reserve requirement is increased to 4.5 per cent from 3.5 per cent for commercial banks and 3.0 per cent for finance companies.

- 16 October 1989: Reserve requirement is increased from 4.5 per cent to 5.5 per cent.

- 16 January 1990: Reserve requirement is increased from 5.5 per cent to 6.5 per cent.

- 16 August 1991: Reserve requirement is increased from 6.5 per cent to 7.5 per cent.

- 16 September 1991: All outstanding ringgit received through swap transactions with nonresidents, including offshore banks, is to be included in the eligible liabilities base and be subject to statutory reserve requirements.

- 2 May 1992: Reserve requirement is increased from 7.5 per cent to 8.5 per cent.

- 3 January 1994: Reserve requirement is increased from 8.5 per cent to 9.5 per cent. The reserve requirement is extended to cover foreign currency deposits and transactions (such as foreign currency borrowing from foreign banking institutions and interbank borrowing). Previously it applied only to ringgit-denominated transactions.

- 1994: Reserve requirement is increased in two steps to 11.5 per cent.

Philippines (1992)

- 15 August 1994: The reserve requirement is reduced from 19 to 17 per cent (excluding reserves held in the form of government securities) with the objective of inducing a decline in domestic interest rates.

Source: IMF (1995)

BOX 3.4: STERILISATION THROUGH MANAGEMENT OF GOVERNMENT FUNDS

The year next to the country name denotes the first year of the surge in inflows.

Malaysia (1989)

- April 1990: The money market operations (MMO) account of the Accountant-General maintained at Bank Negara is reactivated. Government deposits placed with the banking system that will mature that year (about RM3.7 billion) are withdrawn from the system and deposited in the MMO account.

- 1992–94: Transfer of government deposits and Employee Provident Fund (EPF) deposits to Bank Negara.

Philippines (1992 and 1994)

- The national government issues securities and deposits proceeds with the Central Bank.

Thailand (1988)

- 1987–mid 1992: Government deposits held at the Bank of Thailand are increased from 25 per cent of total deposits at the end of 1987 to 82 per cent by mid 1992.

Source: IMF (1995)

BOX 3.5: STERILISATION THROUGH FISCAL AUSTERITY MEASURES

The year next to the country name denotes the first year of the surge in inflows.

Malaysia (1989)

- 1992–93: Fiscal consolidation. Real public consumption growth reduces significantly (0.4 per cent in 1992). Public sector deficit is reduced to about 1.5 per cent of GDP.

Thailand (1988)

- 1988–91: Moderation of government expenditure. Government budgetary balance (in per cent of GDP) swings from a deficit of 1.4 per cent to a surplus of 4.9 per cent in 1991–92. A value-added tax is introduced.

Source: IMF (1995)

How successful have they been? If we examine the rate of growth of money supply, particularly domestic credit, we find that the sterilisation efforts were not a complete success. As noted earlier, the money supply in a number of economies grew faster than did nominal GNP. Domestic credit grew considerably in almost all economies. Although HPAEs were able to contain inflation rates below 10 per cent, they remained higher than those of their trading partners—as reflected in the appreciation of real effective exchange rates. This is another indication of less-than-successful sterilisation due to the impossible trinity.

To the extent that HPAEs were successful in sterilising via open market operations, domestic interest rates remained higher than the international rates, encouraging more capital to flow in. Even if sterilised fully, the inflow of capital can change the composition of domestic demand. If it falls more on tradable products, it will widen the current account deficit. It can also create inflationary pressure, due to supply lags and asset price inflation, and hence a decline in international competitiveness through real appreciation (see Box 3.1). On the other hand, to the extent that HPAEs failed in sterilisation, domestic credit grew at a faster rate, causing inflation to rise. Thus, in either case, the capital account developments drove the current account developments. As noted earlier, the current account deficits of a number of economies (notably Thailand and Malaysia) grew as a percentage of their GDPs. The market perception of unsustainable current account deficits due to the policy dilemma posed by the eternal triangle eventually led to speculative attacks on the Thai baht and other currencies.

POLITICAL ECONOMY OF MACROECONOMIC MANAGEMENT AND DISMANTLING THE ASIAN DEVELOPMENT MODEL

As the discussion shows, internationalisation or increased capital mobility affected the autonomy of national governments' policy choices. According to the standard open-economy macro models of Mundell-Fleming,[2] in a fixed or pegged exchange rate regime increased capital mobility renders monetary policy less useful domestically: it becomes simply a tool for maintaining the exchange rate. While fiscal policy can have more effectiveness, governments may still be constrained in using it by their commitment to exchange rate stability. For example, if fiscal expansion induces inflationary expectations or budget deficits, pressures on the exchange rate will increase, leading to a devaluation as the foreign exchange reserve declines. In a flexible exchange rate system, the fiscal policy loses its potency due to the response of international capital to interest rate changes. For example, an expansionary fiscal policy raises the domestic interest rate above the world rate. This induces capital flows which put pressure on the exchange rate to appreciate. The appreciation of the exchange rate adversely affects competitiveness and offsets the expansionary impact of fiscal policy. Although monetary policy tends to have more potency under a flexible exchange rate system when capital is mobile, the very size of the impact may deter the monetary authority from using it. This point has been articulated by Alan Greenspan, Chairman of the US Federal Reserve:

> A consistently disciplined monetary policy is what our global financial system increasingly demands and rewards ... While there are many policy considerations that arise as a consequence of the rapidly expanding global financial system, the most important is the necessity of maintaining stability in the prices of goods and services and confidence in domestic financial markets. Failure to do so is apt to exact far greater consequences as a result of cross-border capital movements than those which might have prevailed a generation ago (*New York Times*, 21 June 1995: A-1, D-9).

While the relative effectiveness of fiscal and monetary policies depends on the exchange rate system as the barriers to capital mobility are removed, increased internationalisation constrains governments to a conservative fiscal and monetary policy mix independent of exchange rate regimes. This is also true for small, highly open economies regardless of shades of government (Alesina & Roubini 1992; Alt 1985).

Another important event since the 1980s that has constrained the macroeconomic policy mix is the rapid deregulation of the domestic financial sector, which resulted in unprecedented growth of both financial institutions and financial products. Financial institutions have a vested interest in keeping inflation low because a rise in interest rates reduces the value of fixed-interest securities. Also, an inflation rate that is consistently above that of most other countries is a reliable sign that sooner or later the currency will be devalued, which adversely affects the repatriation of foreign capital income and those with fixed foreign liabilities. This financial market sentiment has been echoed by the former Governor of the Reserve Bank of Australia, Bernie Fraser: 'monetary policy was becoming the hostage of influential financial markets with a vested interest in making the Reserve Bank give greater weight to inflation than unemployment' (*Sydney*

Morning Herald, 16 June 1996). Financial markets also worry about large budget deficits, which they fear may lead to a rise in interest rates or to devaluation.

HPAEs display a progressive government withdrawal from regulation of the real and the financial sides of the economy since the mid 1980s, in line with neo-classical orthodoxy. This meant a substantial dismantling of the Asian growth model in which governments played a vital role both in terms of high infrastructure investment and a strong relationship with business. As noted at the start of this chapter, macroeconomic discipline was essential to the exceptionally rapid economic growth of HPAEs. But prior to becoming hostages to financial markets (both domestic and international), governments maintained fiscal discipline through a virtuous circle of growth. They invested in infrastructure and human capital formation which increased the productivity of private investment and international competitiveness as explained by the new growth theory (Barro 1997; Lucas 1988; Romer 1990). In the repressed financial system, the governments used their close relationships with business to guide private investment towards profitable and internationally competitive sectors (Amsden 1989, 1991; Lee 1992; Rajan & Zingales 1998). This meant that governments were able to maintain fiscal balance (surplus or a small deficit) through growth dividends as their revenues continued to rise with the growing private sector paying increasing tax.[3]

This model of fiscal balance involves substantial lags, as infrastructure investment usually comes to fruition only after a long gestation period. As a result, it has an inflationary bias. Given the vested interest of the financial sector in low inflation, the model becomes inoperative with the increased influence of financial markets. Governments were forced to achieve fiscal balance more quickly and had to reduce tax on capital income, as higher capital tax may encourage capital to leave. The neo-classical orthodoxy also suggests that lower taxes foster entrepreneurial innovation. Thus, governments had to achieve fiscal balance by cutting their expenditure. For example, as shown in Table 3.5, the share of tax revenue in most HPAEs remained stable between 1985 and 1995 and government expenditure as a proportion of GDP fell drastically except in Korea, the Philippines, and Taiwan, where it increased marginally. Since cuts in current expenditure are politically

Table 3.5: Government Finance Indicators (% of GDP)

Economy	Tax revenue				Expenditure				Fiscal balance/deficit			
	1975	1985	1995	1996	1975	1985	1995	1996	1975	1985	1995	1996
Hong Kong	8.6	10.4	11.1	11.6	12.8 (2.7)	15.3 (2.8)	13.9 (3.1)	14.6 (3.2)	1.9	0.4	−0.3	2.2
Indonesia	16.9	18.3	14.1	14.6	21.6 (0.9)	23.5 (1.9)	15.5 (0.6)	15.1 NA	3.9	3.7	−0.4	1.2
Korea	13.8	14.8	16.9	8.6	15.7 (2.2)	16.3 (3.0)	17.6 (3.6)	18.3 (3.1)	2.1	1.2	0.2	0.5
Malaysia	20.5	21.6	19.0	18.9	31.4 (6.1)	32.9 (5.6)	22.4 (4.8)	22.6 (5.0)	8.5	5.7	−0.8	0.7
Philippines	13.2	10.7	16.3	16.7	16.0 (1.9)	14.1 (2.0)	18.2 (3.2)	18.3 (3.4)	1.4	1.9	−0.5	0.3
Singapore	17.1	17.3	16.4	17.7	26.3 (3.1)	39.1 (4.6)	20.8 NA	NA	−0.8	4.4	NA	NA
Taiwan	16.5	8.5	10.8	9.8	21.4 (0.8)	14.0 (1.6)	15.1 NA	14.3 (1.5)	−1.3	0.2	1.1	−1.4
Thailand	11.5	13.7	17.0	17.0	14.9 NA	18.9 NA	15.4 NA	17.8 NA	1.7	4.3	−3.0	0.9

Source: Asian Development Bank, *Key Indicators for Member Countries*, 1997

Note: Figures in parenthesis are expenditure on education as a percentage of GDP difficult as they affect social services (meagre to begin with in HPAEs), governments chose the easier option of cutting infrastructure investment. However, the decline in public infrastructure investment was not offset by a rise in private participation in the sector, as expected within the neo-classical framework. It is also disturbing that there was a decline in expenditure on education in some countries, such as Indonesia and Malaysia, as a percentage of GDP between 1985 and 1995. This led to a vicious circle. The more reductions there were in infrastructure and education, the larger was the decline in productivity, the slower was economic growth, and hence the more pressure on governments to reduce expenditure (Eatwell & Taylor 1998; Taylor 1998).

Moreover, as Rajan and Zingales (1998) point out, when there is surplus capital in relation to opportunities for profitable investment, its efficient allocation requires a financial system which operates at arm's length and is based on a legal framework rather than on relations, as occurs in HPAEs. The domestic financial system could not change as fast as capital flowed in. The problem was compounded by the rapid withdrawal of government, as financial deregulation under the weight of international capital markets and IMF–World Bank pressure was taken as synonymous with *laissez-faire* or no regulation. The financial system remained relations-based and lacked prudential regulation. This meant that when the increased flow of capital was channelled through the banking sector, banks could venture into risky loans and thereby increase the fragility of the financial system. Inefficient use of capital also had adverse effects on productivity. As productivity of investment fell, people increasingly directed their high savings to the speculative financial investment facilitated by financial deregulation. The incentive for short-term speculative investment also arose from lack of confidence in the economy, as the prospect for long business cycle swings increases with governments' withdrawal from their stabilisation role. The shift to short-term speculative capital had further adverse effects on productivity. As the productivity-driven economic growth slowed, governments needed to encourage more foreign capital to drive demand-led growth—a slow-down in economic growth would threaten their legitimacy. Governments increasingly became hostage to financial markets, especially international capital, which constrained their ability to respond to macroeconomic shocks, for which they had once gained reputation.

BOX 3.6: RISKS AND BENEFITS OF CAPITAL ACCOUNT LIBERALISATION

Increasing international mobility of financial capital is a major aspect of the global economy, and the volume of international financial transactions far exceeds that necessary to finance ordinary trade in goods and services. For example, the ratio of foreign exchange trading to world trade rose from 10:1 in 1980 to 70:1 in 1995 (Bank for International Settlements 1996).

With the sharp rise in cross-border transactions of foreign exchange, there has been a fundamental shift in the assessment of the value of capital control. Thus, the International Monetary Fund (IMF) amended its Article VI and endorsed an eventual move to capital account convertibility. The World Bank has actively encouraged capital market liberalisation. The International Finance Corporation (an affiliate of the World Bank) fosters stock market developments in developing countries and encourages them to open their capital market to foreign portfolio investments. The argument for capital account liberalisation is very simple: free trade in capital will eliminate efficiency losses and, like trade in goods and services, generate mutual gains for trading partners.

Capital account liberalisation and financial sector deregulation are likely to generate the following benefits (Eatwell 1996).

- Savings will be directed to the most productive investments regardless of national boundaries (capital will flow from capital-rich countries to capital-poor countries).

- Increased competition will create a more efficient financial system, offering better opportunities for savers and lower costs for borrowers.

- New financial instruments such as derivatives (futures, swaps, and options) help firms to manage financial risks more effectively.

- The long-term result should be higher investment and growth.

- The markets provide a healthy discipline for governments, which encourages better policies and performance.

These points are based on two propositions. First, competitive markets ensure both productive and allocative efficiencies. Second, financial markets operate so as to process information efficiently—certainly better than governments could.

However, according to Bhagwati (1998: 7), a champion of free trade, 'the claims of enormous benefits from free capital mobility are not persuasive. Substantial gains have been asserted, not demonstrated, and most of the payoff can be obtained by direct equity investment'. Rodrik's (1998) findings on one hundred industrial and developing countries for 1975–89 support Bhagwati's position. Rodrik finds that capital account convertibility has no significant effect on economic growth. Eatwell (1996) also finds that there is a substantial gap between the expected gains from capital account liberalisation and the reality.

Bhagwati (1998) points out that trade in capital is not the same as trade in goods and services. Most transactions in capital markets are driven by speculative and financial considerations such as hedging against exchange rate movements, and arbitrage opportunities—an inevitable consequence of the 1973 abandonment of the fixed exchange rate system. Being driven by speculation, unlike equity investment (foreign direct investment), these capital transactions are short-term and volatile in nature. According to Kindleberger (1989), capital flows are characterised by panics and manias. Sudden reversal in capital flows can cause a liquidity crisis, with substantial adverse impacts on real output. The domestic interest rate must be raised to prevent capital outflows, but that causes substantial difficulties for indebted firms and may even cause bankruptcies. On the other hand, a surge in inflows can contribute to the fragility of banks as their credit activity expands. The probability of a banking crisis rises if the financial sector is deregulated at the same time. The external account imbalance due to an investment boom financed by external capital necessitates interest rate increases to slow the activity, but the rising interest rate attracts more capital inflows, adding to the very problem it was supposed to solve. Thus, both the external account problem and the weakening of the banking sector result from excessive capital inflows (Akyuz 1998) (see Box 3.1).

The opening of the capital account and financial sector liberalisation increase the prospect of financial crises, and there is a real danger that the crises will spill beyond one country or region. The danger of contagion is due to the increased trade and financial interdependence between countries (Glick & Rose 1998).

Capital flows also pose a problem for macroeconomic management, known as the open economy trilemma. To attract capital inflows, countries are tempted to peg their exchange rates (or reduce their volatility). As this happens, they lose control of their monetary policy. One way to manage the problem is to follow a contractionary fiscal policy to counteract the impact of monetary expansion due to capital inflows. The demand to produce a conservative budget means abandoning its commitment to full employment, leading to a deflationary tendency in the economy. This encourages short-term investment, which adversely affects long-term growth prospects.

Note: Under IMF Article VI, adopted in 1944, member states are allowed to impose permanent controls to avoid 'restrictions on payments for current transactions'. Keynes, one of the architects of the Bretton Woods system, argued for a much stronger version which would have required the IMF and other countries to assist in enforcing capital controls. Keynes (1933: 236) held the view that finance must primarily remain 'national'. However, that version was compromised under pressure from Wall Street (Helleiner 1994).

CONCLUSION

This chapter provides an account of macroeconomic management in HPAEs during the 1990s and the constraints they faced in the wake of financial deregulation and capital account liberalisation. Although macroeconomic indicators displayed sound fundamentals, beneath them lay weaknesses resulting from an inconsistent macroeconomic policy mix and the withdrawal of governments from regulating the economy. Both were due to pressures from domestic and international financial markets. Bhagwati (1997) claims that the pressure to open the capital market and deregulate the domestic financial sector is a conspiracy of the 'Wall Street–US Treasury–IMF complex'. OECD members (industrialised countries) led by the USA pressed for the liberalisation of the world economy in several dimensions: revision of the IMF Articles to require member nations to remove all controls on capital markets; liberalisation of trade in financial services and suppression of industrial policy interventions under the auspices of the WTO; and an OECD multilateral investment accord.[4] These initiatives are designed to give international financial institutions and transnational corporations unfettered access to markets worldwide. The chapter alludes to the idea that HPAEs happily participated in this 'conspiracy' due to the legitimacy needs of their authoritarian regimes, as they failed to make the transition to a productivity-driven phase of economic growth. They have become hostages to international capital and financial institutions and surrendered their sovereignty over macroeconomic policy-making. This has led to the dismantling of the Asian growth model which served them so well in the past.

Is there any going back? Following the work of Garrett and Lange (1996), it seems not. Internationalisation has led to a process of endogenous political and institutional changes, both domestically and internationally. The HPAEs may follow the lead of Malaysia and temporarily withdraw from international capital markets, and there may emerge an international order which puts some limits on capital mobility. But the influence of the financial sector will remain dominant in the more complex economies of Asia, and they cannot avoid the transition to more transparent and democratic societies. They have to institute a financial sector based on rules, replacing relation-based operations with an arm's length allocation of investible funds. This is already evident in a number of countries, notably Indonesia. Increased globalisation has coincided with an information revolution—people are more aware of what is happening around them. As growth falters there will be increased demand for change, and that demand will become louder with the deepening impact of the financial crisis on poverty and inequality. With the demise of neo-classical orthodoxy and the possible introduction of controls on international capital mobility, the postwar Keynesian consensus may re-emerge, with government assuming its traditional role of stabilisation.

Chapter 4

Financial Liberalisation and Prudential Regulation

INTRODUCTION

> Financial markets ... can be thought of as the 'brain' of the entire economic system, the central locus of decision-making: if they fail, not only will the sector's profit be lower than would otherwise have been, but the performance of the entire economic system may be impaired (Stiglitz 1994: 23).

This quote captures the central role the financial sector plays in an economy, and its validity is borne out by Asia's financial crisis and the resulting economic crisis in the late 1990s.

The early development economists saw underdevelopment as primarily the result of market failure. The conventional wisdom was that, left to itself, the financial market will not generate sufficient savings to lift economic growth rate, nor will it direct investible funds to socially desired sectors. Since underdeveloped countries are capital-scarce, it was argued that, if left to the market, the interest rate would be overly high, which would deter potential investors. The policy prescription was to impose *economic* regulation on the financial market in the form of interest rate ceilings, a situation often referred to as 'financial repression'. When the interest rate is set below the market equilibrium level, an excess demand for credit is created. This allows the government to direct credit to socially desirable sectors or projects.

This was the demand-side story of the financial sector, but the supply side also had a number of arguments. To begin with, the link between savings and interest rates is uncertain, due to opposing *income* and *substitution* effects. For example, a low interest rate policy should result in low savings due to the substitution effect, but high savings due to the income effect. Thus, the effect of an interest rate ceiling on the supply of investible funds is ambiguous. It is argued that the supply of savings could be increased by forced saving. The main instrument of this process is a government budget deficit, financed by money creation (Kalecki 1976). The process of forced saving can work through a number of channels. First, expansionary fiscal-monetary policy increases income via the familiar Keynesian multiplier, which in turn induces savings to rise. Second, the expansionary fiscal-monetary policy will generate inflation. Inflation lowers real return on financial investment (especially when interest rates are administratively controlled), and thereby induces wealth-holders to change their portfolio by investing in physical capital. The resultant rise in capital intensity increases output and hence savings (Tobin 1965). Inflation also changes income distribution in favour of profit-earners with a higher propensity to save (Kaldor 1955–56). Finally, inflation imposes a tax on real money balances. That is, people hold more money to maintain the real value of their money and thereby transfer resources to the government (Friedman 1971), which can be used for financing investment.

Thus, the two dominant features of the orthodox policy stance were an interest rate ceiling and inflation. The combination produced either very low or negative real interest rates in most developing countries. However, this policy stance came under severe criticism with the publication of seminal works by McKinnon (1973) and Shaw (1973). Financial repression was singled out as a cause of the low savings rate and underdevelopment of the financial sector in developing economies. It has been argued that a repressed financial sector and negative (or low) real interest rates have a number of growth-inhibiting effects. First, it encourages people to hold their savings in unproductive assets such as real estate, gold, and other precious metals. This hampers the growth of the financial sector (the brain of the economic system) due to inadequate demand for financial assets. The 'shallow' financial sector adversely affects the savings rate due to a lack of alternative financial assets and hence reduces financial resources for investment. Second, the low and negative real interest rate encourages potential investors to be indulgent. This results in inefficient investment and a capital-intensive industrial structure which is out of line with developing countries' factor endowment. Third, the non-market allocation of investible funds encourages rent-seeking and directly unproductive activities when government tries to pick 'winners' or priority activities. This sows the seeds of crony capitalism. Other symptoms of financially repressed economies include splitting the financial system into regulated and unregulated segments (a black market characterised by high interest rates).

The Shaw–McKinnon contributions generated a new orthodoxy: financial 'deepening' or development is essential in the process of capital accumulation, as reflected in savings and investment ratios and their productivity. This in turn contributes to economic growth. Financial deepening is best facilitated by a competitive financial system in which interest rates are market-determined and there is no (or very little) administratively driven selective credit allocation. The policy message is clear. Both financial and real sector development require a comprehensive package of financial liberalisation that frees interest rates to their market-clearing levels and eliminates administratively determined selective credit allocation.

The hypothesis of financial liberalisation appeared to exert a considerable influence on policy developments in industrialising nations. As Hanna (1994: 1) notes:

> Theories of the link between financial performance and economic growth, particularly as advanced by McKinnon (1973) and Shaw (1973), have been the basis for a series of financial reforms around the world, most prominently in the Southern Cone of Latin America, but also in Turkey, parts of Africa and East Asia.

In the Asia–Pacific region, Taiwan was the first country to introduce a high interest rate policy (in the late 1950s), although in subsequent periods the Taiwanese financial system became heavily regulated. In Korea, interest rate reform was adopted in 1965 as a result of recommendations by Shaw, Gurley and Patrick, which were influenced by the Taiwanese experience (Cole & Park 1983). Indonesia built upon the experience of Korea to institute attempts to revive the financial sector in 1968, although this was reversed after the oil price shock of 1973 (Cole & Slade 1992). Korea too reversed its early efforts at interest rate reform during the heavy and chemical industries (HCI) drive of the 1970s. Both these economies later renewed their quest for financial sector reform. As far as other economies of the region are concerned, Singapore and Hong Kong had long been known as international financial centres. Financial reform in Malaysia and the Philippines started in 1978 and 1980 respectively (World Bank 1993b), and the People's Republic of China (PRC) began experimenting with the process only in the late 1980s (World Bank 1995). Thailand was generally noted for its modest distortions in financial markets (Agarwala 1983; World Bank 1989). The available data suggest that, compared with other regions, financial repression was moderate and that real interest rates exhibited less variability (World Bank 1993a).

The enthusiasm that greeted the financial liberalisation hypothesis turned out to be optimistic and somewhat naive. The empirical foundation of the Shaw–McKinnon paradigm appears less robust than anticipated—for example, the evidence about the interest rate–savings link is ambivalent (Hossain & Chowdhury 1996; Islam & Chowdhury 1997). A study by Bandiera et al. (1998: 21) concludes, 'it would be unwise to rely on an increase in savings as the channel through which financial liberalisation can be expected to increase growth'. Further, the disastrous results of financial reform in the 1970s in the Southern Cone countries highlighted the need to avoid severe macro-imbalances as a precondition for the beneficial effects of financial liberalisation and to pay more careful attention to the sequencing of reforms (see Edwards 1984 for a review). Advocates of the early version of the financial liberalisation hypothesis have modified their position and support a more nuanced version of the view (McKinnon 1982, 1984, 1988).

There is a trend in the literature to question the analytical foundations of the financial liberalisation hypothesis by arguing that what is perceived to be financial repression is really a case of efficient internal capital markets (Lee 1992). Variants of this argument can be found in Wade (1988) and Amsden (1989). The Korean experience of the 1970s and that of Japan in the early phase of its industrialisation are often marshalled as evidence in favour of this intriguing view.

However, the financial crisis in Southeast Asia has made it clear that too much attention was given to the allocative aspects of the financial system and too little to prudential, organisational, and protective regulation—an issue of central significance in the market failures that characterise financial systems (Stiglitz & Weiss 1981; Stiglitz 1989). The events in Southeast Asia and financial crises in liberalising countries have exposed the limitations of both the naive view of financial liberalisation and its nuanced version. In particular, they indicate that financial liberalisation increases the fragility of the banking sector. The problem becomes more acute in the absence of a proper *prudential* regulatory framework, and is compounded by increased capital flows. Even a repressed financial sector can become stressed with increased capital flows.

This chapter focuses on the pitfalls of financial sector liberalisation and reflects on the lessons of the financial crisis in the Asia–Pacific economies. It also provides a critical evaluation of the internal capital market hypothesis and its variants. It maintains that both a liberalised system and a repressed system can be efficient under different sets of circumstances, and the capital account must not be liberalised before an effective *regulatory* and *supervisory* framework is in place.

FINANCIAL LIBERALISATION: SOME COMPLICATIONS

Shaw (1973) has made the important point that 'financial repression is part of a package'. Such a package entails distortions in foreign exchange markets, in the trade regime, and in labour and product markets in general, and macreconomic instability. The observation has an important implication that was insufficiently emphasised by the early writers on financial liberalisation. Removing distortions in the financial system without reforming distortions in other markets and restoring macroeconomic stability is a ratification of the classic 'theory of the second-best': removing one source of distortion while leaving others intact does not necessarily constitute a welfare-improving move (Lipsey & Lancaster 1956–57).

The naive version of the financial liberalisation hypothesis does not generally discuss problems of market failure that could affect financial systems. Market failure stems from a number of sources, such as externalities, the exercise of monopoly power by dominant banks, and information asymmetries between borrowers and lenders (Kay & Vickers 1988). Examples of externalities include the risk of systemic failure (the notion that bank failures may be correlated, with actual or threatened failure in one case raising the risk of failure of another) and the 'infection effect' (lowering of product and price standards through excessive competition). Concern has also been expressed that financial liberalisation might unleash dominant firms that could exercise monopoly power (through excessive price-cost margins and erection of entry barriers) to the detriment of dynamic and static efficiency (see Vittas 1992 for a fuller discussion).

Stiglitz (1989) has emphasised the central role of information asymmetries in the market failure of financial systems. In essence, the argument is that banks do not have perfect information about the creditworthiness of borrowers. Moral hazard and adverse selection problems could emerge: borrowers have an incentive to assume more risky projects when the cost of credit increases; the banks' reliable clients may be replaced by less solvent debtors because the former are indistinguishable from the latter. In such a context, interest rate 'overshooting' (rising to excessive levels to cover default risk) could occur, thus crowding out low-risk projects with high, *ex ante* social rates of return. It is plausible that in the early stages of development information asymmetries are more acute, partly because of the lack of institutions that collect and disseminate credit information.

Macroeconomic instability could exacerbate problems of moral hazard, as a key advocate of financial liberalisation, McKinnon (1984), has recognised. This represents a sophisticated variant of the fallacy of the second-best alluded to above. Macroeconomic instability exacerbates the moral hazard problem because of the risk of systemic failure. This makes it difficult for the monetary authorities to sanction the imprudence of a particular bank, thus creating incentives for interest rate overshooting. In a significant departure from his original position, McKinnon (1988) has suggested the need to impose con-trols on interest rates to cope with cases of moral hazard and argues that the failure of authorities to recognise the problem of interest rate overshooting was partially responsible for the 1970s financial collapse of the Southern Cone countries.

In another attempt to provide a more nuanced version of the original financial liberalisation hypothesis, McKinnon (1982) has argued the need to pay attention to the sequencing of reforms. This is a significant departure from the 'big bang' approach advocated by Shaw (1973)—the notion that all microeconomic reforms should be attempted simultaneously. The revisionist view seems to be that deregulation of the financial system should follow a sequential path (Edwards 1984). Reform should start with the trade and exchange rate regime, followed by financial sector reform. Once domestic financial liberalisation is complete, liberalisation of the capital account can be implemented. The World Bank (1989: 127–8) has reaffirmed this dogma by observing that: 'until [domestic financial] reforms are well underway, it will probably be necessary to maintain controls on the movement of [foreign] capital'.

The logic of the sequencing approach is driven by the concern that a country undergoing domestic financial liberalisation could be vulnerable to destabilising capital flows, based (again) on the experience of the Southern Cone countries. However, the financial fragility and banking crises experienced by liberalising countries and the financial crisis in East Asian economies which generally had a reasonably stable macroeconomic environment have led to a need for another kind of sequencing. Events indicate that achieving macroeconomic stability before financial and capital account liberalisation may bring an important independent source of financial instability under control, but it does not completely eliminate the problem of moral hazard and other sources of instability. As mentioned earlier, financial liberalisation may encourage perverse behaviour on the part of financial institutions, and thus enhance the risk of banking and financial crisis in an otherwise well-functioning economy. The study by Demirguc-Kunt and Detragiache (1998) shows that banking crises are more likely to occur in liberalised financial systems. Furthermore, the risk of banking crises is much higher in countries where the institutional and regulatory framework is weak and corruption is widespread. Therefore, institutional and legal reform for strengthening the regulatory and supervisory environment of the financial sector must precede financial sector reform and capital account liberalisation (see Box 4.1).

Elek and Wilson (1999: 2) argue that the free flow of capital could magnify existing distortions in the financial sector in the absence of an effective institutional and regulatory framework. According to them, capital controls should remain as a 'third-best' measure, but only temporarily while the distortions are removed through 'first-best' policy instruments. This is in line with Krugman (1998d).

Cole and Slade (1999: 108) take a much grimmer view of the liberalisation–globalisation model:

> Painful as it may seem for those of us who have advocated this model, [the] recent crises compel us to reconsider whether it is possible to create in a few years the essential preconditions for a safe and sound, privately owned financial system, operating in a

free-wheeling globalised world, especially in developing countries that are still in the early stages of establishing effective, democratic political and legal systems.

At the very least, [the Asian] crisis should provoke a searching re-examination of the risks inherent in the pursuit of the strategy of liberalisation and globalisation, as well as exploring alternative approaches that might produce better results over the longer run for countries in different stages of the economic and political development process.

The discussion so far has raised a number of complications that affect the naive version of the financial liberalisation hypothesis. Its advocates have been acutely aware of some of these complications and have sought to revamp the basic theory to fit the changing context of developing economies. Despite the modifications, some believe that, under conditions of market failure, financial liberalisation is an untenable proposition. More importantly, what is construed as financial repression can in fact be interpreted as a mechanism that is able to resolve market failure and thus facilitate growth. This topic forms the substance of the next section.

BOX 4.1: FINANCIAL SECTOR REFORM AND FINANCIAL CRISIS

Many developing countries experienced financial crises after introducing financial reform programs in the mid 1970s (World Bank 1989; Capiro & Klingebiel 1996; Lindgren, Garcia & Saal 1996). There seems to be a close relationship between financial liberalisation and financial crisis. Financial liberalisation reform may increase the fragility of financial and non-financial firms and set the stage for a financial crisis through the following channels.

- Financial liberalisation reform may lead to excessive risk-taking by financial institutions through increasing the freedom of entry into the financial sector and the freedom to bid for funds through interest rates and new financial instruments, unless tempered with regulation and prudential supervision. The lack of effective prudential regulation and supervision is often a major cause of financial crisis.

- An implicit or explicit guarantee of government bailout of deposits and bankers may also encourage unsound lending patterns and trigger excessive risk-taking by financial institutions following financial deregulation.

- The liberalised structure may lead to concentration of market power through interlocking ownership and lending patterns. Such a financial structure may create market failures because of moral hazard, adverse risk selection, and oligopolistic pricing.

- Interest rate deregulation results in an excessive rise in interest rates, especially when euphoric expectations generate an artificial demand for credit. This may have a number of adverse effects: it raises the prospect of market failure as high interest rates attract risky borrowers; it may affect banks and other financial institutions if they have large exposure to long-term assets at fixed interest rates funded by short-term liabilities; and it may lead to distress borrowing by firms with high debt:equity ratios.

- If interest rates above a certain level are considered risky due to adverse risk selection, financial institutions may want to hold interest rates down and ration credit. Credit rationing can cause bankruptcies of firms which in turn may affect banks.

- The monetary authority may lack adequate and effective instruments of monetary control to influence the interest rates or may follow a hands-off policy in the belief that the domestic interest rate will automatically converge with foreign interest rates through arbitrage.

- If the capital account is liberalised at the same time, the high domestic interest rate may attract short-term foreign capital which increases the risk of sudden reverse flows and financial crisis.

- An open economy with a fixed exchange rate system and a liberalised capital account faces the 'impossible trinity'—it cannot simultaneously control money supply, maintain a fixed exchange rate, and encourage capital flows. It generates expectations of devaluation and hence speculative attacks on domestic currency (see chapter 3).

CAN FINANCIAL REPRESSION BE GOOD FOR GROWTH?

Can a repressed financial system actually facilitate rapid economic growth? Proponents of financial repression point out that the empirical evidence in favour of financial liberalisation is dominated by large repressions and hence does not invalidate the hypothesis that mild repression enhances economic growth. This is the conclusion of the World Bank study (1993a) which finds that financial repression in the high-performing Asian economies (HPAEs) has been mild, unlike that in many other developing economies.

Lee (1992) provides the most comprehensive rationale in favour of the hypothesis that financial repression can promote growth. Variants can be found in Wade (1988), Wade and Veneroso (1998), Amsden (1989, 1991), and Amsden and Euh (1993). In developing this argument, it would be useful to start with the distinction that Zysman (1983) makes between a capital market-based and a credit-based financial system.

In a capital market-based financial system, securities (stocks and bonds) are the main sources of long-term business finance. Borrowers can choose from a broad spectrum of capital and money market instruments offered competitively through a large number of specialised financial institutions. In a credit-based system, the capital market is weak and firms rely heavily on credit to finance investment. This makes them very dependent on banks, to the extent that banks are the main suppliers of credit. However, if banks are themselves dependent on the government, then firms are heavily dependent on the government. It is thus a state-controlled credit-based financial system. In such an institutional environment, financial repression (in the form of government control of credit allocation) becomes the norm and firms exhibit high debt:equity ratios.

Wade (1988) and Wade and Veneroso (1998) maintain that Korea and Taiwan exhibit the classic features of government-dominated credit-based systems. During the 1970s, debt:equity ratios were 300–400 per cent in Korea and 100–200 per cent in Taiwan. The corresponding figures in Latin American countries such as Brazil and Mexico were 100–120 per cent; in industrialised countries the figures were below 100 per cent. Wade (1988) attributes this to higher domestic savings rates (30–40 per cent of GDP) in Asia as opposed to 15–20 per cent in industrialised countries. Mostly, households who prefer less risky bank deposits to equities make these savings. In situations where households and governments are not significant net borrowers, bank loans are biased to the corporate sector. Furthermore, in Taiwan, until very recently virtually the entire banking system was government-owned. In Korea the same was true until 1980–83 and, even after the financial deregulation of the mid 1980s, the government exercised de facto control of the banking system through personnel policies, appointment of senior managers, range of services, and the like.

According to its advocates, distinct advantages flow from the operation of a state-dominated credit-based system. Wade (1988: 134), for example, identifies two alleged advantages. First, 'a credit-based system permits faster investment in developing country conditions than would be possible if investment depended on the growth of firms' own profits or on the inevitably slow development of a securities market'. More importantly, productive investment is less affected by speculative stock market booms and busts. Second, a credit-based system tends to avoid the bias towards short-term profitability that often appears to be associated with a stock market system. This stems from the argument that lenders of long-term finance are interested in borrowers' ability to repay loans over the long term. Hence, long-term performance becomes the dominant consideration, entailing a focus on such issues as the ability of organisations to develop new products, cost competitiveness, and so on. Managers are concerned with these criteria rather than with short-term performance in the stock market.

According to Wade and Veneroso (1998), such a financial structure requires cooperation between banks and firms and considerable support from the government. The government must be ready to buffer firms' cash flow and supply of capital against systemic shocks, while not protecting firms from the consequences of bad judgment. In Korea, for example, inefficient companies were often penalised, either by being required to undertake managerial or financial restructuring, or by allowing them to go into bankruptcy (Chang 1998). A state-dominated financial system provides the government with the political clout necessary to implement its industrial strategy. As Wade (1988:134) puts it: 'firms are dissuaded from opposing the government by knowledge that opponents may find credit difficult to obtain'.

The notion that a credit-based financial system can be seen as a political device to assist governments in implementing industrial strategy is the crux of Amsden's (1989, 1991) argument that financial repression is an essential feature of 'late industrialisation' (of which Korea and Taiwan are classic examples). In her model of late industrialisation, governments deliberately use selective credit allocation to speed the process of industrialisation. However, industrialising nations run the risk that the costs of financial repression can outweigh its alleged benefits, in the sense that it can provoke a subsidy mentality and induce wasteful rent-seeking behaviour. Governments can circumvent this difficulty by ensuring that abuse of preferential credit allocation is minimised, through imposing strict performance standards. If such standards are based on good approximations of *ex ante* social rates of return, politically determined credit allocation will lead to socially profitable investments in desirable industries and sectors. Hence, financial repression will lead to rapid growth.

A more sophisticated argument in favour of financial repression stems from transactions cost economics, which relies heavily on the notion of information asymmetries. This view is closely associated with the work of Lee (1992) and can be characterised as the 'internal capital market hypothesis'.

As noted earlier, when information asymmetries between borrowers and lenders are high and pervasive they can be a potent source of market failure. Under such circumstances, reliance on the internal capital market (reliance on finance generated through retained earnings or depreciation charges) can resolve market failure by reducing or eliminating the incidence of information asymmetries.

Lee (1992) has tried to adapt this argument to the East Asian case by suggesting that a state-dominated credit-based system operates as a de facto internal capital market. The state cultivates a long-term and close relationship with borrowing firms. The atmosphere of trust and cooperation created as a result of the close relationship allows 'lender monitoring' to be carried out effectively and efficiently, so that information asymmetries (and transactions costs) are minimised. Hence, what is apparently considered a phenomenon of financial repression is in effect an internal capital market that is more efficient than private capital markets—an interpretation endorsed in Dalla and Khatkhate's evaluation (1995) of Korean financial reforms in the 1980s and 1990s.

While these arguments are suggestive and interesting, it is possible to construct cogent counter-arguments. First, one should be careful not to confuse a credit-based system with a state-controlled credit-based system. Financial repression is a necessary feature of the latter, not the former. More importantly, the major advantages of a credit-based system as identified by Wade do not require the existence of state control (and hence financial repression). The only way in which financial repression can contribute to economic growth in this framework is to presuppose that a strong-willed government has the capacity to overcome the inadequacies of private capital markets without the corresponding risk of government failure.

The hypothesised superiority of lender monitoring in a state-controlled financial system is also questionable when one takes account of the interactions between formal and informal credit markets. This point can be developed using an argument expounded by Cole and Patrick (1986). When formal financial institutions are regulated, informal credit markets expand. Such markets provide funds to those who cannot obtain credit from formal sources. In addition, privileged borrowers in regulated markets have an incentive to re-lend to users in unregulated markets (and hence profit from arbitrage). The outcome is that informal credit markets act as a channel for diverting official (regulated) credit to more profitable investment opportunities, thus invalidating the notion that the state can effectively monitor the behaviour of borrowers. Some evidence can be offered to substantiate these arguments, using the Korean experience. In 1972, approximately 50 per cent of commercial firms in Korea financed their investment needs through the informal credit market. In addition, credit diversion was quite extensive (Cole & Patrick 1986).

However, the Asian financial crisis of the late 1990s seems to have given some credibility to the view that financial repression is good for the economy. Although financial liberalisation in the form of interest rate deregulation began in many Northeast and Southeast Asian economies, their financial sector remained heavily regulated until the late 1980s. For example, according to Park (1994: 57), 'Almost every financial activity in Korea, including access to the banking sector, the determination of interest rates, and the allocation of credit, has been heavily regulated by the government'. The pace of liberalisation accelerated in the 1990s, marking a significant departure from the Asian development model implied by the growth-promoting financial repression view (Brownbridge & Kirkpatrick 1998). In at least two areas the departure has been crucial: control over external borrowing and state guidance of investment. For example, in Korea, deregulation of the financial sector in the early 1990s included removing restrictions on corporate debt financing and cross-border flows. Local companies and banks were allowed to raise money overseas without the traditional supervision and control. Likewise, the Thai government relaxed foreign exchange controls, granted offshore banking licences, eased the rules governing non-bank financial institutions (NBFIs), and allowed finance companies to fund equity purchases on margin. With the removal of interest rate controls or ceilings, the scope for investment guidance also diminished as market-determined interest rates were increasingly relied upon for allocation of investible funds. It is argued that the financial crisis did not result from the long-term and close relationship between government, business, and main banks (a salient feature of the Asian development model) which has come to be known as crony capitalism; rather, the departure from the model precipitated the crisis. In support of their argument, advocates (for example Stiglitz 1998a) point to bank failures in the 1990s in fully transparent countries such as the USA and Sweden. Not long ago, the US financial system was criticised for ignoring longer-term corporate prospects and there were repeated calls by economists (for example Porter 1992) for it to move towards a more relationship-based Asian or Japanese model.

BOX 4.2: FRAGILITY OF THE BANKING SECTOR IN INDONESIA

The internal weaknesses of the Indonesian banking sector played a major role in exacerbating the financial crisis arising from the exchange rate collapse during 1997–98. These included weak management, excessive credit concentration, moral hazard, inadequate and lack of transparency in reporting the financial condition of banks, and ineffective supervision by Bank Indonesia.

Management weakness was manifested in the ineffective internal control and limited information system. As a result, implementation of the self-regulatory banking system proved ineffective, contributing substantially to the abuse of authority that exposed the risk of failure in the banking system. It also contributed to a more concentrated credit expansion to a limited number of debtors, particularly individuals or business groups that had close ties with the banks. This meant the banks were heavily reliant on the resilience of the business activity being financed. Consequently, once the crisis affected the business activity it worsened the banking performance.

The absence of a deposit insurance scheme necessitated an implicit guarantee by the central bank for the survival of commercial banks, to preclude systemic failure in the banking sector. This induced moral hazard and led to a high-risk attitude among bankers.

The supervision and guidance by Bank Indonesia were ineffective because of weak law enforcement and lack of independence and the situation was worsened by incomplete public information on the financial condition of banks. Violations of prudential regulation were widespread.

Table 4.1 provides selected indicators of the banking sector prior to the crisis. As can be seen, funds in both deposits and loans expanded rapidly, loans to the property sector rising by more than 50 per cent. Excessive expansion also occurred in the liabilities side denominated in foreign currency, as reflected in the worsening net open position. On the asset side, non-performing loans rose. Prior to the crisis, the Indonesian banking sector was very vulnerable.

Table 4.1: Selected Banking Indicators in Indonesia (Rp billions)

Indicator	1995	1996	1997	1997–98
Deposits	214764	281718	357613	452937
Credits	234611	292921	378134	476841
Property	42793	58797	68318	70112
Consumer	25310	35579	39769	39061
Non-performing loans	24400	27957	30802	109780
Foreign asset/foreign liabilities (%)	57.7	42.9	50.5	22.2
Off-balance sheet accounts				
Claims	76213	121853	478813	174574
Liabilities	178423	208903	1060349	439343
Operating cost/operating income	0.92	0.92	0.95	1.01

Source: Bank Indonesia, *Report for the Financial Year* 1997/98, 86–7

RELATIONSHIP VS ARM'S LENGTH FINANCIAL SYSTEMS

Rajan and Zingales (1998) have attempted to synthesise both views. They offer a theoretical rationale for a relationship-based financial system at an early stage of development and a market-based system later. Their starting-point is the dual primary roles of a financial system—resource allocation and return to the financer. In an underdeveloped economy with a poor legal structure, a relationship-based system which limits competition ensures a return to the financer by granting some control over the firm being financed. Without such assurances, funds would not flow in sufficient quantity to productive investment. Financers attempt to secure a return on their investment by retaining some kind of monopoly over the firms they finance. The opacity (or lack of transparency) is a barrier to entry required for the maintenance of monopoly power.

A relationship-based system, which restricts competition, does not always yield sub-optimal results. It allows financers (banks) to take a longer perspective in investment decisions, as they can use their monopoly power to charge above-market rates in normal circumstances in return for an implicit agreement to provide financing at below-market rates when firms face short-term cash-flow difficulties. That is, the relationship-based system allows banks and firms to internalise joint surplus by trading short-run losses for longer-run gains. This is borne out by examples such as the Sumitomo Bank guaranteeing Mazda's debts after the first oil-price shock and its rescue effort, exhorting employees within its *keiretsu* to buy Mazda cars.

However, when the supply of capital increases with economic growth and the number of profitable projects declines, price signals become essential in the selection of projects. And the price signal or a market-based system cannot work well unless there are well-developed institutions for enforcement of property and contractual laws and strong disclosure legislation as a guarantee of protection. Thus, two factors determine which system works better: the ratio of available capital to profitable investment opportunities and the degree to which institutional development facilitates contracting. Figure 4.1 summarises outcomes of the two systems. Both systems can work well when the available capital:investment opportunities ratio is low, but there is a strong legal system. Neither system works when the availability:opportunity ratio is high, but the legal system is very weak.

Figure 4.1: Conditions for Efficiency of Relationship-based and Arm's Length Financial Systems

	Low capital: opportunity ratio	High capital: opportunity ratio
High contractability	Both	Market-based
Low contractability	Relationship-based	Neither

This explains why the relationship-based system worked in the early stage of HPAEs' development, and why it failed at a later stage. When capital was scarce compared to profitable investment during the initial phase of development, it was not difficult to determine projects with positive net present value without a well-functioning price signal. The relationship-based system did reasonably well in selecting profitable projects. It allowed firms to expand without being too sensitive to their operating cash flow, and to reap economies of scale and scope. Furthermore, since the relationship-based system allows cross-subsidisation, banks could finance younger firms at below-market rates, compensated by above-market rates for mature firms.

However, institutional development lagged behind financial deepening with economic growth[1] and the pace at which the financial system moved towards a market-based system. As a result, the situation in HPAEs in the 1990s can be described in terms of the lower right-hand corner of Figure 4.1—high availability:opportunity ratio and low contractability. The problem was compounded by the huge and rapid inflow of foreign capital. Foreign lenders (especially of short-term capital) do not have a long-term relationship with the local borrowers, and their ability to monitor loans effectively was impeded because of lack of transparency in published accounts as banks and NBFIs in Indonesia, Korea, and Thailand did not use international accounting standards when compiling audited accounts.

This does not mean, however, that HPAEs mistook financial sector deregulation as a move towards a *laissez-faire* system or confused between *economic* and *prudential* regulation. A number of countries did implement prudential regulation while removing economic regulation, but failed to enforce it due to political interference from the groups which benefited from the former relationship-based system. It is appropriate to now examine the political economy of financial sector liberalisation.

BOX 4.3: FINANCIAL SECTOR REFORM IN KOREA

Korea's financial system suffers from excessive policy loans, a high ratio of non-performing loans, and non-transparent regulations. Following the financial crisis, the government has undertaken reform measures.

- A Financial Supervisory Commission was launched in April 1998. By January 1999, it absorbed the securities and insurance supervisory commissions to become the only financial sector supervisory body. It has been active on issues such as prudential standards, bank recapitalisation, debt reduction of corporations, speeding the work-out process for non-viable banks, and general financial deregulation.

- Non-performing institutions are being weeded out. By September 1998, ninety-four financial institutions had operations suspended. Commercial banks were asked to meet the Bank for International Settlements (BIS) standard capitalisation ratio of 8 per cent. Those who failed had to submit restructuring plans. This has resulted in liquidation of the five weakest banks through purchase and acquisition by other banks.

- The Korea Asset Management Corporation was established to buy non-performing assets from banks. It was expected to write off 32.5 trillion won of bad financial assets in 1998–99.

- The Korea Deposit Insurance Corporation has been allocated 31.5 billion won for bank recapitalisation.

- New accounting and prudential arrangements are being put in place. The International Monetary Fund (IMF) work program has a strict timetable for the implementation of these arrangements.

Source: Department of Foreign Affairs and Trade (Australia), *Country Economic Brief: Korea*, December 1998

POLITICAL ECONOMY OF PRUDENTIAL REGULATION IN EAST ASIA

Following the move towards financial liberalisation in the early 1980s, almost all East Asian economies experienced banks and NBFI failures (Capiro & Klingebiel 1996). These episodes made the liberalising economies aware of the need for prudential regulation and supervision. For example, in the 1990s Indonesia, Korea, Malaysia, and Thailand all raised capital adequacy requirements and imposed the Basle capital adequacy ratio of 8 per cent of risk-adjusted assets. Restrictions were also imposed on large loan exposures, insider lending, and foreign exchange exposures. As observed by Folkerts-Landau et al. (1995: 51–5), these regulations were generally stronger than in other developing countries. According to Brownbridge and Kirkpatrick (1998: 17), 'Prudential regulations in Indonesia, Korea, Malaysia and Thailand were reasonably strong by international standards in many respects'.

However, as Reisen (1998) and Fane (1998) have pointed out, enforcement of regulation was weak. The enforcement of insider lending restrictions was difficult due to a lack of transparency in accounts and political pressure on regulators (Folkerts-Landau et al. 1995). For example, in Indonesia and Korea insider transactions were extensive because many large corporations had affiliated financial institutions from which credit could be obtained on preferential terms. These loans could be rescheduled and further credit extended even when existing loans were not serviced (Rahman 1998: 7). Thus, in Indonesia and Korea several banks did not comply with capital adequacy ratios and other regulations (UNCTAD 1998: 64). Also, political interference was pervasive in Indonesia where Bank Indonesia had little effective independence to impose discipline on the banking industry (*Far Eastern Economic Review* 1998). The Thai Central Bank has little independence, and had to extend $US25 million to support politically connected finance companies in 1997 (*Far Eastern Economic Review* 1998). Moreover, regulatory requirements forced banks to allocate a nominated minimum share of their loan portfolio to preferred sectors (small and medium-size business in Indonesia and Korea, the Bumiputera community in Malaysia, and agricultural and rural industries in Thailand). Thus there was a conflict of interest between the role of central banks in enforcing economic regulations (such as the requirement to lend a minimum share of loan to priority sectors) and their role in enforcing prudential regulations (Brownbridge & Kirkpatrick 1998: 18).

Although a market-based system required governments to adopt an arm's length approach and allow bankruptcies of insolvent companies, governments continued to bail them out. For example, Thailand supported failed financial institutions by establishing the Financial Institutions Development Fund, which provided funds to rehabilitate the failed Bangkok Bank of Commerce in 1996. The Thai government also established the Property Loan Management Organisation (PLMO) to purchase non-performing property loans from financial institutions and arrange for property loans to be restructured. These acted as implicit insurance schemes and the amalgam of a market system with the *modus operandi* of a relationship-based system created the worst kind of financial market failure by inducing moral hazard.

Unlike the crisis economies of Indonesia, Korea, Malaysia, and Thailand, Hong Kong and Singapore were largely free of political interference. In both, regulators adopted a much stricter approach to checking and enforcing compliance with the banking laws. Singapore imposed higher capital adequacy ratios (12 per cent) than those of the Basle standards (8 per cent) and Hong Kong enacted strong banking regulations covering areas such as insider lending, investment in equities, and disclosure requirements (Dodsworth & Mihaljek 1997). Table 4.2 summarises the quality of prudential regulation in East Asia.

Table 4.2: Quality of Prudential Regulation and Supervision in Selected East Asian Economies

Economies	Bank regulatory framework	Enforcement of regulations	Quality of bank supervision
Hong Kong	Very good	Good	Good
Indonesia	Satisfactory	Weak	Weak
Korea	Weak	Weak	Fair
Malaysia	Satisfactory	Weak	Weak
Singapore	Very good	Strong	Very good
Thailand	Weak	Weak	Weak

Source: Brownbridge & Kirkpatrick (1998)

BOX 4.4: FINANCIAL SECTOR REFORM IN THAILAND

On 14 October 1997 the Chavalit government took several major policy steps to give authorities greater scope to deal with the financial sector.

- The Financial Restructuring Agency (FRA) was established to manage the asset disposal of the fifty-eight suspended finance companies and the Asset Management Corporation (AMC) was created to manage their bad debts.

- The Bank of Thailand liberalised ownership restrictions to allow foreign financial institutions to hold more than 50 per cent equity in financial institutions for a period of ten years. This is likely to encourage foreign banks to recapitalise ailing local institutions.

- In response to the first IMF program review in November 1997, new measures included closing fifty-six of the suspended companies. The FRA was required to dispose of assets from those closed finance companies by the end of 1998. Asset disposal commenced in February 1998. A 'good bank', called Radhanosin Bank, was established to bid for the good assets of the closed finance companies.

- In February 1998, the Bank of Thailand seized control of four ailing banks. Existing shareholder funds were written down and central bank liquidity support was converted into equity, effectively nationalising them.

- During the second program review, in February 1998, the IMF sought to accelerate the process of financial sector restructuring. To strengthen the capital base of all remaining domestic financial institutions, loan classification and provisioning rules had to be in line with international standards by 2000. All financial institutions had to accelerate recapitalisation plans by the end of 1998 to meet stricter rules on loan classification and provisioning requirements. The government was to reduce its ownership of the four nationalised banks as soon as possible. An independent commission was

Table 4.3: Types of Financial Regulation: Objectives and Key Policy Instruments

Type of regulation	Objectives	Examples of key policy instruments
Macroeconomic	Maintain control over aggregate economic activity Maintain external and internal balance	Reserve requirements, direct credit and deposit ceilings, interest rate controls, restrictions on foreign capital
Allocative	Influence the allocation of financial resources in favour of priority activities	Selective credit allocation, compulsory investment requirements, preferential interest rates
Structural	Control the possible abuse of monopoly power by dominant firms	Entry and merger controls, geographic and functional restrictions
Prudential	Preserve the safety and soundness of individual financial institutions and sustain public confidence in systemic stability	Authorisation criteria, minimum capital requirements, limits on the concentration of risks, reporting requirements

Table 4.3: Types of Financial Regulation: Objectives and Key Policy Instruments

Type of regulation	*Objectives*	*Examples of key policy instruments*
Organisational	Ensure smooth functioning and integrity of financial markets and information exchanges	Disclosure of market information, minimum technical standards, rule of market-making and participation
Protective	Provide protection to users of financial services, especially consumers and non-professional investors	Information disclosure to consumers, compensation funds, ombudsmen to investigate and resolve disputes

Source: Adapted from Vittas (1992: 63)

appointed to identify ways to improve the effectiveness of the
Bank of Thailand, including its supervisory role.

Source: Department of Foreign Affairs and Trade (Australia), *Country Economic Brief: Thailand*,
August 1998

MANAGING THE FINANCIAL SYSTEM DURING DEVELOPMENT: TOWARDS AN APPROPRIATE REGULATORY FRAMEWORK

The preceding discussions have shown that both the naive version of the
financial liberalisation hypothesis and strident advocates of (East Asian-
style) financial repression pay insufficient attention to the fact that the
resolution of market failure that afflicts financial systems needs an
appropriate regulatory framework. An internal capital market—or
financial repression more generally—can, in theory, resolve the problem
of market failure, but the emerging conventional wisdom is that prudential and other regulation is essential for a stable, efficient, and fair financial system and for economic growth. It is now generally agreed that
inappropriate regulations and supervisory standards not only retard a
country's long-term economic growth but increase the likelihood of a
financial crisis that could spread beyond the country's border.

Table 4.3, which draws heavily on Vittas (1992), provides a simple
framework that shows the importance of prudential and related regulations in the efficient management of financial systems.

Table 4.3 makes it clear that the liberalisation/repression debate has
focused primarily on the allocative aspects of the financial system. This
reflects the fact that in developing countries prudential, organisational,
and protective regulations were hardly considered, largely because
information problems were given insufficient attention. However, this
is beginning to change. As Vittas (1992: 79) puts it:

In both developed and developing countries financial regulation is
now moving toward the elimination or substantial reduction of
macroeconomic, allocative, and structural controls and toward
the adoption and substantial strengthening of prudential, organisational and protective controls.

Although Table 4.3 shows the different types of financial regulation
as seemingly mutually exclusive categories, in reality the different regulations have effects that cut across their designated domain. For example,

global credit controls that stem from macroeconomic objectives also fulfil a prudential function to the extent that they restrain banks from imprudent expansion of credit. Furthermore, as Barth, Capiro and Levine (1998) point out, there is relatively little empirical evidence to support advice on specific and comprehensive regulatory and supervisory reforms, because detailed country comparisons of financial regulatory and supervisory systems for developing countries do not exist. However, based on their preliminary study of fifty countries and other studies, Barth, Capiro and Levine (1998: 6) suggest that the following initial steps could reduce significantly the likelihood of banking crises:

• develop and improve legal systems and information disclosure

• impose rate ceilings on bank deposits

• establish limits on the rate at which banks can expand credit or on the rate of increase in their exposure to certain sectors, such as real estate

• require greater diversification of bank portfolios

• reduce the restrictions on the range of activities in which banks can engage.

Barth, Capiro and Levine maintain that it is not possible to determine *a priori* which combinations are most appropriate for countries at different stages of development. Despite this caveat, it would be fair to maintain that the central purpose of prudential and organisational regulation is to deal with market failure associated with moral hazard, while protective regulation focuses on the need to design a fair financial system that protects the interests of users of financial services.

BOX 4.5: PRUDENTIAL REGULATIONS IN MALAYSIA

The Malaysian government responded to the financial crisis by implementing a series of prudential regulations.

• Rules relating to classification of non-performing loans were tightened, beginning in financial year 1998/99. A loan which has been in arrears for three months will be classified as non-performing (the previous standard was six months).

• Banking institutions are required to disclose greater information on their financial position, including information on non-performing loans, exposure by sector, and movements in their provisions for bad and doubtful debts, including interest rate in-suspense.

- A real-time gross settlements system for large interbank funds transfers was to be implemented in January 1999.

- Banks have to raise their general provisions from 1 per cent of total outstanding loans net of interest-in-suspense and general provisions, to 1.5 per cent, effective from financial year 1998/99.

- Financial institutions are required to meet minimum risk-weighted capital adequacy requirements (8 per cent) on a quarterly basis, instead of the former annual requirement, and the framework will be expanded to incorporate market risks.

- Single customer lending guidelines have been tightened, with the limit on single customer exposures reduced to 25 per cent of total capital of banking institutions, from the former level of 30 per cent.

Source: Department of Foreign Affairs and Trade (Australia), *Country Economic Brief: Malaysia*, November 1998

BOX 4.6: HOW DID THE PRC AND VIETNAM AVOID THE FINANCIAL CRISIS?

All the causes identified as contributing to the financial crisis in the region, such as a lack of effective regulatory and supervisory framework and weak macroeconomic fundamentals, were present in the PRC and Vietnam. The distortions arising from the banking sector's subsidy of state-owned enterprises and politically determined investment projects were potentially destabilising for the financial sector, yet both the PRC and Vietnam were reasonably unaffected by the regional financial crisis. One reason why they could avoid the financial crisis was that they maintained tight controls on short-term capital flows.

It should, however, be pointed out that the ratio of available capital to investment opportunity was quite low in those countries, and hence a repressed or relationship-based system could operate efficiently. But with economic growth and the flow of long-term capital in the form of foreign direct investment, the ratio of available capital to investment opportunity will rise to a point where the relationship-based system will become inefficient. The PRC and Vietnam must liberalise their financial sectors and strengthen their supervisory and regulatory frameworks. The sooner they take measures towards doing so, the better it will be.

CONCLUSION

This chapter has argued that the key challenge facing developing economies is nurturing an appropriate regulatory framework for managing the financial system. In applying this to the Asia–Pacific economies, it would be useful to set the context by summarising the core issues raised so far.

The starting-point in any discussion of financial systems in industrialising economies is the notion that removal of policy-induced distortions in financial markets will generate sustained real effects by enhancing the national saving rate and improving investment efficiency. The core ideas were developed by Shaw and McKinnon and appeared both radical and refreshing in an intellectual environment where digirisme in development economics was still fashionable. In retrospect, the first-generation version of the financial liberalisation hypothesis appears somewhat naive. Critics could point out that the interest rate–saving link—a key element of the Shaw–McKinnon framework— lacked a robust empirical and analytical foundation. More importantly, the positive view of financial liberalisation is clouded by the marked increase in financial fragility experienced by liberalising developing countries, especially the East Asian economies which generally had a sound macroeconomic environment. These experiences suggest that the benefits of financial and capital account liberalisation may have to be weighed against the cost of increased financial sector fragility. Some (Capiro & Summers 1993; Stiglitz 1994) have gone further, arguing that financial repression can be seen as a mechanism for facilitating growth, an argument that can be rationalised by appealing to information asymmetries that in turn sow the seeds of market failure.

The financial crises in Asia and in other liberalising economies show the importance of sequencing liberalisation as a second-best or third-best solution, in the absence of the first-best or big-bang removal of all distortions. It is generally agreed that legal and institutional reform to strengthen supervisory and regulatory environment must precede financial liberalisation, and the capital account must not be liberalised before a well-functioning financial system is in place. This does not ignore the importance of macroeconomic stabilisation prior to capital account liberalisation—a lesson learned from the liberalising Southern Cone economies.

In sum, domestic financial reform cannot be seen independently of the problems posed by capital mobility. An efficient, well-regulated financial system can be resilient against the volatility of 'hot money'. However, it takes time, possibly decades, to build such a system. More importantly, such a system may require a certain degree of political and institutional development—that is, the consolidation of democratic governance with transparent and accountable institutions. Without such political development, an open capital account may pose more risks than benefits—as the Asian crisis testifies.

The chapter has discussed the crisis experience and the operation of financial regimes in the HPAEs in light of the different trends in the literature. Although some economies in the region—Korea, Taiwan, and Indonesia—experimented with a high interest rate policy in the mid to late 1960s, the experiments were later dropped. Large-scale systematic changes in the interest rate regime and credit allocation policies began in earnest towards the end of the 1970s and financial liberalisation gathered pace in the 1990s. Thus, the HPAEs had more than ten years' experience with financial sector reforms. In general, interest rates were above the inflation rate and the degree of volatility in real rates was lower than other regions. There is general agreement that much of the impressive growth record of HPAEs was due to their vigorous financial liberalisation.

However, the onset of a more liberal financial regime in East Asia led to bank failures and financial fraud (see Fry 1990 for comparative data, Lau 1990 on Taiwan, Sheng 1992 on Malaysia, and Hanna 1994 on Indonesia). The precise nature of these problems varied from country to country, but common elements were large-scale accumulation of non-performing loans and corruption through insider trading. In many cases, the problems were large enough to jeopardise public confidence in the banking system (Lau 1990: 207). Faith in the financial liberalisation–globalisation model was severely shaken by the massive banking and financial crises that swept the region in 1997. Within a year, the costs of the financial crisis in terms of lost output and increased human misery wiped away the gains of the previous decades. For a while, there was a danger of reverting to a regime of financial repression, when Malaysia imposed controls on short-term capital flows in a desperate attempt to stabilise its currency and financial sector.

Given the experience of unprecedented and costly financial crisis, what can one say about the future evolution of financial systems in the East Asian economies and the normative criteria for managing such systems? It seems that the financial liberalisation–repression debate has outgrown its topicality in the East Asian economies. Concern over the volatility of short-term capital flows, information asymmetries, and moral hazard problems suggests that the choice is not between a *laissez-faire* approach and financial dirigisme but the development of an efficient, sound, and fair system within a regulatory framework that builds on prudential, organisational, and protective regulations. It would be fair to maintain that the initial focus of financial sector reforms in East Asia was on allocative aspects. Little attention was given to the need for developing and enforcing prudential and related regulations. For example, the financial reforms in Indonesia, which started in 1983 and were regarded as among the most comprehensive in the region, entailed attempts to improve prudential supervision only in 1989. The most comprehensive measures in that area were announced in 1991—nearly a decade after the onset of reforms (Hanna 1994: 27).

The Asian financial and banking crisis has highlighted the urgency of designing and implementing appropriate regulatory and supervisory frameworks. Most countries have taken steps to strengthen their institutional and legal frameworks to minimise the moral hazard and incentive problems at the heart of the crisis. In the November 1998 meetings in Kuala Lumpur, Asia–Pacific Economic Cooperation leaders agreed to adopt internationally recognised principles for financial sector management and supervision. More importantly, most countries have not chosen the Malaysian path of reimposing capital controls, and it seems that Malaysia's selective capital and exchange controls are likely to be temporary. The moves towards political reform with a view to achieving a more transparent and democratic system in Indonesia, Thailand, and Malaysia can only enhance the prospect of a safe and sound financial system compatible with the free flow of capital.

Chapter 5

Labour Rights and East Asian Economic Development: Which Way Now?

INTRODUCTION

Labour 'rights' or labour 'standards' stem from the notion that workers are entitled to pursue 'their material and spiritual development in conditions of freedom, dignity, economic security and equal opportunity' (International Labour Organisation (ILO), Declaration of Philadelphia, 1944). This basic entitlement is often expressed in conventions as freedom of association, the right to organise and bargain collectively, prohibition of forced or compulsory labour, and so forth. Admittedly, some observers reject the notion of universal labour rights and imply that they are culturally specific constructs. This chapter opposes such a relativist interpretation. It maintains that it is possible to promulgate internationally acceptable guidelines on labour standards and that the welfare of workers in specific countries or regions can be evaluated against such norms. Such a perspective introduces a key debate in East Asia in particular and development policy in general. To what extent does the need to maintain unfettered labour markets during the process of industrialisation entail benign neglect or even wilful suppression of worker rights? Does such a trade-off matter for economic growth?

Advocates of competitive labour markets distinguish between 'processes' and 'outcomes'. They would acknowledge that East Asian governments infringed labour rights, but that was compensated by exemplary outcomes in the form of rapid growth in real wages and full employment in the pre-crisis period. Progressive affluence and the gradual process of democratisation in the region have led to improving labour standards to meet international norms.

Critics of East Asian labour market policies emphasise that the failure to uphold basic worker rights was a glaring weakness of the pre-crisis period that cannot be overlooked by focusing on outcomes. They also contend that the need to upgrade labour standards to international norms is not merely a morally virtuous goal, but an economically rational one as well. Future growth prospects in the region depend significantly on the extent to which its labour market institutions can be reformed in a humane way.

The nature of the debate on worker rights in East Asia is the regional equivalent of the broader debate on the link between globalisation and labour standards. Indeed, the issue of labour standards re-emerged in the Seattle round of global negotiations on international trade under the World Trade Organization (WTO), held between 30 November and 3 December 1999. The chapter sets the discussion of labour rights in a global context. It also notes the growing convergence of views between the advocates of unfettered labour markets and proponents of labour rights. This, the chapter suggests, is an auspicious development, as it provides an appropriate intellectual climate in which the governance of labour market institutions in post-crisis East Asia can move forward.

LABOUR MARKET AND ECONOMIC DEVELOPMENT: TWO VIEWS

What kind of institutional arrangements facilitate the smooth functioning of the labour market and thus the rapid industrialisation of developing economies? Reflections on this issue have, according to Freeman (1993a, 1993b), generated two views on the role of the labour market in economic development. One is classified as the 'distortionist' model (called the 'neo-liberal view' in this chapter). This, he claims, is typically associated with the work of the World Bank—although in more recent contributions the Bank has offered a much more qualified view of its position (World Bank 1995: ch. 12). The alternative is the 'institutionalist' view associated with the work of the ILO.

In the neo-liberal view, labour market interventions such as minimum wage legislation, mandated contributions to social security, job security legislation, large-scale unionisation, and collective bargaining impair the growth process through a variety of routes. These interventions, while 'intended to raise welfare and reduce exploitation ... actually work to raise the cost of labour ... and reduce labour demand ... and labour incomes where most of the poor are found' (World Bank 1990: 63). The ILO (1991a: 5), on the other hand, claims that 'over the long run suppression of free industrial relations jeopardises prospects for economic development' and that there is a 'need to re-regulate the labour market' (ILO 1991b: 65).

In a later report, the ILO (1995: 72–3) extends this theme, maintaining that the process of globalisation has actually weakened the resolve and ability of governments—in both developed and developing economies—to protect labour rights. Thus, globalisation creates a context where governments have an incentive to 'dilute, or fail to enact, measures intended to protect the welfare of workers'.

It is necessary to review these competing ideas on the role of the labour market in economic development to set the appropriate context for appreciating the issues in the governance of the labour market institutions of East Asia.

Labour market institutions as impediments to growth: The neo-liberal model

The neo-liberal view interprets organised labour as the source of both market failure and government failure. Trade unions represent monopoly imperfections in labour markets. They also form part of protection-seeking distributional coalitions. Indeed, some models of trade union behaviour consider them 'insiders' primarily interested in seeking benefits for employed members and unconcerned about the interests of 'outsiders' (unemployed, new jobseekers) (Carruth & Oswald 1987).

Minimum wage legislation and job security regulations may also cause unemployment, by creating wage rigidities. In the context of developing economies, the impact of such institutional variables needs to be placed in their proper context. In a typically poor, labour-surplus economy characterised by subsistence wages, attempts at fostering strong unions, minimum wage legislation, and job security legislation are likely to engender perverse results rather than boost the welfare of workers. These institutional variables end up being primarily responsible for the existence of entrenched dualism in labour-surplus economies: a 'fix-wage' formal sector consisting of a 'labour aristocracy' and a 'flex-wage' informal sector consisting of casual, low-paid jobs. In other words, sectoral wage differentials are higher in the presence, rather than in the absence, of labour market institutions. It is also alleged that organised labour leads to restrictive practices that impede job flexibility, constrain the capacity of management to cope with external shocks, and retard technological innovation. The effect is to impede dynamic efficiency.

An important element of the neo-liberal model is the notion that labour market rigidities impair international competitiveness. By increasing labour costs above market-clearing levels and by retarding productivity, high union density, minimum wage legislation, and related regulations lead to adverse shifts in unit labour costs (nominal wages adjusted by productivity)—a standard measure of trends in international competitiveness. More importantly, pro-labour legislation can offset the salutary effects on export competitiveness that can be generated by exchange rate policy. For example, devaluations typically enhance export competitiveness by engineering a fall in real wages. This presupposes the absence of real wage resistance by workers—an assumption that may not be valid in the presence of strong unions and wage indexation.

Competitive labour market or labour subordination?

If labour market regulation leads to adverse consequences for competitiveness, does this mean that coercive labour legislation (ban on unions, organised industrial action, elimination of minimum wage legislation, and job security regulations etc.) is the price that industrialising economies must pay? According to some radical scholars of the 'labour subordination' hypothesis, the answer is yes. They abhor the attenuation of labour rights associated with rapid industrialisation (as in the case of East Asia), but accept the economic logic underpinning it.

The labour subordination hypothesis has static and dynamic versions. Representative examples of the static version include Deyo (1987, 1989) and Frobel, Heinrich and Kreyo (1980). It is characterised by the observation that 'foreign and local investors have an especially strong interest in low wages ... in labour peace and a minimum of union interference in managerial autonomy' (Deyo 1987: 46). In other words, the radical position maintains that state-imposed labour discipline is vital to the success of export-oriented industrialisation and draws on the East Asian experience to validate that view. Interestingly, such an argument is largely inseparable from the position taken by Bhagwati (1986)—an eminent economist with impeccable neo-classical credentials and presumably a natural ally of the neo-liberal model. Bhagwati (1986: 100), also drawing on the experience of the East Asian newly industrialising economies (NIEs), accepts the point that 'authoritarian methods to keep trade union wage demands under control' can pay substantial dividends in the form of low inflation and general macroeconomic stability.

The dynamic version of the labour subordination hypothesis is evident in the more recent contributions of Deyo (1998), who argues that state control of the labour movement changes over time. Deyo uses this framework to explain the evolution of labour subordination in East Asia. In the early phase of export-oriented industrialisation, centralised control or cooption of the labour movement is dominant. In the more mature phase of export-oriented industrialisation and closer integration of national economies with the global economy, the governance of labour market institutions shifts to the enterprise level via mechanisms such as enterprise unionism and enterprise-level bargaining. In reality, shifting the focus of labour control from state to the enterprise level entails 'fragmenting and dispersing the workforce to a greater extent than in the earlier period' (Deyo 1998: 220). Thus, there is 'continued labour subordination'.

There are, however, a number of strategic advantages to the devolved nature of labour market management. First, enterprise-level labour subordination is compatible with 'international demands for increasing recognition of labour and human rights' (Deyo 1998: 221). Second, it creates regimes of 'exclusionary democracies' in industrialising economies in which business finds a critical political base through parliamentary institutions, but at the same time labour is unable to exploit the opportunities created by political liberalisation. The latter is the outcome of enterprise-level labour subordination that effectively dilutes the collective action capacities of workers (Deyo 1998: 221).

Managing the labour market: Institutionalist view

The institutionalist view does not simply rely on a critique of the neo-liberal model or decry various modes of labour subordination. It develops an alternative framework for analysing the appropriate role of the labour market in economic development. This may be seen as a conscious attempt to oppose—or at least qualify—the notion that attenuation of labour rights is a necessary price to pay for East Asian-style industrialisation.

How can one characterise the institutionalist view? Standing (1992: 327) depicts it as a school of thought that interprets:

> unions as a source of 'dynamic efficiency', obliging enterprises to pay efficiency wages rather than 'market clearing' wages and inducing management to raise productivity by technological innovations and cost-saving practices rather than reliance on low-cost labour.

Sengenberger (1991: 249) makes a very similar point when he argues that labour standards and other legally mandated benefits create pressures on employers to 'overcome the misguided preoccupation with cost-cutting ... and [focus] attention to the strengthening of productive power (via training, technical innovation etc.)'. Piore (1990) emphasises that economic development is characterised by multiple equilibria. A sweatshop strategy can lock an economy into a low-wage, low-tech equilibrium, but an upgrading of core labour standards pushes an economy into a high-wage, high-tech equilibrium (see also Rodrik 1996a).

To justify labour market interventions, one could also invoke the notion of the market's failure to provide training. Interventions in the form of mandated benefits or minimum standards for labour training, for example, could be seen as producing positive externalities that cannot be internalised by firms. Profit-maximising employers do not provide such socially desirable benefits. Labour market interventions in such a situation could be regarded as a response to market failure rather than as undesirable microeconomic distortions.

The argument that key labour market institutions, such as unions, can play a productive role in economic development is also reflected in the voice/exit model of Freeman and Medoff (1984). Unions can provide a 'voice' through which workers can air any grievances. The weakness or absence of unions may induce workers to take the 'exit' option, leading to an increase in labour turnover—and high labour turnover impedes firm productivity.

Pencavel (1995: 23), in a careful review of the role of unions in economic development, reaches a conclusion that is similar in spirit to the institutionalist perspective:

> unions have the potential to help raise productivity in the workplace by participating with management in search of better ways of organising production. It is important for workers also not to feel alienated from the economic and social system and to believe they have a stake in it. Process matters: even if outcomes were identical, employees value the fact that they or their agents help to shape their working environment.

Nelson (1991) has emphasised that if trade unions are structured as peak associations within a framework of democratic corporatism, evidence from Europe shows that an economy can achieve the twin blessings of low inflation and low unemployment. Using OECD data, Chowdhury (1994) has shown that such a system also yields higher investment rates. A theoretical rationale can be provided in terms of game theory. A well-known result from this analytical framework is that if bargaining partners—the government, peak employers, and worker associations—plan for the long term, induced by repeated strategic interaction, they may arrive at cooperative solutions (such as collective wage restraint in the face of external shocks) that can take account of societal interest instead of sectional interests. Such a rationale resonates with Axelrod's (1984) theory of the evolution of cooperation in a context of repeated 'prisoner's dilemma' games.

One should, as Freeman (1993b: 135–9) emphasises, take account of a range of political economy considerations when interpreting the appropriate role of the labour market in economic development. The concept of corporatism noted above is part of this repertoire of political economy arguments. The point is that inclusive politics—where organised labour is given access to the policy-making process as part of a tripartite dialogue between government, business, and labour—may engender responsible unionism. There are also other ways in which organised labour can play a productive role in the political management of economic policies.

It is now widely recognised that policy-makers trying to implement a structural adjustment package (trade liberalisation, macroeconomic stabilisation) need political support to sustain their program. One way of engendering such support is by providing compensatory labour market measures, such as severance pay or job retraining, to enhance workers' capacity to cope in the post-reform phase. Other possibilities include worker ownership rights through profit-sharing in public-sector enterprises undergoing privatisation, as a means of reducing resistance to privatisation. Finally, organised labour can contribute to the effective implementation of a structural adjustment package by offering feedback to the government on social and income distribution effects—a point emphasised by Birdsall (1995: 442).

An important element of the institutionalist perspective of the labour market is incorporating the impact of product market imperfections on firm-level wage and employment decisions. It is well-known that in the presence of monopoly imperfections in the product market, labour demand will be lower than would otherwise have been the case. More importantly, employers operating in markets with monopoly imperfections may share rents with unionised workers or insiders (Geroski et al. 1996). Under such circumstances, making product markets more competitive, for example through trade liberalisation and increased domestic competition, may encourage both employers and unions to abandon rent-sharing proclivities and be more responsive to economy-wide employment and wage considerations. This is an important implication because it means that there are ways of enhancing labour market performance without resorting to labour subordination.

Finally, it is worth noting that institutionalists are likely to be inspired by Rodrik (1999), who has argued, on the basis of cross-country data, that countries which respect labour rights (typically associated with well-functioning democracies in poor and rich nations) generate a better distribution of the enterprise surplus in the manufactiring sector than do countries where political freedom is restricted. As he puts it:

> There is a robust and statistically significant association between the extent of political participation and wages received by workers, controlling for other ... possible determinants. The association

exists both across countries and over time within countries. Countries with greater political participation than would have been predicted from their income levels ... also have correspondingly higher wages relative to productivity (Rodrik 1999: 32).

GLOBALISATION AND LABOUR RIGHTS: REVISITING THE DUAL VIEWS ON THE LABOUR MARKET IN INDUSTRIALISING ECONOMIES

At several points in the discussion, references have been made to the implications of globalisation for the debate on the appropriate role of the labour market in economic development. In recent years, the relationship between globalisation and labour rights (or labour standards) has become a key policy and political debate—see Lee (1997) and Golub (1997) for comprehensive surveys. Several aspects of the debate are germane to a fuller understanding of the neo-liberal vs institutional perspectives on the labour market in developing economies in general, and East Asian economies in particular.

To start with, there is the contentious question of inserting a social clause in international trade relations. This would entail a link between core labour standards as defined by the ILO (pertaining to such conventions as the freedom of association and right to collective bargaining, discussed below) and trade liberalisation. This has been a major issue in trade talks under the auspices of the WTO (see Box 5.1 for details).

BOX 5.1: LABOUR STANDARDS AND GLOBAL NEGOTIATIONS ON INTERNATIONAL TRADE

Trade ministers from 135 countries met at Seattle, USA, between 30 November and 3 December 1999 for a round of global negotiations under the WTO, to resolve a range of thorny issues. One was the issue of including a 'social clause' on the WTO agenda.

The USA proposed setting up a working group to study the incorporation of labour standards in WTO rules. The proposal received a sympathetic response from the European Union (EU). The proposal was apparently inspired by the US trade unions and the International Congress of Free Trade Unions (ICFTU), who argued that 'unless WTO member states agreed to tie core labour standards to WTO rules, they would face a major backlash from workers around the world'.

Developing countries resisted the US-backed proposal on labour standards, fearing that it could lead to barriers to their exports, because rich nations, such as the USA, could maintain that factory conditions in developing countries did not meet the prescribed labour standards.

The developing countries received vigorous support from the United Nations Conference on Trade and Development (UNCTAD). In a handbook for trade negotiators from the world's forty-eight least-developed states, UNCTAD urges negotiators to resist any 'consideration/discussion of a social clause with trade sanctions imposed through the WTO'. Kofi Annan, the UN Secretary-General, supported UNCTAD's position. He maintained that the WTO meeting was not the appropriate forum to negotiate labour, environment, and other social issues. Instead, he argued that UN agencies dealing with these issues should be strengthened to avoid giving industrial nations a pretext for protectionist policies.

Sources: Reuters as reported in *Jakarta Post* (30 November 1999, 'WTO Meeting Hopes to Bridge Gap on Trade Rounds', 'UNCTAD Urges Poor Nations to Keep Labour Off the Agenda'); *International Herald Tribune* (30 November 1999, 'Trade Envoys Vow to Listen to Critics')

Advocates of the social clause in international trade negotiations maintain that trade sanctions should be invoked when internationally recognised labour standards are violated. This view embodies the strong moral message that trade sanctions are effective in alleviating exploitative labour conditions in the global economy, and is part of the broader belief that nations should argue in the international arena for improvements in human rights.

Scholars who are sympathetic to the institutionalist perspective on the role of the labour market in economic development normally subscribe to the notion that all countries—both rich and poor—should aspire to attain and sustain core labour standards. In other words, there should be international harmonisation of labour standards. However, they are likely to emphasise the economic rationale underpinning the objectives (core labour standards) rather than particular instruments (such as trade sanctions) to achieve those objectives.

One argument in favour of harmonising labour standards across countries stems from the proposition that countries with low labour standards (usually developing economies) will have an undue cost advantage over trading partners that comply with core labour standards (usually developed economies).[1] As Box 5.1 shows, this is no longer an academic debate but an integral part of a contentious global agenda.

It was noted earlier that globalisation can generate a zero-sum game among countries, leading to a relentless dilution of labour standards. The pressures stemming from globalisation may impel policymakers to cut costs, including labour costs, to stay ahead of competitors. In addition, the increased mobility of capital means that host nations feel compelled to provide incentives, including the availability of a low-cost and compliant workforce, to attract and retain foreign investment. Unfortunately, such competitive strategies are easily replicable, leading countries into a bidding game in which all participants are worse off because they impair labour standards in order to gain market share of trade and foreign direct investment (FDI) at each other's expense. The harmonisation of labour standards can thus be seen as a mechanism for fostering a cooperative solution to a zero-sum competitive game.

Some scholars hold that 'most people attach value to processes as well as outcomes' (Rodrik 1997: 5). Labour standards pertain to processes, while wages and employment represent outcomes. People care about both. Hence, the case for attaining core labour standards across countries can be justified on the grounds of procedural fairness.

It could be argued that attaining a satisfactory international standard of labour rights is a global public good (because labour rights are kin to universal human rights), but like all public goods it is prone to underprovision and free-rider problems. Although some countries may be good international citizens and diligently maintain the core ILO conventions, others may simply free-ride, leading to a global underprovision of the public good. International mechanisms for attaining universal compliance may thus be seen as an attempt to cope with the free-rider problem that leads to sub-optimal attainment of labour standards across nations.

Advocates of competitive labour markets would object to some of the above arguments on the ground that economic growth is the most effective vehicle for gradual improvement of labour standards (Srinivasan 1990). Competitive labour markets, in conjunction with other appropriate micro- and macro-policies, will bring widening opportunities for unskilled workers in terms of rising real wages and productive employment. Over time, progressive affluence will lead to demands for improvements in working conditions. Imposing developed country labour standards on developing countries will impair their comparative advantage based on low labour costs and ultimately defeat the purpose of a social clause, namely, sustained improvements in the welfare of workers.

The notion of a social clause could also be described as an implicit instrument of protectionism. Trade liberalisation exposes sunset industries in the developed world (such as textiles and footwear) to competitive pressures from similar industries in the developing world. As old-fashioned protectionism is much more difficult to sustain in the post-Uruguay Round of trade liberalisation, the linking of labour standards to international trade is thus a veiled attempt by politically powerful producer lobbies in industrialised countries to reinstate the agenda of protectionism. There is also the contentious issue of the universality of labour rights or standards. Is it possible to define labour standards that are not culture-bound? Does the issue of a social clause or harmonisation mean cultural imperialism—an undue imposition by the West on the developing world and hence an infringement of national sovereignty? This politically charged issue often crops up in international forums, as the tension between the OECD countries (notably the USA) and some East Asian governments over the Universal Declaration of Human Rights testifies. Some economists appear sympathetic to this critique of core labour standards. Bhagwati (1994: 59) observes:

> The diversity of labour practices and standards is widespread in practice and reflects ... diversity of cultural values, economic conditions, and analytical beliefs and theories concerning the economic consequences of specific labour standards. The notion that labour standards can be universalised, like human rights such as liberty and habeas corpus, simply by calling them 'labour rights' ignores the fact that this easy equation between

culture-specific labour standards and universal human rights cannot survive deeper scrutiny.

Even if widely shared concepts of labour rights were developed, and even if arguments pertaining to unfair competition, the progressive dilution of labour standards driven by globalisation, and the underprovision of a global public good were valid, critics would question whether a legislative approach is the most efficient solution. Ultimately, international cooperation on core labour standards may require legislative sanctions in order to be effective. But legislative instruments may have undesirable side effects, such as impairing labour market flexibility that in turn may impair employment opportunities. Hence, some observers have advocated voluntary consumer boycotts, and ethical product labelling and voluntary codes of conduct by multinational companies, as more efficient alternatives (Freeman 1994;). However, Lee (1997:17) has argued that 'it is difficult to accept that purely voluntary action can be a substitute for intergovernmental action', for a number of reasons. Purely voluntary action to provide for a public good can be undermined by free-rider problems. Voluntarism and product labelling can be effective against particular types of infringement of labour standards that have emotional appeal (such as the use of child labour), but may be less effective against others (such as suppression of trade unions). Lobby groups seeking implicit instruments for protecting domestic industries may manipulate product labelling and voluntarism to suit their ends. Finally, it is difficult to guarantee the reliability of the information on which product labelling is based.

The debate on core labour standards is contentious. However, it has extended the discourse on the role of the labour market in industrialising economies in a number of directions and has provided a framework for interpreting developments in the East Asian region.

LABOUR RIGHTS AND EAST ASIAN ECONOMIC DEVELOPMENT

It is generally agreed that East Asia has been characterised by labour market flexibility, particularly in comparison to other regions. In terms of key indicators, such as real wage growth and employment, pre-crisis East Asia was a shining exemplar of sustained improvements in the welfare of workers. The issue is whether that entailed either benign neglect or wilful suppression of labour rights, and whether such costs can be justified by eventual labour market outcomes.

Labour rights and East Asia: An optimistic view

It is possible to paint a fairly optimistic picture of the East Asian experience with labour rights. Such a perspective starts from the premise that labour subordination did occur in the past for political reasons, because of the perceived association between organised labour and communist dissidents. However, developments suggest a move away from the dubious practice of labour subordination.

Korea and Taiwan both witnessed waves of industrial unrest after the political liberalisation of the late 1980s that enabled them to break away from a historically entrenched tradition of strict controls on the labour movement. The role and power of unions in the two countries have been substantially enhanced (Galenson 1992). Changes in labour market institutions in South Korea show that it is on the way to adopting a 'social accord' model (see Box 5.3).

In Southeast Asia, Malaysia was conspicuous for banning unions in the export-oriented, FDI-dependent electronics sector, but agreed to allow unionisation in 1988 (Standing 1992: 329). Minimum wage legislation in Thailand and Indonesia has been increased (Islam & Chowdhury 1997).

Union densities are not necessarily lower in East Asia than in other economies in the developing world. Frenkel (1993), for example, estimates union density at 17 per cent in Singapore, 19 per cent in Hong Kong, 33 per cent in Taiwan, 24 per cent in South Korea, 14 per cent in Malaysia, and 6 per cent in Thailand. In Pakistan and India union density is below 10 per cent (World Bank 1995: 82), although for India Joshi and Little (1994) suggest a higher figure.

If union wage differentials indicate a regulated labour market, East Asia is not an outlier. For example, in Malaysia the union wage premium is 15–20 per cent compared with 10 per cent in Mexico and 5–20 per cent in the USA, United Kingdom, and Germany (World Bank 1995: 81).

Several commentators (Lee 1984; Manning & Pang 1990; Addison & Demery 1987) have noted that there is no evidence that the East Asian economies deliberately tried to suppress wages in the export-oriented sectors in order to maintain and prolong their competitive advantage in labour-intensive manufacturing. In other words, suppression or control of the union movement did not entail attempts to regulate the wage determination process.

Evidence compiled by Golub (1997, drawing on Golub 1995, 1996) also maintains that there is no deliberate suppression of wages in developing countries, including East Asia, to gain an unfair advantage in international trade. The inference is based on the behaviour of wages and productivity. If wage growth progressively falls behind productivity growth, wage suppression may be taking place. The cross-country evidence seems to suggest instead a good correlation between wages and productivity growth.

Other studies, such as Fields (1995), Fields and Wan (1989), and Lim (1990) acknowledge the infringement of labour rights in East Asia, but emphasise that labour market outcomes are more important. As Lim (1990: 154) observes:

In Malaysia, labour organisation has been restricted in the export-oriented electronics industry for more than twenty years. Singapore has virtually outlawed strikes for thirty years, and its unions are controlled by the government ... Neither country has ever had a minimum wage ... Yet ... wages, hours of work, working conditions, fringe benefits and social protections are superior by developing-country standards.

Fields (1995) makes similar points in emphasising the fact that high-growth high-wage outcomes in East Asia occurred despite infringements of labour rights and weak labour standards.

Views that emphasise the primacy of labour market outcomes at the expense of infringements of labour rights presume that attempts to uphold labour rights are deleterious to economic efficiency and growth. Many studies have shown that the presumption is not justified. Freeman (1993a: 134) highlights the fact that 'extant studies reject the claim that unions are a general impediment to macro adjustments or to enterprise performance in developing countries, although they may be so in particular cases'.

The general theme of Freeman's conclusions has been upheld by an OECD study. After reviewing evidence on the relationship between labour standards and competitiveness in a sample of developing countries, the OECD (1996b:105) emphasises that 'any fear on the part of developing countries that better [labour] standards would negatively affect either their economic performance or their competitive position on world markets has no economic rationale'.

Rodrik's study of the relationship between labour rights and competitiveness in developing countries is worth discussing. Its conclusions are mixed. Relaxed labour standards seem to boost the competitiveness of developing countries in labour-intensive products, but the benefit is crucially impaired by the fact that 'countries with poor labour standards received less foreign investment than would have been predicted on the basis of their other characteristics' (1997: 46).

It is worth noting that at least one study maintains that what matters for labour market performance in terms of wages and employment is greater coordination among social partners (government, business, and labour) in the wage-bargaining process (Scarpetta 1996). The study, based on a sample of OECD economies, shows that both highly centralised and fully decentralised bargaining systems are beneficial to labour market performance. The implications support the inclusive approach to management of the labour market and raise doubts about the ideological presumption that enhancing labour market performance must rely on an enterprise-level focus.

Standing (1992) is one of the very few studies in an Asian context that tests the role of unions in affecting enterprise performance. It relies on firm-level data from a large-scale 1988 survey of Malaysian establishments. Standing (1992) arrives at the following conclusions about the relationship between unionisation and labour market outcomes.

• Unionised firms are more likely to engage in training and thus improve worker productivity.

• Product innovations and work reorganisation are much more prevalent in unionised firms.

• There appears to be a positive correlation between unionisation and labour productivity.

• There is no clear evidence that unions represent a source of employment rigidity.

In sum, there is a case for rejecting the view that coercive labour legislation to remove or alleviate distortions in the labour market is the necessary price of improved outcomes in terms of wages and working conditions. Such legislation probably represents an avoidable infringe-ment of human rights. The World Bank, often considered an advocate of the neo-liberal view, ratifies these ideas. The Bank observes (1995: 86): 'Denial of workers' rights is not necessary to achieve growth of incomes'—a theme that will be discussed again later.

Labour rights and East Asia: A circumspect view

Critics maintain that, despite clear evidence of improvements in the welfare of workers in terms of some key indicators, and despite an emerging consensus that the preservation of labour rights is compat-ible with the objective of rapid economic growth, East Asia continues to represent a troubling case of labour subordination (Deyo 1998; Human Rights Watch 1998). The ILO generally supports the view that labour rights in East Asia were neglected in the past and that this neglect was one of the key weaknesses of the pre-crisis period. It high-lights future directions in this area:

> There had been a relative neglect of labour rights and social protec-tion in the pre-crisis period of high growth. Social progress lagged far behind the spectacular economic progress achieved in the decades that preceded the current crisis ... There [is] no doubt that key elements for correcting this deficiency [are] the full respect for basic labour standards and the fostering of a strong and free labour movement. This would ensure constant democratic pressure to im-prove working conditions and levels of social protection. It would also be invaluable in ensuring smooth adjustment to structural change, in coping with economic and social crises, and in raising productivity and competitiveness (ILO 1998a: 2).

The theme of a need for a new social contract model for East Asia is a major preoccupation of the ILO, reflected in a recent report on the East Asian crisis (Lee 1998). Eddy Lee, the principal author of the report, observes that the protection of labour rights is fundamental to the emergence of a social contract model. He rejects the view that the notion of labour rights—as a manifestation of political and civil liber-ties—is a culturally specific construct and incompatible with 'Asian values'.

As noted earlier, there is growing convergence between the advo-cates of worker rights and those who emphasise deregulated labour markets as the most effective vehicle for promoting the welfare of workers. The World Bank (1998c: 7), in its study of the consequences of the East Asian crisis of 1997, notes:

> Even before the onset of the crisis, three major vulnerabilities already existed, but they were masked by widespread growth: protracted poverty and rising inequality; *concerns about labour rights*; and rising demands for formal mechanisms to offset household insecurity. The crisis has aggravated conditions underlying each of these issues. These ... have to be addressed in order to build the foundations for a caring and competitive society (emphasis added).

Elsewhere, the Bank (1998c: 11–12) observes:

> Countries in the region sought to maintain relatively unfettered labour markets during the early stages of economic development at the expense of granting workers' rights to bargain collectively ... Failure to modernise worker–management relations in countries with sophisticated economic and political structures can become costly, as Korea's experience in the late 1980s has shown. If there is no industrial relations system to allow workers to air grievances and resolve disputes, strikes and other forms of ... actions, sometimes violent, can become common. One of the challenges facing maturing economies in East Asia is that of managing industrial relations to protect workers' legitimate rights, but avoid granting entitlements that result in resource inefficiencies.

Other commentators, such as Pang (1998) and Manning (1998), who were formerly sympathetic to the neo-liberal model, hold a more circumspect view about labour rights in East Asia. Pang (1998: 69), in his review of Manning's (1998) monumental work on the Indonesian labour market, observes:

> while restrictions on labour rights may have been necessary in the early stages of Indonesia's development, they need to be relaxed to meet the rising aspirations of workers and to sustain productivity growth. This relaxation would have been difficult to manage even if growth had continued to be robust. But with the economic setback ... it must be confronted. The challenge for the government is to do so while maintaining the competitiveness of Indonesian exports and the confidence of investors.

Progress in labour rights: Recent evidence from East Asia

It is clear that the 1997 crisis paved the way for a consensus that the management of labour rights is one of the key challenges facing the East Asian region. One way to evaluate the current state of play on worker rights in East Asia is to find internationally recognised benchmarks against which judgments can be made. Despite concerns that labour rights represent culturally specific conceptions, such benchmarks exist. The ILO has played a key role in promulgating them and others, such as the OECD and the US government, have endorsed them (Golub 1997: 18).

Since 1930, there has been a range of core ILO conventions. They pertain to freedom of association, the right to organise and collective bargaining, suppression of forced labour, elimination of discrimination in employment and occupation, equal remuneration for men and women for work of equal value, and the prevention of child labour through the stipulation of minimum age for employment (Conventions 29, 87, 100, 105, 111, and 138)—collectively, these may be taken as representing internationally recognised core labour standards. In fact, the ILO calls them 'fundamental human rights' (ILO 1998b:1). With the exception of Convention 138 (minimum age for employment), all have been ratified by well over one hundred countries. The ILO has stepped up its campaign for universal ratification since May 1995, following its seventy-fifth anniversary and the World Summit on Social Development held at Copenhagen. Between then and 1998, more than eighty ratifications were registered and various governments notified the ILO that at least thirty were under active consideration (ILO 1998c: 2). At the 'jobs summit' in London, the G-8 (the G-7 plus Russia) governments reiterated their belief in 'global progress towards implementation of internationally recognised core labour standards' (Taylor, R. 1998).

Given these developments, one way of monitoring worker rights in East Asia is to establish the extent to which the ILO conventions are ratified by governments in the region. Admittedly, ratification does not amount to effective enforcement of pro-labour legislation. However, if governments refuse to formally endorse ILO conventions and international covenants, it may be construed as evidence that they need the latitude to interfere in labour markets, even though such interventions may impair labour rights. This is not mere conjecture: some East

Asian governments have actively opposed the protection of human rights through binding commitments to international covenants on the ground that they entail a Western imposition on developing nations (*Australian*, 'Great Divide on Human Rights', 29 July 1997).

Given the above caveats and clarifications, Table 5.1 provides pertinent evidence on the issue of labour rights in East Asia.

Table 5.1: Ratification of Core ILO Conventions: East Asia (as at late 1999)

Country	No. 29	No. 87	No.98	No. 100	No.105	No. 111	No. 138
China	No			Yes			
Indonesia	Yes	Yes	Yes	Yes	Yes	Yes	Yes
Japan	Yes	Yes	Yes	Yes	No	No	No
Korea			No	Yes	Yes	Yes	Yes
Malaysia	Yes	No	Yes	No	Yes	No	No
Philippines	Yes	Yes	Yes	Yes	Yes	Yes	No
Singapore	Yes	No	Yes	No	Yes	No	No
Thailand	Yes	No	No	No	Yes	Yes	No

Sources: ILO, ILOLEX database 1998 (International Labour Standards and Human Rights database); ILO 1999, Jakarta office. Information correct as at 11 October 1999

Notes: Yes = ratified, No = not ratified

China has notified the ILO that Conventions 87 and 98 remain applicable to Hong Kong Special Administrative Region (SAR)

ILO Convention 29 (Forced Labour) requires the suppression of forced or compulsory labour in all its forms with the exception of military service, properly supervised convict labour, and emergencies such as war and earthquakes (1930, ratified by 145 states)

ILO Convention 87 (Freedom of Association and the Protection of the Right to Organise) establishes the right of all workers to form and join organisations of their own choosing without prior authorisation, and lays down a series of guarantees for the free functioning of organisations without interference by the government (1948, ratified by 121 states)

ILO Convention 98 (Right to Organise and Collective Bargaining) provides for protection against anti-union discrimination, protection of workers' and employers' organisations against acts of interference by each other, and measures to promote collective bargaining (1949, ratified by 137 states)

ILO Convention 100 (Equal Remuneration) pertains to equal pay for men and women for work of equal value (1973, ratified by 62 states)

ILO Convention 105 (Abolition of Forced Labour) prohibits the use of any form of forced or compulsory labour as a means of political coercion or education, punishment for the expression of political or ideological views, workforce mobilisation, labour discipline, punishment for participation in strikes, or discrimination (1957, ratified by 130 states)

ILO Convention 111 (Discrimination) calls for national policies to eliminate discrimination in access to employment, training, and working conditions, on grounds of race, colour, religion, political opinion, national extraction, or social origin, and to promote equality of opportunity and treatment (1958, ratified by 130 states)

ILO Convention 138 (Minimum Age) aims at the abolition of child labour, stipulating that the minimum age for working shall not be less than the age of completion of compulsory schooling (1973, ratified by 62 states)

Once ratified, these conventions are regarded as binding commitments. Even in the absence of ratification, the ILO conventions serve as a standard of reference for national law and practice. For further details, see ILO (1998c: 2–3)

A new convention on the elimination of the worst forms of child labour (no.182) was adopted by the ILO following the 1999 International Labour Conference

As Table 5.1 indicates, Indonesia is the only country in the sample that has a full ratification of core ILO conventions. All the others fall short of full ratification of the fundamental labour standards. China and Korea have the fewest ratifications. Korea appears to be an odd case. It has made considerable progress since the democratisation movement that started in 1987, but seems to drag its heels on full ratification the core ILO conventions. Based on the current record of ratification of the core conventions, the ILO (1998c:1) laments that 'freedom of association ... remains elusive in much of East and South-East Asia'.

The evidence provided in Table 5.1 can be complemented by some country summaries on worker rights in East Asia, drawing on Deyo (1998), Human Rights Watch (1998), and ILO (1998c). The focus is on the economies most affected by the financial crisis—Indonesia, Malaysia, Thailand, and Korea.

Indonesia is an intriguing case, as during 1998 it became the first country in East Asia to join fifty-four other countries (of the 174 that are members of the ILO) with the distinctive status of full ratification of the core ILO conventions. The background to this achievement is shown in Box 5.2.

BOX 5.2: POLITICS OF LABOUR MARKET REFORM—INDONESIA

In June 1998, the Indonesian government ratified ILO Convention 87 on Freedom of Association and Protection and of the Right to Organise. In May 1999, the government ratified Convention 105 on Abolition of Forced Labour, Convention 111 on Discrimination in Employment and Occupation and Convention 138 on Minimum Age. Within a year, Indonesia acquired the distinctive status of becoming the only nation in Asia to ratify all core ILO conventions.

Reform of the governance of labour market institutions was not limited to the ratification of the core ILO conventions. It unleashed a momentum that led to the release of trade union activists from imprisonment and the breaking-up of the state-sanctioned sole trade union that had been widely perceived as a thinly veiled goverment instrument for attenuating labour rights. Ten trade unions were formed immediately, and eventually twenty-six were registered by the government. A new Trade Union Bill is awaiting approval from the government. There have been developments in other aspects of labour legislation and an ILO-assisted Tripartite Indonesian Task Force has been set up as an instrument for social dialogue on labour issues. The task force played an important role in an awareness-raising campaign throughout Indonesia to advise employers, workers, and provincial governments about the core conventions and the implications of their ratification by Indonesia.

The government also decided to defer the controversial 1997 Manpower Act that was due to be implemented by October 1999. The Act was widely perceived as inimical to the cause of labour rights.

In order to understand the politics of labour market reform in Indonesia, it is necessary to revisit the 1997 financial crisis. The crisis unleashed a 'people's movement' that swept from office the authoritative Soeharto regime that had ruled Indonesia for three decades. The transitional government under B.J. Habibie, that replaced Soeharto in May 1998, found itself in a political environment characterised by widespread demands for change. '*Reformasi*' was the rallying cry, along with calls to end KKN (the Indonesian abbreviation for 'corruption, collusion, and nepotism'). The government found itself championing the cause of improving its tarnished record on human rights, restoring basic freedoms, and nurturing democratic processes in general.

The suddenly liberalised political atmosphere combined with the crisis-ridden economy to lead the government to a position where it felt the need to rely heavily on assistance from international organisations. The international financial institutions (IMF and World Bank) that spearheaded the rescue effort for Indonesia shifted the former emphasis on technical issues of implementing their prescribed agenda for reform, to the need for progress in human rights and democratic processes. They thus provided a window of opportunity for the Indonesian government and the ILO (through its technical assistance facility) to work closely on the issue of labour rights.

Doubts remain, however, about the efficacy and sustainability of the reform of the governance of labour market institutions. Was it largely an opportunistic response by a transitional government eager to be returned to power in Indonesia's first democratically held elections (although it failed in that bid)? Did the international organisations, in their zeal to see human rights upheld and democracy nurtured in the world's fourth most populous nation, push through change too quickly? As national laws can supersede the ratification of international treaties in Indonesia, can a later government undermine the apparent progress, given the wide gap that typically exists between ratification and enforcement? Only time will tell how these issues will be resolved, but one reason for optimism is that the reform of labour market institutions in Indonesia occurred in a carefully designed process of social dialogue.

Source: ILO (1999, Jakarta office)

Consider now the case of Malaysia. Although, as shown in Table 5.1, it has ratified some ILO conventions, its *Trade Union Act 1959* and *Industrial Relations Act 1967* place considerable restrictions on union activities. The restrictions apply particularly to pioneer enterprises, such as the electronics sector where unions have been banned since the early 1970s. A small number of in-house unions have been operating in electronic companies but, as in Indonesia, genuine enterprise unionism has not taken root. The government continues to maintain that plant-level unions are more appropriate in the electronics sector than are industrial unions, aided by foreign firms that have used the threat of relocation to more investor-friendly countries as a strategy to stall the development of unionism in the electronics industry.

Other forms of legislation relating to attenuation of labour rights fall within the purview of laws that affect human rights in general. The most conspicuous ones are the Internal Security Act, the Officials Secrets Act, the Printing Press and Publications Act, and the Sedition Act.

In Thailand, there are discrepancies in the application of labour legislation to state enterprises and the private sector. State employees do not have the right to form unions or to strike; in the private sector, strikes must be registered in advance with the Ministry of Labour. The government is attempting to achieve parity between the state and private sectors in terms of entitlements such as unionisation. The degree of unionisation in Thai industry is low, but non-unionised workers can seek redress for grievances through the Tripartite Labour Relations Committee for private-sector workers and the State Enterprise Labour Relations Committee for state-enterprise workers.

Unlike Malaysia, there is no attempt to apply separate legislation to export-processing zones. However, the idea that deregulated labour markets are necessary for international competitiveness certainly prevails in the business community. This is reflected in a 1997 proposal by the Federation of Thai Industries for enactment of a special economic zone convention in close proximity to the Myanmar (Burma) and Cambodian borders. It would be staffed by migrant workers at below-minimum wages and presumably insulated from the application of the core ILO conventions. The current status of this proposal is unclear, given the upheaval of the 1997 financial crisis.

We will now discuss Korea (analysed in greater detail in Box 5.3). During its high-growth era, Korea had a notoriously poor record of labour rights. Two events—one internal, the other external—have shaped current attempts to reform labour laws in Korea. The democratisation process since 1987 has paved the way for labour organisations to air grievances of past injustices, and Korea's admission to the OECD in October 1996 entailed a government commitment to amend labour laws in line with international standards. The new labour law of March 1997 allowed for the formation of competing trade union federations from 2002 and legitimised dissident organisations, such as the Korean Conderation of Trade Unions. The militant teachers' union *Chonkyojo* was granted legal status from late 1999. In return for greater labour market flexibilities such as lay-offs and redundancies, trade unions will, in the future, be able to form political parties. A notable achievement is the establishment of a mechanism for tripartite dialogue between government, labour, and business. It appears that the Kim Dae Jung government is serious about developing a model of social partnership for managing the labour market.

BOX 5.3: POLITICS OF LABOUR MARKET REFORM—KOREA

The contentious issues in the domain of labour rights in East Asia can be illustrated by focusing on the case of Korea. Prior to 1987, Korea was characterised by systematic attempts to suppress labour rights. Some observers maintained that state-sanctioned gender discrimination enabled Korea to sustain its export-led growth because wages lagged behind productivity growth in the export sector, where many workers were female. The process of democratisation that started in 1987 coincided with an outburst of historically unprecedented industrial disputes (see Table 5.2). This was widely seen as a violent reaction by the labour movement to past repression—a bitter legacy that could not be removed even by full employment and sustained increases in real wages. In fact, the exhaustion of the labour-surplus phase of Korean development gave more assertive elements in the trade union movement the opportunity to flex their bargaining muscle.

Table 5.2: Industrial Disputes in Korea, 1970–97

Year	Unionisation rates (%)	Number of disputes
1970	12.6	4
1975	15.8	52
1980	14.7	206
1985	12.4	265
1987	12.3	3749
1989	18.6	1616
1995	12.7	88
1997	NA	78

Source: Databank of the Korea International Labour Foundation, 1998

Although (as Table 5.2 shows) the wave of industrial unrest in the post-1987 phase was short-lived, many within the business community felt that the pendulum had swung too far in favour of labour and that it was deleterious to Korea's international competitiveness. Indeed, there is evidence that the surge in industrial conflicts after 1987 impelled some large Korean firms to relocate some labour-intensive operations abroad. This mindset was at least partly behind an attempt in the mid 1990s to restrain the assertive voice of the labour movement. There were debates on a range of issues: the restriction on multiple unions, the difficulty of lay-offs without government approval, the denial of union rights to engage in political activities, and the lack of third-party intervention to resolve industrial disputes. These issues highlighted the tussle between a peak business association—the Korean Employers Federation (KEF)—and a militant labour organisation—the Korean Confederation of Trade Unions (KCTU)—that was not recognised by the government. In addition, there was the issue of public sector unionism as manifested in the controversy over the recognition of the Teachers Union.

Korea's attempt to modify its labour legislation in the mid 1990s started with the Presidential Commission on the Reform of Labour-Related Laws. Unfortunately, the Commission was unable to resolve the impasse between the KCTU and the KEF. The government tried to break the deadlock by passing new labour laws in December 1996. The passage of what many regard as crucial legislation occurred under rather controversial circumstances—the National Assembly met in secret for only ten minutes, without the presence of any opposition members. The revised labour laws still banned multiple unions in the workplace, deferred recognition of the KCTU to 2001 and maintained the status quo on the non-recognition of the Teachers Union. There were sensible provisions in the new labour laws, such as more flexible working hours with the mutual consent of labour and management, and the ability of employers to engage in lay-offs with prior notification and union consent. However, the controversial manner in which the labour laws were amended, the postponement of the recognition of the KCTU, the continued ban on multiple unions, and the failure to deal with public-sector unionism tarnished the government's impartial image. It was widely seen as having succumbed to the KEF's agenda, which stubbornly opposed the legitimacy of the assertive KCTU in the industrial relations realm. There was public uproar and widespread strikes. Externally, the government faced criticism from the ILO that Korea had broken its pledge to the world community that it would align national labour laws with international norms as part of its entry to the OECD.

The 1997 crisis and its aftermath, together with the change in government, provided opportunities for Korea to renew its attempt to reform its labour laws. There was pressure from the IMF through conditionalities attached to its bailout package that Korea needed to enhance labour market flexibility as a means of coping with the economic crisis. A major achievement of the Kim Dae Jung regime is its formal adoption of the social accord model. A Tripartite Commission comprising representatives from government, business, and labour reached a landmark accord in February 1998. The highlights of the accord were:

- the government would establish a fund of 5 trillion won for unemployment benefits

- public servants would be allowed to form work councils from January 1999 and teachers could organise a trade union from July 1999

- political activity by trade unions would be permitted from the first half of 1998

- labour laws would permit lay-offs under stipulated conditions.

The accord was evaluated by an OECD team that visited Korea in September 1998. It lauded the role of the Tripartite Commission, but felt that the entrenched legacy of distrust between labour and business was still prevalent. The ILO also highlighted the role of the Tripartite Commission but expressed disappointment that, as a result of deferring the recognition of the Teachers Union and the KCTU, Korea was dragging its heels on the ratification of Conventions 87 and 98.

Sources: KEF Quarterly Review, March 1998; Seguino (1998); Deyo (1989); Park Jong-Kew (1997); Watson (1998); Tcha (1998); ILO (1998c)

1997 FINANCIAL CRISIS AND ITS IMPACT ON VULNERABLE GROUPS IN THE EAST ASIAN LABOUR FORCE

In summarising the discussion on labour rights in East Asia, it would be useful to highlight the impact of the 1997 financial crisis and its aftermath on vulnerable groups in the workforce in East Asia, particularly women and migrant workers.

The World Bank (1998c: 15) focuses on gender issues in its analysis of the social consequences of the East Asian crisis and observes that 'there is evidence that women are disproportionately targeted for lay-offs as societies regress to traditional perceptions of men as primary bread-winners'. This occurs in Korea (Human Rights Watch 1998: 11), where employers often resort to casualisation of the workforce in an attempt to cope with the financial crisis. Workers are fired and rehired as 'despatched' labour through despatch agencies at 60–70 per cent of their previous wage. These casual workers have no union rights and no access to unemployment benefits. Non-government organisations and unions fear that the despatch system is hitting women workers hardest—they are usually the first to be fired as they generally fill unskilled positions. The situation has so alarmed the Korean National Council of Women that it has prepared a list of discriminatory dismissals in order to petition the Korean president.

As Davis Lamb (1998) notes, migrant workers were a ready source of cheap labour during the economic boom in the region, but in the post-crisis phase the mood has soured and they are perceived as an economic burden.

In the pre-crisis period, the pattern and scale of migration in the Asia–Pacific region inspired some observers to regard the region as the 'newest international migration system' (OECD 1992; Salt 1992). In a comprehensive survey of the phenomenon, Athukorala (1993) estimated the total number of migrants in the region at the beginning of the 1990s as at least one million. He distinguished between pure labour-importing countries (Japan, Hong Kong, Singapore, and Taiwan); countries that import and export labour (Thailand, Malaysia, and South Korea), and three pure exporters of labour (Indonesia, Philippines, and the PRC). It is estimated that by 1997 the total number of migrants had increased to seven million (Lamb 1998). Singapore hosts 500 000 migrants from the region, Malaysia is host to as many as two million migrants (mainly from Indonesia), and

Thailand has over one million migrants, mainly from Burma, Cambodia, and Laos.

Although such migrants were tolerated during the rapid-growth era, there is now a xenophobic reaction against them. A leading Malaysian newspaper enthusiastically supported the government's decision to repatriate large numbers of Indonesian workers: 'Malaysians will no doubt support such policy, for clearly we are now in the throes of being swamped by foreign workers, bringing with them social, economic, political and security problems for the country' (editorial, *New Straits Times*, quoted in Lamb 1998). A Malaysian minister added: 'We must make sure there are jobs available for Malaysians. Charity begins at home' (*Jakarta Post*, quoted in Human Rights Watch 1998: 2). The Thai government announced that it would expel more than one million illegal workers by the end of 1999. The bulk (approximately 75 per cent) of the target group were Burmese, costing one third of a Thai worker's wages (*Bangkok Post*, 20 January 1998; *Nation*, 18 February 1998). Media reports suggest that maltreatment of migrant workers in detention centres is widespread.

The fundamental problem of migrant workers in East Asia is that they are stripped of labour rights even if they are legally employed. They engage in dirty, difficult, and dangerous jobs ('3D' jobs) spurned by locals. Because of their nationality, they do not have access to any kind of social safety net or union protection. They are not even covered by international covenants. There is, of course, the UN Convention on the Protection of the Rights of all Migrant Workers and their Families, but it is not legally binding because an insufficient number of countries have ratified it (Human Rights Watch 1998: 4). In East Asia, only the Philippines has ratified the convention. Indonesia has indicated willingness to sign, but none of the major labour-importers in the region have shown any inclination to deal with the contentious issue of the rights of migrant workers.

CONCLUSION

A primary issue of this chapter is that benign neglect and even wilful suppression of labour rights accompanied unfettered labour markets in East Asia during its rapid-growth phase. Advocates of competitive labour markets have condoned the practice by highlighting exemplary market outcomes in terms of real wage growth and full employment.

They also emphasise that, in recent years, economies in the region have been moving towards upgrading labour standards to recognised international benchmarks. This may be seen as a 'stages' approach to labour issues, in which poor economies, characterised by subsistence wages and a plentiful supply of unskilled workers, initially rely on free labour markets for development. Once the labour-surplus phase is over, governments can afford to tackle the contentious issue of labour standards.

Advocates of labour rights, such as the ILO, take a more circumspect view. They emphasise that the infringement of labour rights was a glaring weakness of the pre-crisis period and that its legacy has made adjustment to the trauma of the 1997 crisis rather difficult. The economies of the region generally have a long way to go in upgrading labour standards. Most have not fully ratified the core ILO conventions. Organisations such as Human Rights Watch have drawn attention to the plight of vulnerable groups in the labour force in the region, such as women and migrant workers, in the post-crisis period.

One promising development is the growing convergence of views between the advocates of unfettered labour markets, such as the World Bank, and the advocates of labour rights, such as the ILO. Studies from both organisations suggest a degree of consensus on the need for East Asian policy-makers to pay much greater attention to labour rights. Both theory and international evidence suggest that upgrading labour standards to international norms is both a morally virtuous goal and an economically sensible strategy. The fact that some countries, such as Korea and Indonesia, are seriously experimenting with social accord models involving government, business, and labour in dealing with the issue of worker rights, implies that substantial progress in this area may occur.

Chapter 6

Poverty, Inequality, and Economic Growth

INTRODUCTION

The link between poverty, inequality, and economic growth has intrigued both economists and policy-makers. On the one hand there have been concerns about whether the benefit of economic growth does 'trickle down' to have any noticeable effect at the level of poverty. On the other hand, following Kuznets' work (1955), there has been a belief that inequality inevitably rises with economic growth before it falls. It seems, however, that the Northeast and Southeast Asian economies have defied pessimism. There is general agreement that their spectacular economic growth was accompanied by rapid and sustained improvement of both poverty and inequality. The Asian Development Bank (ADB 1994: 35) expresses the conventional wisdom when it notes: 'A remarkable feature of economic growth in East Asia is that it has been accompanied by a reduction in income inequality'. The World Bank (1993a: 3) offers an identical observation about the high-performing Asian economies (HPAEs): 'The HPAEs' low and declining levels of inequality are ... a remarkable exception to historical experience and contemporary evidence in other regions'. Fields (1995: 84) observes: 'The most outstanding examples of broad-based economic improvements over a sustained period of time are the ... NIEs [newly industrialised economies] ... Their income distribution experiences ... present a picture of extraordinary improvements'.

We can see glimpses of this extraordinary achievement in the fact that the number of absolute poor in East Asia declined from an estimated 400 million in 1970 to about 180 million in 1990, while the population grew by some 425 million during the same period

(Johansen 1993). World Bank (1998b) estimates show that between 1975 and 1995, poverty in East Asia dropped by two-thirds according to the region's head-count index using the constant $US1-a-day poverty line (in 1985 purchasing power parity terms). This meant that people living in poverty fell from 60 per cent in 1975 to only 20 per cent by 1995. The two most populous countries of the region—China (the PRC) and Indonesia—made the greatest progress (Johansen 1993). For example, rural poverty in the PRC fell from 33 per cent in 1978 to 11.5 per cent in 1990; in Indonesia, rural poverty declined from 33.9 per cent to 14.3 per cent over the same period (ADB 1994: Table 3.3, 190). Between 1975 and 1995 overall poverty in the PRC and Indonesia dropped by 63 and 82 per cent respectively.

The regional gain in poverty reduction is more impressive in terms of absolute food poverty.[1] For example, Singapore, Hong Kong, and Taiwan seem to have eliminated absolute food poverty. Absolute food poverty has almost disappeared in Korea and Malaysia, where it fell from 18 per cent in 1980 to 2 per cent in 1990. Absolute food poverty in the PRC declined from 28 per cent in 1978 to only 8 per cent in 1988. Furthermore, larger and regionally diverse countries such as Indonesia and the PRC have sharply reduced regional disparities of poverty (ADB 1997: 270). Their gains in improving income distribution have been equally impressive, although there are some signs of growing inequality in recent times.

These spectacular achievements have prompted the World Bank (1993a) to label the HPAEs examples of 'shared growth'. This concept has two dimensions: changes in absolute poverty and trends in relative income inequality.

More recent trends in inequality, however, suggest a complex picture, with inequality rising in some cases. One could argue that the focus of the concept of shared growth is reduction in absolute poverty. But one could also argue that adverse perceptions of relative income inequality could affect the social and political cohesion that characterised the rapidly growing economies of the region. Indeed, Alesina and Rodrik (1994) argue—and provide evidence—that inequality in land and income ownership is negatively correlated with subsequent growth.

It thus appears that the concept of shared growth needs to be carefully scrutinised. This involves understanding the broad forces that led to the reduction in absolute poverty in the region, and focusing on later trends in income inequality. This in turn entails a brief reflection on the contemporary relevance of well-known paradigms on the growth–equity nexus, such as the 'Kuznets hypothesis' (Kuznets 1955) and Sen's 'entitlement approach' (Sen 1981).

WHAT IS SHARED GROWTH?

As mentioned earlier, the idea of shared growth was first mooted by the World Bank (1993a) to identify a common, defining feature of East Asian dynamism. However, the Bank did not define the concept and tended to conflate it with the 'developmental state' paradigm. What is the pedigree of shared growth? Is it an innovative notion or simply a case of putting new wine in an old bottle? In what way is it related to the earlier literature on the growth–equity trade-off? These are issues that need to be clarified before the concept of shared growth can be applied to the HPAEs' experience.

One starting-point is specifying a social welfare function that captures, in an *ad hoc* manner, the key performance indicators of economic development.

$$W = W\,(Y, I, P)$$

where Y is real per capita income, I is an index of inequality, and P is an index of absolute poverty. Thus, I measures relative gaps across the population, while P focuses on a subset of the population, that is, those who fall below a designated poverty line. It seems plausible to argue that increases in Y with decreases in I and P will lead to an increase in the value of W. Shared growth can readily be interpreted in terms of this general proposition: the concept states that a sustained increase in Y will not translate into a sustained increase in W if there is a simultaneous increase in I and P. This is simply another way of putting the familiar refrain that economic growth (increases in Y) is not synonymous with economic development. The latter requires the benefits of growth to percolate down to the masses.

The concept of shared growth is straightforward, even banal, if I and P are perfectly correlated and if there is prior knowledge that Y, I, and P will behave in a systematic manner. However, I and P can move in different directions. A rise in I is compatible with a fall in P and a sustained rise in Y. Thus, while the average income of the poor could rise, the rich could still get richer at a faster rate. In such a case of ambiguity it is important to distinguish between the 'weak' and 'strong' versions of shared growth.

In the strong version of shared growth, the value of W in the context of a growing economy can only rise if I falls (or at least remains constant) and P falls. In the weak version, the value of W in the context of a growing economy can rise even if I goes up, provided P falls. This can be regarded as the 'absolute poverty' approach.

It is possible to argue that the weak version of shared growth was implicit in the early literature on the growth–equity trade-off. The classic study by Kuznets (1955) utilised longitudinal data on industrial countries to show that inequality rises then falls during the process of economic growth. This bred the 'U-shaped' hypothesis and inspired a generation of development economists to verify its existence by utilising cross-country data. Robinson (1976) concluded that the Kuznets hypothesis acquired the force of an 'iron law'. The U-shaped hypothesis also enabled many to realise that there was an inevitable trade-off between growth and equity (Adelman & Morris 1973). There were critics of this literature (Beckerman 1977; Lal 1976), but they apparently overlooked the key fact that Kuznets (1955) never implied that P would rise then fall during the process of economic growth. His explanation, which focused on a progressive transfer of population from a low-income agricultural to a high-income, urban-based industrial sector, clearly implied that the average living conditions of the poor would progressively improve during the industrialisation that accompanied economic growth, despite transitional increases in inequality.

It is also worth emphasising that the first-generation development economists and policy-makers never considered growth the only objective of development (Bhagwati 1984; Arndt 1987). Their primary concern was that sustained growth should eventually lead to sustained reductions in poverty—the 'trickle-down' theory—although they conceded that 'some degree of inequality ... was an essential part of the structure of incentives in any growing economy' (Pant 1962, quoted in Arndt 1987: 101). Later evidence clearly substantiates the point that progressive increases in Y are negatively correlated with P for any given level of inequality (Squire 1993). In sum, the weak version of shared growth epitomised the early literature on the growth–equity trade-off. Figure 6.1 shows the weak version of shared growth in diagrammatic form.

Figure 6.1: Weak Version of Shared Growth (Kuznets hypothesis)

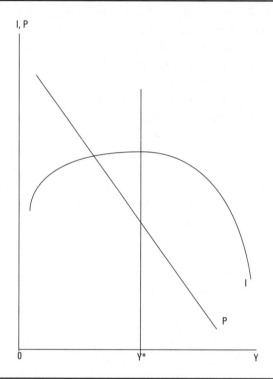

Notes: Both I and P can be expressed in values that fall in the unit interval (0, 1). For example, it is possible to fix the initial value of I at 0.2 (as measured by the Gini ratio) and P at 0.7 (as measured by the head-count ratio)

As can be seen from Figure 6.1, I rises (in accordance with the Kuznets hypothesis), but P falls progressively. Shared growth takes place in this case, provided one accepts the weak version (or, equivalently, the absolute poverty approach). Shared growth unequivocally takes place beyond Y*.

Is it possible to have short-run increases in both I and P, until the turning-point Y*? Anand and Kanbur (1984) have developed a Kuznets-type model which shows that it can happen. However, Chowdhury and Islam (1993) have argued that the Anand–Kanbur version of Kuznets assumes that the population progressively migrating to an urban-based industrial sector cannot be absorbed into gainful employment because of wage rigidity in that sector. This expands the size of the low-income, urban informal sector. Given the considerable evidence of both real and nominal wage flexibility in developing countries (Freeman 1993a), this seems to be a rather dubious assumption.

The strong version of shared growth can be shown diagrammatically as in Figure 6.2.

Figure 6.2: Strong Version of Shared Growth

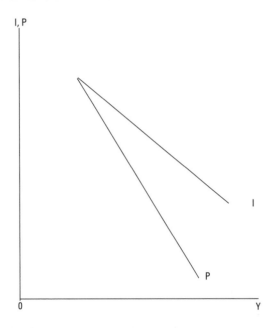

Notes: Both I and P can be expressed in values that fall in the unit interval (0, 1). For the sake of simplicity of exposition, we will fix the initial value of I at 0.5 (as measured by the Gini ratio) and P also approximately at 0.5 (as measured by the head-count ratio). Typically, I falls over a small range (e.g. 0.5–0.4), while P can vary over a large range (e.g. 0.5–0.1), hence the difference in the slopes

Figure 6.2 shows that Y, I, and P are systematically correlated and reinforce each other. To explain this, it would be useful to introduce the concept of the 'growth elasticity of poverty reduction', which refers to an X per cent reduction in poverty due to a 1 per cent increase in the growth rate. This reflects the slope of the 'poverty function'. Research (for example Ravllion & Sen 1994) has noted that the growth elasticity of poverty reduction depends on prevailing levels of inequality. If a 1 per cent increase in the growth rate is accompanied by a fall in inequality, this will lead to a fall in poverty that exceeds X per cent. In graphical terms, this means either a steeper slope of the poverty function ('pivot effect') or a parallel downward shift of the poverty function ('shift effect').

Figure 6.3: The Pivot Effect of Inequality Reduction on the Growth–Poverty Relationship

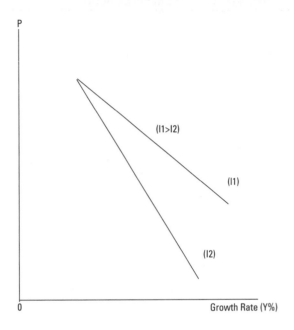

Figure 6.3 shows the pivot effect and Figure 6.4 shows the shift effect. Exactly which effect dominates is a matter for empirical verification, but in any event poverty level falls significantly when economic growth is accompanied by a decline in inequality.

It is possible to use political economy arguments to explain why inequality matters for growth and poverty reduction. This view relies on the notion of distributive politics (Alesina & Rodrik 1994), which holds that when inequality becomes a major social concern, it sows the seeds of demand for redistributive measures which in turn retard growth through policy distortions such as macroeconomic populism (see Dornbusch & Edwards 1990).

This epitomises the so-called East Asian miracle. As Birdsall (1995: 440) puts it: 'What was common across East Asia was the ... idea of "shared growth" ... [there] was an emphasis on ... policies and

Figure 6.4: The Shift Effect of Inequality Reduction on the Growth–Poverty Relationship

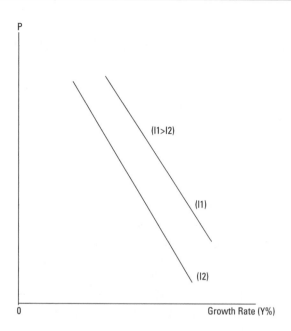

programs … for ensuring that the working class, the non-elite, would benefit from growth'.

How can one explain the occurrence of the strong version of shared growth in Northeast and Southeast Asia? What were these 'programs and policies' that ensured that the 'non-elite' would participate vigorously in the growth process? The next section will focus on policies and programs, and we end the above discussion by stating that, in sum, the notion of shared growth varies. In its weak version, it can be linked to the early literature on the growth–equity trade-off as embodied in the Kuznets hypothesis and the trickle-down theory. The strong version can be linked to more recent research which argues that inequality is important in a number of ways for both growth and poverty alleviation. Such research highlights the possibility of implementing policies and programs that are both pro-growth and equitable, and warns of the dangers of distributive politics. This chapter argues that Northeast and Southeast Asian political economies exhibit elements of the strong version of shared growth. In particular, they try to overcome the problem of distributive politics by emphasising growth-oriented redistributive strategies such as export-oriented development and the expansion of education.

PUBLIC POLICY AND SHARED GROWTH

As evident from the discussion of shared growth, both poverty and inequality are determined by structural and policy variables. Although in reality it is difficult to isolate the effects of structural factors from those of policy variables, as structure and policy interact continuously, some practitioners such as Bigsten (1989) and Sundrum (1990) have offered a checklist of structural factors which affect income distribution. These include intersectoral labour allocation, population pressure, asset distribution, technology, and factor market performance. However, as Lal (1976) has warned, it is not enough to have a checklist. It is necessary to show how the various structural factors interact.

Research has also identified programs and policies that lead to reductions in inequality and poverty, and that simultaneously promote productivity and growth. Birdsall (1995) and Birdsall and Sabot (1994) have highlighted two such policies: labour-intensive, export-oriented industrialisation and heavy public investment in universal basic education. Export-oriented industrialisation increases the demand for low-skilled workers and drives up wages and employment, while aggressive investment in public education enhances the human capital endowment of such workers. These forces interact to create the happy outcome of shared growth. Sen (1981), in his 'entitlements' approach, tells a similar story, although he emphasises the need for labour-intensive industrialisation rather than export-oriented industrialisation. He also highlights the need for public action to provide basic needs, such as education and housing. The thrust of Sen's position is thus sympathetic to the strong version of the shared growth hypothesis.

It would be fair to maintain that a robust and general model of income distribution is yet to be constructed. Sen (1981), however, makes an ambitious attempt with his entitlements approach. In a later contribution, Sen (1985) conceptualises poverty as the lack of certain basic capabilities, such as avoiding hunger and illiteracy, which is different from income-based approaches to poverty. As will be argued in greater detail later, the advantage of Sen's work lies in the fact that it allows the prevailing policy environment to be considered a major influence on income distribution.

As Sen (1981: 308) puts it:

Each economic and political system produces a set of entitlement relations governing who can have what in that system. For a market economy, the determining variables of entitlements can be broadly split into:

(i)   ownership vector ...
(ii) exchange entitlement mapping.

The former pertains to each individual's portfolio of physical and human capital assets; the latter to the individual's ability to acquire, given his or her ownership bundle, alternative bundles of commodities through production or trade.

Sen maintains (1981: 311) that 'Poverty removal ... is ultimately dependent on a wide distribution of effective entitlements, and this—for any given level of per capita income—would tend to be reflected in the low level of inequality in the distribution of income'.

What causes a 'wide distribution of effective entitlements'? There are two main forces corresponding to Sen's distinction between ownership vector and exchange entitlement mapping. Thus, any factor or set of factors which affects the ownership vector would directly influence both poverty and inequality. Common examples are a sustained increase in the overall volume of assets and asset redistribution, such as land reform. Similarly, any factor or set of factors which influences the exchange entitlement mapping will in turn affect poverty and inequality. Examples include the shifts in terms of trade faced by poor peasants, the availability of employment opportunities for semi-skilled and unskilled workers, and the direct provision of basic needs (primary education, basic health care services, and low-cost housing) by the state.

The entitlement approach does not make neat predictions about the time-path of inequality and poverty during economic growth, as do models that belong to the Kuznets genre. All it suggests is that the key structural determinant of inequality in a market economy is the set of entitlement relations. Any market economy at any stage of development will experience either a decline or a rise in poverty and inequality, depending upon the nature of changes in its set of entitlement relations.

Critics of the entitlement approach may consider its lack of predictive capacity a weakness. It could also be argued that the distinction between ownership vector and exchange entitlement mapping is rather stylised and not always helpful. For example, rapid expansion of primary education affects both the exchange entitlement mapping and the ownership vector. This chapter maintains that, despite these alleged limitations, the entitlement approach is a marked improvement on Kuznets-type views on income distribution in developing economies. The simplicity of the Kuznets model occurs at the expense of analytical content, and it does not allow for the prevailing policy environment playing any explicit and important role in determining income distribution. The entitlement approach, however, assigns public policy an explicit and significant role in terms of its impact on poverty and inequality. Public policy is thus the next subject of discussion.

Policy measures which influence both the ownership vector and the exchange entitlement mapping will in turn influence outcomes on poverty and inequality. This seems to be the key message of the entitlement approach. An obvious example of a policy measure which directly affects the ownership vector in a developing economy is asset redistribution through land reform. Since land is a key asset in many if not most developing countries, land reform has understandably been the subject of much discussion in the development literature. However, land reform is politically costly and is thus not a useful policy option in most cases. This suggests the need to consider more feasible policy alternatives with the potential to alleviate poverty.

There are two broad policy measures which have considerable relevance in influencing the set of entitlement relations in a market economy: employment creation and direct provision of basic needs by the state. It could be argued that employment creation affects both the ownership vector and exchange entitlement mapping. Thus, the principal asset of the poor is their labour services. Employment creation, by enhancing the value of this asset, would influence the prevailing ownership vector. At the same time, the enhanced purchasing power of the poor generated by employment creation allows them to acquire the preferred bundle of alternative commodities, thus affecting the exchange entitlement mapping. As employment creation works through both channels, it is a powerful redistributive tool.

What is the most effective way to create sustainable employment of the labour services of the poor? The concept of export-oriented industrialisation now becomes very relevant. Export-oriented industrialisation allows developing economies to intensively utilise a key resource which is in plentiful supply: semi-skilled and unskilled workers. Given that such workers are typically represented in poverty groups, the enhanced purchasing power of such groups reduces poverty. At the same time, the strategy has an equalising influence on income distribution by increasing the income share of poorer groups. Fields (1995) has added the important observation that, to generate favourable income distribution effects, export-oriented industrialisation must operate in the context of relatively undistorted labour markets, free of institutional impediments that raise wages above the market-clearing level.

It is worth pointing out that, according to Sen, the key issue is labour-intensive industrialisation rather than export-oriented industrialisation. Employment creation is a means of entitlement-raising: whether it is generated via the domestic or the export market is a secondary issue (Sen 1981: 299). This point has some appeal but it should be treated with caution. While large economies may rely on domestic markets to foster labour-intensive industrialisation, it is unlikely to occur in economies with a limited domestic market. Furthermore, monopoly imperfections which inhibit the growth of labour demand are more likely to crop up in narrow domestic markets than in the global terrain of export markets.

Employment creation may be seen as an indirect means of entitlement-raising. It operates through the labour market to enhance the purchasing power of the poor, who then acquire their preferred bundle of commodities. A more direct method of entitlement-raising is the selective provision of basic needs to the poor by the state (Streeten et al. 1981). Primary education, basic health delivery systems, low-cost housing, and sanitation facilities may all be seen as basic needs which enhance the endowments of the poor as well as their exchange entitlement mapping. Advocates of basic needs would emphasise that, as a strategy, it is consumption-oriented in appearance but productivity-enhancing in substance. In other words, there are large human capital components in the various basic needs items. The productivity-enhancing effect of education is well-known, but it has also been argued that improved nutritional standards and better health facilities raise the productive potential of individuals and generally enhance adaptability and capacity to change. Thus, the basic needs strategy alleviates poverty both by boosting the current consumption bundle of the poor and by raising their productivity.

Strands of the literature have gone beyond the claim that public spending on basic needs is an essential component of poverty alleviation to offer ways of designing targeted spending programs with maximum poverty-reducing effects. This literature has yielded reasonably robust conclusions (de Walle 1995).

- Spending on basic services, particularly primary and secondary education and basic health care, almost universally reaches the poor. This implies that the case for expanding the share of public spending on basic needs ('broad targeting') is well-founded, although vigilance is necessary to ensure that the benefits of such spending do not go disproportionately to the better-off.

- Certain interventionist public policies, such as food subsidies and public employment schemes, have at times been quite pro-poor, but there have also been many cases of dismal failure.

- When poverty is widespread and administrative capacity for monitoring public spending programs is low, broad targeting is desirable.

- Generally, what is needed is a combination of universalism in certain spending categories (usually of a basic needs type) and finer targeting in others (providing safety nets, for example). Such a two-pronged approach provides a good basis for policy design.

It would be useful to summarise by deciding whether employment creation or basic needs provisions (broad targeting) is more effective in alleviating poverty and generating a more equal distribution of income. It is best to regard them as complementary rather than competing strategies. As the World Bank puts it (1990: 51):

> Both elements are essential. The first provides the poor with opportunities to use their most abundant asset—labour. The second improves their immediate well-being and increases their capacity to take advantage of the newly created possibilities. Together, they can improve the lives of ... the poor.

ECONOMIC CRISIS, STRUCTURAL ADJUSTMENT, AND POVERTY

While employment creation and basic needs provisions were core policy issues in the 1970s and remain so today, the 1980s added a new dimension to the debate on the impact of the policy environment on poverty and income distribution. This stems from the fact that a number of developing economies experienced serious macroeconomic imbalances manifested in unsustainable fiscal deficits, rising external indebtedness, balance-of-payments problems, and rampant inflation, prompting the governments of those countries to implement orthodox stabilisation measures such as fiscal restraints and tight credit controls in order to restore macroeconomic equilibrium. In addition, many developing economies had to follow structural adjustment policies recommended by key multilateral institutions—the World Bank and the International Monetary Fund (IMF)—as conditions attached to loans dealing with their macroeconomic disequilibrium. These structural adjustment policies usually entail efforts to implement policy reform as a means of boosting aggregate supply. The intention is not only to offset the aggregate demand reduction caused by orthodox stabilisation measures but to provide a basis for future growth. Typically, structural adjustment measures entail minimising distortions in the relative price structure through trade liberalisation, deregulation of product and factor markets, and privatisation. The primary objective is to achieve a more internationalised, private sector-driven economy. Although sound in principle, the practice of macroeconomic stabilisation cum structural adjustment has, according to some critics, led to unanticipated adverse consequences on poverty and income distribution. This has prompted many development observers to seek macroeconomic adjustment with a 'human face' (Cornia, Jolly & Stewart 1988).

Summers and Pritchett (1993: 385) have responded to the critique by offering qualified support for IMF/World Bank-led adjustment programs. As they put it: 'Evidence suggests that the poor fared better on average in adjusting nations though they are often hurt in the stabilisation phase when recession is unavoidable. There is also no evidence that social indicators (e.g., infant mortality) have deteriorated in adjusting countries'.

Why should these stabilisation cum adjustment measures lead to adverse income distribution consequences? The reduction in aggregate demand engenders a rise in unemployment which, in turn, directly affects the living standards of the poor. More ominously, faced with the exigencies of restoring macroeconomic equilibrium, many developing countries cut back public expenditure on essential social services, many of which are critical in maintaining the well-being of the poor. The long-term implications are adverse, as these developments can be seen as de facto divestment of human capital.

It is important, when assessing the link between adjustment measures and poverty, to take a number of factors into account. First, the adverse impact of adjustment measures on poverty is essentially short-term. In principle, adjustment measures should boost output growth in the medium to long term and thus create sustainable employment opportunities for the poor. Second, there are important components of adjustment measures, such as exchange rate depreciation, which have distributional consequences. Exchange rate depreciation typically boosts demand for labour-intensive exports in the manufacturing sector and assists small farmers who produce exportable goods. Third, the income distribution consequences are often complex, creating a range of gainers and losers, so that the net effect is not always clear. For example, deregulating controls on food prices—a favourite item in the adjustment agenda—will boost the living standards of small farmers who are net producers of food, but hurt landless rural workers and the urban poor.

Despite these qualifications, adjustment measures can, under certain circumstances, cause at least a transitional increase in poverty. The policy challenge is to find means of cushioning these unfavourable effects of adjustment. The World Bank (1990: ch. 7) has called for attempts to protect public expenditure on basic needs-type services through a temporary pause in investment and, more importantly, through a restructuring of the government's fiscal position—a conclusion endorsed by Summers and Pritchett (1993). This would entail, as Sundrum (1990: 282) puts it, 'increasing public revenue mainly by taxes falling on the upper income groups, and by reducing public expenditure on services whose benefits accrue mainly to these groups'. Several studies of country-specific experiences have shown that countries which have adopted measures similar to those mentioned were successful in offsetting the adverse effects of stabilisation cum adjustment policies on the poor.

There is a more fundamental lesson from the discussion. Efficient macroeconomic management and correspondingly efficient microeconomic policies may not always be seen as poverty-alleviating and redistributive strategies in the same spirit as measures such as land reform. The financial and economic crises that have swept the Asia–Pacific economies also highlight the fact that high economic growth alone is inadequate. There must be a social safety net to ensure that the gains in poverty reduction do not evaporate due to sudden shocks.

POVERTY, INEQUALITY, AND ECONOMIC GROWTH: ASIA–PACIFIC EXPERIENCE

This section provides an overview of medium-term trends in inequality and poverty in the economies of the Asia–Pacific region. Two measures are used: the Gini ratio for income inequality and the head-count ratio (the proportion of the population below a given poverty line) as a measure of poverty. The latter is supplemented by a social indicator (infant mortality). While the Gini ratio is an acceptable measure of income inequality, it has been recognised for some time that the head-count ratio is a theoretically inadequate measure of poverty (Sen 1976). Nevertheless, when it is not possible to use more robust distribution-sensitive poverty measures, 'it is better to use the ... head-count ratio than to use no index at all' (ADB 1994: 191).

It is important to remember that there is a problem with accessing reliable data, a problem that is particularly acute in the case of income distribution statistics. As Fields (1995) has correctly emphasised, such statistics are not published regularly anywhere and international agencies, such as the World Bank, have been notoriously reticent about providing data in their regular published sources. When attempts are made to construct such data sets, not many countries meet the test of reliability (see Fields 1997). These observations should be borne in mind when interpreting the information provided in the following tables.

Table 6.1: Poverty Indices: East Asia vs Other Regions, 1990s

Region	Head-count index (%), 1990	Infant mortality (per 1000)
East Asia	11	34
Latin America	25	47
Middle East and North Africa	33	80
Sub-Saharan Africa	48	107
South Asia	49	92
Aggregate	30	63

Source: Adapted from Squire (1993: Table 1378)

Note: The head-count index is based on a poverty line in 1985 purchasing power parity (PPP) dollars of $US370 per person per year

Table 6.1 shows head-count ratios for regional aggregates—East Asia versus other regions for a particular year (1990). More country-specific details are shown in Table 6.2. As can be seen, East Asia has a considerably lower level of poverty (11 per cent) than is the average for other developing countries (30 per cent). Another popular measure of social progress (infant mortality) shows that the index of infant mortality in East Asia (twenty-eight per 1000) is well below the developing country average (sixty-three per 1000). What is more germane to the discussion is that East Asia's performance in terms of these basic indices is significantly better than Latin America's—a region with a similar income level.

Table 6.2: Medium-term Trends in Absolute Poverty (head-count ratios): Asia–Pacific Experience

Region	Year	Urban (%)	Rural (%)
PRC	1978		33.0
	1985	1.9	11.9
	1990	0.4	11.5
Indonesia	1970	50.7	58.5
	1980	19.7	44.6
	1987	8.3	18.5
Philippines	1961	50.5	64.1
	1971	40.6	57.3
	1991	36.7	52.4
Korea	1965	54.9	35.8
	1980	10.4	9.0
	1984	4.6	4.4
Hong Kong	1963/64	35.6	
	1973/74	3.5	
Singapore	1972/73	7.0	
	1977/78	1.5	
	1982/83	0.3	

Sources: Selectively extracted from ADB (1994: Table 3.3, 190). Hong Kong and Singapore estimates from Rao (1988: 38). See Rao and ADB for details on methodology and original sources

Table 6.2 provides country-specific details and charts medium-term trends in poverty (as measured by head-count ratios for rural and urban areas) covering, in some cases, a thirty-year time span (1960s–1990s). The story in Table 6.2 is one of unmitigated success as far as poverty alleviation is concerned. Poverty has apparently been virtually eliminated in the city-states of Hong Kong and Singapore. Even in the large, populous economies of the region, such as the PRC and Indonesia, there were rapid and sustained reductions in both rural and urban poverty during the two decades studied. The sorry exception, once again, is the Philippines. Although poverty fell between 1961 and 1991, the rate of progress was slow and the incidence of poverty remained high compared with other economies of the region. The cases of Indonesia and the Philippines are worth noting. Both are island economies with similar income levels: $US670 GNP per capita in Indonesia and $US770 GNP per capita in the Philippines (1992 prices). Yet rural poverty in Indonesia was 18.5 per cent in 1987 and a staggering 52.4 per cent in the Philippines as recently as 1991. Even allowing for different methodologies and ˙˙data, the difference is striking.

Table 6.3 charts medium-term trends in inequality for a number of Asia–Pacific economies. It would be useful to discuss the two groups— the Asian NIEs (Hong Kong, Singapore, Korea, and Taiwan) and the ASEAN-4 (Indonesia, Malaysia, the Philippines, and Thailand)—separately. In the former, the general trend seems to be a fall in inequality for a certain period followed by a perceptible shift towards greater inequality, particularly in the 1980s. The exception is Taiwan, where the sharp decline in inequality between 1964 and 1970 was followed by a phase (1976–90) of relative constancy in the value of the Gini ratio. These conclusions seem to be at variance with the trends reported in Fields (1995: esp. 103).

In the ASEAN-4, Thailand stands out as a case where there was a sharp increase in inequality between 1975 and 1990. In Indonesia, a moderate fall in the value of the Gini ratio between 1976 and 1980 was offset by an equally moderate increase in inequality between 1990 and 1993. In the Philippines and Malaysia inequality was lower in the 1980s than it was in the 1960s and 1970s, but the initial values of the Gini ratio were rather high.

It appears that the conventional wisdom—that the Asia–Pacific economies represent rare cases of rapid egalitarian growth—no longer holds true. It was probably a valid proposition during the 1960s and 1970s, but later trends suggest a different story.

How should these patterns of poverty and inequality be interpreted, in light of the above analysis? To start with, how do the cases

Table 6.3: Trends in Income Inequality (Gini ratio; year)

Indonesia	Hong Kong	Korea	Malaysia	Philippines	Singapore	Taiwan	Thailand
0.34; 1976	0.49; 1966	0.34; 1964	0.50; 1968	0.49; 1961	0.50; 1966	0.36; 1964	0.41; 1965
0.34; 1980	0.44; 1971	0.33; 1970	0.53; 1976	0.49; 1965	0.46; 1973	0.30; 1970	0.43; 1968
0.32; 1987	0.37; 1980	0.39; 1976	0.49; 1979	0.48; 1971	0.41; 1980	0.31; 1980	0.45; 1975
0.32; 1990	0.42; 1986	0.39; 1980	0.46; 1988	0.45; 1986	0.46; 1986	0.32; 1985	0.50; 1986
0.34; 1994	0.45; 1991	0.40; 1988	0.47; 1995	0.45; 1989	0.49; 1989	0.31; 1990	0.50; 1990

Sources: Medhi (1994: Table 1); Shari (1998)

relate to the standard benchmark in international comparisons of income distribution, namely, the Kuznets hypothesis or the Kuznets curve? The first-generation literature on East Asian NIEs often noted that this group of economies defied the pessimistic predictions of the Kuznets curve. They still defy its predictions, but in a different way.

As Medhi (1994: 70) concludes:

> The available data indicate that the distribution of income in the ... Asian NIEs ... has shown a tendency to become more unequal in recent years. This is in contrast to the earlier periods of their development where income inequality declined as the economies grew ... it suggests the reverse of the Kuznets hypothesis, according to which the income distribution gets worse ... before it gets better later.

The facts that must be explained are: the reduction of inequality in the early stages of growth followed by an increase in the NIEs; growing inequality in some of the ASEAN economies, especially Thailand; and sustained and rapid reductions in poverty in all the Asia–Pacific economies.

The entitlements approach can be resurrected at this stage. It views distributional changes as the product of changes in the ownership vector and in exchange entitlement mapping. Changes in a key ownership vector—land ownership in the rural areas of Taiwan and South Korea—have been influenced by historical circumstances. In those countries, land reform programs were implemented at the end of the 1940s, often under foreign (US) supervision. In South Korea, land reforms were instituted between 1947 and 1949, the outcome being a redistribution of land owned by big farmers and absentee landlords. The effect on the distribution of land ownership can be gleaned from the following statistics. In the late 1930s, 3 per cent of all farm households owned over 66 per cent of all land; by the end of the 1940s 'less than 7 per cent of all households were landless' (Amsden 1989: 38, quoting Ban, Moon & Perkins 1980). It must be noted that the destruction caused by the Korean War also had a levelling effect on asset distribution (Choo 1975).

In Taiwan, land reform involved rent reduction, the sale of public land, and the 'land to the tillers' program. The effect was that between 1949 and 1957, owner-farmers as a proportion of all farmers increased from 36 to 60 per cent (Kuo 1975). In both Taiwan and South Korea, early land reforms were important in generating a relatively equitable distribution of income in the initial stages of rapid economic growth.

Although asset redistribution in South Korea and Taiwan explains the trend towards higher equality in the early stages of their rapid economic growth, the same analysis cannot be applied to Singapore and Hong Kong. Moreover, even in South Korea and Taiwan, durable factors—rather than a once-off asset redistribution—must be considered when explaining long-term trends in inequality and poverty. As the entitlement approach emphasises, in a developing, labour-surplus economy, the utilisation and returns to labour services are the major mechanisms for reducing poverty and generating more equitable growth. From this perspective, labour-intensive industrialisation, entailing the utilisation of semi-skilled and unskilled workers, is the key route to lower poverty. All four NIEs are characterised by labour-intensive industrialisation fostered by an export-oriented regime. This produced full employment and rapid growth of real wages within a decade.

Labour-intensive industrialisation loses some of its significance in light of the increases in inequality in East Asian NIEs during the 1980s. The very success of export-oriented industrialisation in eliminating labour surplus conditions in East Asia provided the momentum for a policy shift towards industrial restructuring. Growing labour scarcity led to upward pressure on labour costs which, without a compensating increase in productivity, posed a threat to the NIEs' competitive advantage in labour-intensive products. This was the driving force behind the adoption of restructuring policies in East Asia. The timing, scale, and intensity of these policies varied. In Singapore, restructuring policies were pursued vigorously between 1979 and 1984; in Korea, they were particularly evident between 1973 and 1979. Restructuring efforts in Taiwan and Hong Kong were less intensive and vigorous, and were primarily effective in the financial sector of Hong Kong.

The impact of restructuring on income distribution works largely via income adjustments in the labour market. Incentives to guide resources toward capital- and skill-intensive sectors tend to increase the demand for skilled and professional workers at the expense of semi-skilled and unskilled workers. Efforts to increase the supply of skills through the education and training system take time to catch up with the changes in labour demand patterns. A probable outcome is that income distribution turns against workers with lower human capital endowments. Suggestive evidence for this proposition can be found in Chowdhury and Islam (1993: ch. 12).

Specific policies associated with the restructuring process and the transition to a labour-scarce phase probably contributed to the worsening inequality in South Korea and Singapore. In the former, the government explicitly tried to favour large firms, particularly the *chaebols* (large diversified business groups), by offering preferential credit so that they could play a leading role in moving the economy toward heavy, capital-intensive industries. This led to a sharp increase in industrial concentration and offset the relatively equitable asset distribution of the 1950s (Amsden 1989; Kim 1986). In Singapore, selective immigration policy caused labour market segmentation and contributed to rising inequality. It is necessary to add that the selective immigration policy was pursued as an adjunct to the process of industrial restructuring.

BOX 6.1: TRADE AND INEQUALITY

The phenomenal decline in income inequality in HPAEs during their early phase of development (1960s–1980s) gave rise to the conventional wisdom that greater openness to trade in developing countries reduces inequality. This happens as the gap in wages and employment rates between skilled and unskilled workers narrows with the increase in demand for unskilled labour. However, the rise in inequality in HPAEs in the later phase and the experience of Latin America has challenged this optimistic view. There are at least two ways in which increased openness could increase wage inequality in middle-income countries. First, the low-skilled sector may contract due to import competition from low-income countries. That is, although greater openness raises the wages of unskilled workers in low-income countries, it may lower the wages of unskilled workers in the middle- and high-income countries. Second, when middle-income countries adjust to greater competition from low-income countries by restructuring towards high-tech activities the demand for skilled workers may rise, which may mean higher premiums for specific skills. Both factors then contribute to wider wage dispersion between unskilled and skilled workers in middle-income countries.

Source: Wood (1997)

For Hong Kong, Lin (1985) has noted that the worsening income distribution between 1976 and 1981 coincided with an increase in the size of the service sector, particularly financial services. Lin (1994) has also pointed out that the shift of resources toward the service sector ('deindustrialisation') was accompanied by a shift of the most labour-intensive industries from Hong Kong to the PRC, reducing the demand for low-income workers and depressing wage levels.

An important aspect of inequality in the NIEs that has been insufficiently studied is the implications of the demographic transition that occurs in tandem with the transition to a labour-scarce phase. There is a decline in fertility, implying that, over time, such societies will have a relatively high cohort of older people. Deaton (1995) has shown that, in such situations, inequality tends to increase largely because consumption and income among the old are more unequally distributed (the 'within cohort' effect), but also because inequality between age groups tends to rise (the 'between cohort' effect). Deaton pro-vides evidence from Taiwan to support these propositions.

We will now consider the case of the ASEAN-4. Three of the economies (Indonesia, Malaysia, and Thailand) are widely regarded as recent examples of export-oriented, labour-intensive industrialisation leading to rapid and sustained reductions in poverty. The impact on income distribution is, however, more complex. While inequality in Malaysia has fallen, Thailand represents the opposite extreme, with a sustained phase of growing inequality. The contrast could be partly explained by the fact that since 1969 Malaysia has had a strong commitment to redistributive policies in the form of its New Economic Policy (NEP), intended to improve the economic well-being of the Malay population. Commentators generally agree that this redistributive strategy at least partially explains the improvement in income distribution (Medhi 1994; World Bank 1993a). The NEP was conceived as a positive-sum game: improving the economic well-being of the Malays, but not at the expense of others and in the context of a growing economy (see Chowdhury & Islam 1996).

Thailand stands out as a case of successful labour-intensive industrialisation which, although reducing overall poverty, has not apparently had a commensurate impact on income inequality. Medhi (1994), drawing on the contributions of Atchana and Teerana (1989) and Pranee (1997), maintains that relative income standards of workers and households in industrial and service sectors grew more rapidly than those of workers and households in the agricultural sector. This presumably reflects benign neglect of the agricultural sector—the reverse of what happened in Indonesia (see Thorbecke 1991).

The entitlement approach emphasises that the direct provision of basic needs by the state is an effective mechanism for reducing poverty and inequality. Dreze and Sen (1990) are strong advocates of the view that economic growth may not lead to broad-based improvement in standards of health and education, reflected in indicators such as life expectancy, child mortality, primary enrolment rates, and adult literacy, unless they are accompanied by public provision of basic services. They approvingly cite particular countries (such as Sri Lanka) and particular states (such as Kerala in India) to substantiate their argument.

The common perception is that the mechanism of basic needs provision was less important in East Asia. The process of the poor acquiring their basic needs occurred via the market rather than through deliberate public action. In other words, the higher income generated through labour-intensive industrialisation gave large segments of the population the purchasing power necessary to acquire basic needs.

This view is not valid when one extends the sample of Asia–Pacific economies to include the PRC. Given its political ideology, the PRC is committed to an interventionist basic needs strategy (see, for example, Ahmad & Wang 1991; World Bank 1992). The ADB (1994: 198) summarises the PRC experience:

> Through its efforts to provide improved health, education, disability and retirement benefits, China has achieved a much lower rate of poverty than would be expected given its level of national income. China has also attained levels of social indicators which exceed those of much wealthier countries.

Even in the market economies of the Asia–Pacific region, elements of both broad targeting (the universal provision of basic services) and narrow targeting (income transfers focusing on particular services and segments of the population) can be found. For example, in Hong Kong, apparently the epitome of *laissez-faire* policies, Lin and Ho (1984: 50) note:

> the government spends something approaching one-fourth of the national income providing various sorts of physical infrastructure ... compulsory primary education, extensive medical and health services, subventions for numerous social welfare agencies, and public low-cost housing for well over 40 per cent of the population.

An ambitious low-cost public housing program is also a key feature in Singapore (Lim et al. 1988). In addition, all the East Asian NIEs have made large-scale public investments in education and training, ranging from basic to tertiary levels. Thus, in many respects the NIEs followed a basic needs strategy that not only improved social well-being but was also investment-oriented in the sense of augmenting the productivity of human resources. This aspect of public policy is being replicated in the NIEs of Southeast Asia. In summary, labour-intensive industrialisation, the transition to a labour-scarce phase in the NIEs, and public spending on basic needs have been the driving forces behind medium-term trends in income distribution in the Asia–Pacific region.

BOX 6.2: ECONOMIC CRISIS OF THE 1990s, POVERTY, AND INEQUALITY

In 1975 people in roughly six out of ten East Asian countries lived on less than $US1 a day. By 1995 it was down to roughly two out of ten. Although we do not have precise estimates, tens of millions of people have been dragged back into poverty by the current crisis (Stiglitz 1998e).

This quote reflects the general observation on the impact of the 1990s financial crisis. The IMF and the World Bank made tentative estimates of its likely effects on poverty and human welfare. The financial crisis was considered likely to adversely affect the living standards of low-income households predominantly through two channels: price increases, and hence a reduction in real income and consumption; and the loss of jobs.

Table 6.4: Poverty in Indonesia, Korea, and Thailand (% of population)

	Indonesia	*Korea*	*Thailand*
Poor before the crisis	11.3	15.7	15.1
Additional poor due to:			
real income decline	4.8	1.6	2.3
unemployment	0–6.4	0–10.5	0–9.3
Total additional poor	4.8–11.2	1.6–12.1	2.3–11.6

Table 6.4 presents the IMF's estimates of the impacts of the Asian crisis on poverty. The combined effect of real income decline and unemployment on the number of poor in Indonesia was estimated to increase by between 9.2 million and 21.5 million persons (5–11 per cent of population). The number of poor in Korea was projected to rise between 0.7 million and 4.7 million persons (2–12 per cent of population), and in Thailand the estimated corresponding figure was between 1.5 million and 6.7 million persons (3–12 per cent of population). Of the three countries, Indonesia suffered the largest reduction in real GDP and highest unemployment. However, the impact of rising poverty was estimated to be less in Indonesia because households affected by job losses were relatively further from the poverty line and could absorb a larger decrease in consumption before becoming poor.

The World Bank used two scenarios to simulate the impact of the Asian crisis on poverty. The first assumed a 10 per cent decrease in aggregate consumption or real income between 1997 and 2000. The second scenario took into account the most likely growth prospect during 1997–2000. In both scenarios, simulations were conducted with and without any change in inequality. A poverty line of $US1 a day was applied for Indonesia and the Philippines, and $US2 a day was used for Malaysia and Thailand. The results are presented in Table 6.5.

Table 6.5: Poverty Projections with –10% Growth and Changing Inequality (% of population)

Country	1997	2000 (–10% growth)	
		No change in Gini	10% increase in Gini
Indonesia ($US1 per day)	6.7	13.9	19.8
Malaysia ($US2 per day)	13.6	19.2	25.9
Philippines ($US1 per day)	23.5	31.7	36.3
Thailand ($US2 per day)	11.1	16.8	24.6

In the first scenario, with no change in inequality, it was estimated that the incidence of poverty in Indonesia would double and that it would increase by 35–50 per cent in the Philippines, Thailand, and Malaysia. The impact on poverty increases considerably if a 10 per cent worsening of inequality (a rise in the Gini coefficient) is assumed, thus confirming the powerful effect of inequality on poverty.

For a comprehensive survey of the social impact of the Asian crisis, see Booth (1999).

ADJUSTMENT WITH A HUMAN FACE: INDONESIA AND MALAYSIA

To what extent are short-term changes in inequality and poverty in the region's economies due to 1980s macroeconomic stabilisation and structural adjustment? This is a contentious issue: some critics believe that macroeconomic stabilisation and structural adjustment have, in many cases, worsened inequality and poverty. Have the economies of the region suffered a similar fate? This section studies Indonesia and Malaysia briefly, then offers broad reflections on the NIEs.

As shown in Table 6.6, both Malaysia and Indonesia experienced unanticipated external shocks in 1982–83—the OECD recession and deteriorating terms of trade. Buoyed by the 1979 commodity and oil price boom, Malaysia had entered a path of unsustainable fiscal expansion, while Indonesia was unable to restructure its economy from its dependence on the oil sector. Yet, faced by the adverse external shocks of the early 1980s, policy-makers in both economies responded swiftly with a combination of macro-stabilisation and structural adjustment measures. Indonesia, in particular, embarked on wide-ranging fiscal, financial, and trade reform. What is most germane to this discussion is that both economies managed to maintain their momentum of poverty alleviation and apparently did not experience any adverse trends in inequality throughout the period of adjustment. Indonesia and Malaysia have thus defied the pessimistic claims of those who maintain that adjustment in the 1980s has led to immiserisation in many developing countries.

The information provided in Table 6.6 provides clues to this happy outcome. First, both economies had access to foreign funds at a time

Table 6.6: Macro-stabilisation, Structural Adjustment, and Income Distribution: Malaysia and Indonesia, 1978–89

Country	Year/origin of crisis	Particular characteristics	Main macro policies	Poverty indicators
Malaysia (1978–87)	1982–83 OECD recession Expansionary fiscal policy Deteriorating terms of key primary commodities (rubber, tin, oil)	No recourse to IMF NEP during 1970s Foreign borrowing 1984 Persistent large fiscal deficits	Devaluation (1984) Cuts in public expenditure	Urban poverty up slightly Rural poverty down Distributional shift to Malays maintained Annual increase in expenditure on education (5.7%) and health (3.7%)
Indonesia (1979–89)	1982–83 decline in terms of trade (oil) OECD recession	No recourse to IMF Balanced budget (constitutionally required) Continued access to foreign funds	Devaluation Interest rate liberalisation Trade reform Tax reform Fiscal restraint	Poverty fell Urban and rural income distribution stable Cuts in social expenditure (schools, clinics starting in 1986)

Sources: Extracted from Bourguignon et al. (1991: 1493) which draws on Demery & Demery (1991) (Malaysia) and Thorbecke (1991) (Indonesia)

when many developing economies did not. This reflects the perceived credibility of their domestic polices. Significantly, the access to foreign funds served as a very important cushion in dealing with the external shocks of the early 1980s. Second, both economies had rather favourable initial conditions—rapid, investment-driven growth. Third, Malaysia maintained its commitment to social expenditure, which grew in real terms during the adjustment phase. Fourth, Indonesia maintained its commitment to rural development even during the difficult period of the 1980s, although it did start cutting down on social expenditure around 1986. Finally, both economies combined fiscal contraction with expenditure-switching policies.

In sum, Indonesia and Malaysia represent clear examples of economies that offset the adverse distributional consequences of macroeconomic austerity through a policy package advocated by those who claim that adjustment measures need a 'human face'. Using simulation exercises, Thorbecke (1991) and Demery and Demery (1991) have shown that these economies would not have yielded markedly better outcomes with alternative policy packages.

The case studies of Indonesia and Malaysia confirm what is known in general terms about the NIEs, which have been remarkably successful in resuming rapid growth after every recessionary phase. This has occurred primarily because policy-makers have taken quick and decisive action in pushing through macroeconomic stabilisation measures, ensuring that expenditure on social services is protected during the recessionary phase and maintaining the momentum of export-oriented policies, for example through exchange rate devaluations. These favourable policy developments ensure that the adverse impact of cyclical factors on poverty is quickly reversed.

BOX 6.3: FINANCIAL CRISIS, WOMEN, AND CHILDREN

In Asia, women have normally held the most precarious forms of low-skilled jobs. As a result, they were the first to face lay-offs and bore a disproportionate share of the brunt of the financial crisis (see chapter 5). For example, in Indonesia, the textile industry, which employed mostly women, laid off half a million workers by March 1998; in Thailand, women comprised 80 per cent of the unskilled workers laid off in the manufacturing sector by February 1998. In Korea, the unemployment rate of women rose from 1.8 per cent to 5.8 per cent during the crisis. Furthermore, the average wage of women workers was lowered in Malaysia and Thailand.

As family income fell drastically, many housewives in the middle class were forced to look for jobs in household trade, massage, or domestic service. There was an increase in prostitution. For example, according to the Jakarta-based foundation Yayasan Kusuma Burana, the red-light districts absorbed fifty to 100 newcomers every month in 1998.

The crisis also led to an increase in child labour—one study estimated that it increased by 0.35 million in Thailand. In poorer areas of Jakarta, enrolment of boys in Year 1 of primary school dropped by 8.3 per cent and in secondary schools by 14.4 per cent. The enrolment of girls in secondary school fell by 19.4 per cent.

Sources: World Bank (1999); ESCAP (1999)

CONCLUSION

This chapter has critically evaluated the conventional wisdom that the economies of the region, particularly the NIEs, are remarkable examples of shared growth. While it is certainly true in terms of poverty reduction, the evidence is less clear when it comes to trends in inequality. There are episodes of rising inequality in the NIEs and in some ASEAN economies, such as Thailand and Malaysia. Possible reasons include the effects of transition to a labour-scarce phase, economic reforms, the dynamics of demography, and country-specific factors. The chapter also evaluated the debate on the impact of stabilisation cum structural adjustment policies in East Asia and concluded that countries have been successful in quickly reversing the adverse impact of cyclical factors on income distribution. Whether they can do the same in the wake of the 1997 economic crisis is yet to be fully decided.

Given the remarkable record of sustained and rapid reductions in poverty (primarily the product of basic needs provision and labour-intensive industrialisation) and the ability of policy-makers to successfully manage the stabilisation cum adjustment policies with a 'human face', is it nit-picking to highlight the episodic increases in inequality?

If we accept that the NIEs have experienced a full-scale transition to a labour-scarce phase and that there has been an irreversible decline in fertility, they have become what Deaton (1995) calls 'ageing and growing economies'. Deaton (using data from Taiwan and selected developed economies) has shown that overall inequality tends to increase in such economies. Thus, both measured and observed inequality is likely to become a significant social concern in the future. This could adversely influence the dynamism of these economies through the mechanism of 'distributive politics' (Alesina & Rodrik 1994). In other words, when inequality becomes a major social concern it sows the seeds of demand for redistributive measures, which in turn retard growth through policy distortions. Indeed, in Korea at least, there is some evidence of the emergence of distributive politics. As Leipziger et al. (1992: xi–xii) put it:

> The perception that the economic gains of Korea's rapid growth have not been fairly enough distributed is causing difficulties in the labour market, where workers ... are trying to appropriate a portion of the gains they feel have eluded them in the past ... Government has indicated that dealing with this perception is one of the highest priorities because it is complicating the task of economic management.

It thus appears that policy-makers in the 'miracle economies' can no longer rely on an outdated belief that inequality has been eliminated through rapid growth. The 1997 financial and economic crisis has added an uncomfortable dimension to the problem—the crisis has pushed millions of people back into poverty. In Indonesia, for example, the number of poor rose from 11 per cent in 1997 to nearly 40 per cent by mid 1998, and the number in Malaysia rose from 6.8 per cent to more than 8 per cent during the same period. In Thailand the incidence of poverty increased from 11.4 per cent in 1996 to 15.3 per cent in 1998 (ESCAP 1999).

This sudden rise in poverty poses a serious challenge to the durability of East Asian growth. If governments fail to provide safety nets for people who fall into the poverty ditch, there is a real possibility of increased social unrest, which may adversely affect economic growth.

The economic crisis has adversely affected growth prospects and there have been severe pressures to cut government expenditure. Thus, governments are faced with the dilemma of cutting social expenditure while there is an increased need to provide social safety nets. If social expenditure is cut and there is a rise in social unrest, the economies are likely to enter into a vicious circle: poverty—social unrest—low economic growth—poverty. Thus, protecting social expenditure at a time of increased pressure to reduce government expenditure in the face of declining economic growth and revenue is not just a moral issue. It is also justified on economic grounds. Hence, the durability of the Asian miracle largely depends on the ability of East Asian governments to handle the pressure. The immediate challenge is to provide emergency support to the hardest-hit section of the population, and the longer-term challenge is to establish cost-effective and fiscally sustainable safety nets that do not create the types of large labour market disincentives found in many industrialised countries.

Chapter 7

Governing East Asia in the 21st Century: Towards a Post-Washington Consensus?

INTRODUCTION

The East Asian crisis has wreaked havoc in the lives of millions of people in the region; it has also caused unprecedented turmoil in thinking on development policy. Should the fact that a prevailing paradigm is in disarray be a source of concern or a cause for celebration? It should be the latter, according to Joseph Stiglitz, chief economist of the World Bank.[1] In a series of speeches and papers, Stiglitz has led the way in pronouncing the demise of the conventional wisdom, or the 'Washington consensus' as he prefers to call it, in the domain of development policy.[2] That reflected the intellectual imprint of Washington-based institutions—the US Treasury, the IMF, and the World Bank. It emphasised a constellation of virtues—free markets, free flow of trade and capital across the globe, macroeconomic management characterised by sound money, fiscal prudence, and limited government—that was regarded as the source of sustained economic prosperity for poor and rich nations. It was an important set of ideas and operationally powerful because of its simplicity. However, the East Asian crisis has exposed its limitations and demonstrated that, in important respects, it is misguided.

The stage is set, argues Stiglitz, for the forging of a 'post-Washington consensus' on the need to be cautious about globalisation both as a concept and as a strategy. It means the need to reform global capitalism. It calls for a renewal of trust in Keynesian demand management policies as a cornerstone of macroeconomic stabilisation, and it urges the need to broaden policy goals to reflect emerging social concerns on democratic governance, social equity, and sustainable development more fully than in the past. These are the fundamental lessons of the East Asian crisis.[3]

The notion of a paradigm shift in the domain of development studies is an apt theme for this concluding chapter in a study of leading issues in East Asian political economy. The core elements of what could become the post-Washington consensus in development policy are briefly discussed, and the chapter focuses on the irony that a major threat to the emergence of a post-Washington consensus may well be Washington itself. The transition to a new paradigm in post-crisis Asia is likely to face considerable challenges, despite the fact that elements of a post-Washington consensus are already in place.

LIMITS OF THE WASHINGTON CONSENSUS

Appreciating the post-Washington consensus requires a brief evaluation of its predecessor, the Washington consensus, the intellectual evolution of which was discussed in detail in chapter 1. It is pertinent to note that the contrasting experiences in the 1980s of debt-ridden Latin America and the historically unprecedented growth of East Asia provide the empirical context in which the Washington consensus evolved. Key Latin American economies suffered high inflation, outright recession and slow growth, no major progress in poverty alleviation, and unsustainable fiscal deficits and money creation, and followed the inefficient protectionist policy of import-substituting industrialisation. This was in sharp contrast to East Asia, which experienced low inflation, fiscal prudence, outward-oriented industrialisation, robust growth, and sustained declines in poverty. The dismantling of the Soviet Russia and the embrace by Eastern Europe in general of a market economy reinforced the ideological supremacy of neo-classical economics over its dirigiste counterparts. It was in such an atmosphere that the 'The so-called "Washington consensus" of US economic officials, the International Monetary Fund [IMF] and the World Bank was formed'.[4] It made sense to consider sound money and fiscal prudence as the pillars of macroeconomic policy, to argue the case for privatisation and limited government, and to extol the virtues of globalisation epitomised by free trade and unrestricted capital movements.

In the wake of the East Asian crisis, we should re-examine the prevailing orthodoxy in development policy. The success of the Washington consensus as an intellectual doctrine rests on a number of factors. 'It focuses on issues of first-order importance, it sets up an easily reproducible framework ... and it is frank about limiting itself only to establishing the prerequisites for development' (Stiglitz 1998a: 6). Despite its global influence, the Washington consensus could not satisfactorily explain growth in pre-crisis Asia nor explain why such economies were, almost overnight, thrust into a crisis of such magnitude. After all, they were paragons of macroeconomic stability and embraced globalisation as the centrepiece of their economic strategy. Even in Latin America, countries such as Argentina and Brazil successfully pursued stabilisation, but the returns—in terms of sustainable and equitable growth—were somewhat disappointing. The answer to these puzzles lies, it seems, in an undue faith in the virtues of globalisation that made macroeconomic policy subservient to the interests of international money markets. The construction of a post-Washington consensus must be based on awareness of the limits of its predecessor.

CORE ELEMENTS OF A POST-WASHINGTON CONSENSUS

As Stiglitz (1998a: 6) notes, the ideas embedded in a post-Washington consensus are 'unfortunately not simple. They are not easy to articulate as dogma nor to implement as policy'. Nevertheless, they must be articulated and their central relevance in engineering a sustainable recovery in East Asia must be demonstrated. One way of embarking on this challenging task is to couch the complex ideas in a set of core propositions. Below is an attempt to develop such propositions.[5]

1 At the core of the East Asian crisis was the failure to appreciate the fatal risks of globalisation in a context of weak domestic institutions, particularly in the financial and corporate sectors, and inadequacies in international capital markets. The appropriate response is neither deglobalisation nor the speedy sequencing of economic liberalisation. As it takes time to build up institutions, the appropriate response is selective globalisation. This entails an approach that steers an economy away from the addiction of domestic entrepreneurs to 'hot money' or short-term capital flows, but

maintains the trust in free trade and the virtues of foreign direct investment (FDI).

2 The East Asian crisis has shown that it is far too costly, in terms of lost output and blighted lives, to try to play the 'confidence game' where macroeconomic policy was subordinated to winning the confidence of speculators and purveyors of hot money. Developing economies must be allowed to renew trust in the Keynesian compact—the notion that it is the legitimate role of government to engage in countercyclical policies to fight recessions that can follow from an externally driven financial crisis.

3 The reform of global capitalism should entail the reform of the Bretton Woods institutions (IMF and the World Bank). They are overly influenced by the US Treasury and Wall Street and have probably become a burden on the capacity of the development policy community to articulate genuine alternatives to the Washington consensus.

4 East Asian policy-makers must also take the blame for being so vulnerable—after decades of wonderful and equitable growth—to an externally driven financial crisis. It is important to develop an inclusive social model that fully recognises the weaknesses of the past without jettisoning its strengths. This involves greater commitment to democratic governance, issues in social equity, and sustainable development. Institutional development along these lines may provide an environment which enables the East Asian economies to respond to the challenges of the twenty-first century.

The rest of the discussion in this chapter expands on these propositions.

THE CASE FOR SELECTIVE GLOBALISATION

Globalisation can be fostered through many channels: flows of goods and services, movement of labour, movement of short-term capital, and FDI. In both economic theory and political economy, the advocacy of globalisation is selective. There is near-universal consensus among professional economists on the virtues of free trade entailed in the unfettered movement of goods and services. It is widely accepted that the East Asian miracle was primarily the product of export-oriented industrialisation. However, a free trade theorist would hardly advocate the unfettered movement of people across the globe. The social and political costs of unregulated cross-border migration would be accepted as outweighing the benefits that, in principle, could accrue from unrestrained international migration.[6]

The logic of circumspection also applies to free flows of hot money, although it is possible to demonstrate the benefits for national economies from an open capital account. Free access to international capital markets can theoretically achieve multiple outcomes. It can allow countries to borrow abroad to engage in 'consumption-smoothing' in the face of exogenous shocks; it can finance productive investment in the presence of low domestic savings; and it can allow risk-pooling better than exclusive reliance on domestic finance can. [7] These benefits, as Elek and Wilson (1999: 4) emphasise, are feasible only as long as 'there are no distortions in international and domestic capital markets'—in the presence of such distortions, open capital accounts can pose more risks than benefits. This is the key logic behind the case for circumspection on capital account liberalisation.

Hardly anybody disagrees with the notion that domestic capital markets in the crisis-affected economies of East Asia were distorted. The concept of 'crony capitalism' is merely a popular way of describing the presence of such distortions. The absence of, or at best insufficiently enforced, prudential regulation as well as the lack of transparency and accountability in financial and corporate governance, were manifestations of such distortions. Few disagree that international capital markets are also prone to market failure. As McKinnon and Pill (1996) argue, unregulated hot money can generate an 'over-borrowing' syndrome. It is widely accepted that hedge funds and short-term money managers can exhibit herd behaviour. Irrational exuberance can drive them *en masse* into emerging markets; self-fulfilling panic can also drive them *en masse* out of such markets. Self-regulation by professional financial institutions has not been effective enough to engender prudent decisions. The outcome is a dramatic volume of destabilising capital flows that can devastate societies even with apparently sound economic fundamentals.

The same arguments—fatal risks and alleged benefits—do not apply to FDI. 'The benefits', as Griffith-Jones (1998: 1) notes, 'are especially clear for foreign direct investment, which are not only more stable, but also brings technological know-how and access to markets'. Indeed, 'FDI flows to the five most affected [East Asian] economies remained positive in all cases and declined only slightly for the group, whereas bank lending and portfolio equity investment flows declined sharply and even turned negative in 1997' (Mallampally & Sauvant 1999: 3).[8] This is perhaps not surprising because FDI is driven by multinational corporations that seek to control assets and production facilities in overseas locations. Such decisions are influenced by long-term profit considerations. Short-term capital, on the other hand, exploits transient profit margins that are heavily influenced by movements in the interest rate, exchange rate, and asset prices.

This does not mean that FDI is without problems—a voluminous literature focuses on its costs and benefits. There is considerable wariness among national governments that national sovereignty may be compromised if there is excessive reliance on foreign firms. In particular, the notion of 'fire-sale FDI' has become a major concern in the wake of the Asian crisis (Krugman 1998c)—many East Asian firms became available at fire-sale prices to foreign investors as a result of dramatic declines in net worth following the collapse of asset prices and sharp exchange rate depreciations. Whether this will improve the efficiency of the corporate sector in East Asia depends on how well they were managed in the pre-crisis period. If the corporate distress is due to mismanagement and corruption (as is popularly believed), fire-sale FDI represents an efficiency-enhancing and cleansing process. However, if the corporate distress in East Asia is largely due to an external shock over which even well-managed domestic firms had little or no control, the benefits flowing from the forced transformation of national ownership of firms in the region are, at best, uncertain.

Despite such caveats about FDI, one point remains valid: FDI is by no means as volatile as hot money. It is this lack of volatility that is most pertinent in discussions about the impact of unregulated capital mobility on the welfare of national economies.

The uncertainties surrounding the benefits of short-term capital flows to a developing economy have been reflected in empirical work. Rodrik (1998), in a cross-country study, does not find any conclusive evidence that countries with open capital accounts have grown faster, invested more, or achieved lower inflation. However, that conclusion is offset by another study (Quinn 1997) that claims to find a strong positive correlation. In the presence of such uncertainty it is best to advocate a circumspect approach to capital account liberalisation. Some critics, such as Bhagwati (1998), are more forthright and are keen to debunk the 'capital myth' while extolling the virtues of free trade and FDI.

Critics could argue that the concept of selective globalisation as interpreted here is indistinguishable from the concept of deglobalisation as advocated by Bello (1999: 61). In his view:

> The way out of chronic and continuing crisis is the deglobalisation, albeit limited, of the domestic economy—that is reorientation toward greater reliance on the internal market; greater reliance on domestic capital resources; closer cooperation with neighbouring economies to create protected regional markets; a lower rate, and more benign pattern of growth that would generate less income inequality and inflict less harm on the environment; and income distribution and political reforms to underpin controlled development.

It is obvious that there are points of agreement with the views espoused in this chapter—as in the references to more equitable and environmentally friendly growth. But selective globalisation differs from deglobalisation when the cornerstone of such a strategy is the 'creation of protected regional markets' or the vague notion of 'controlled development' reminiscent of the discredited dirigiste doctrine of the past (see chapter 1). This is inconsistent with the ethos of selective globalisation that maintains trust in free trade and FDI. It is also inconsistent with the broad fact that Asia–Pacific regionalism in the pre-crisis period was characterised by market-driven regional integration that did not discriminate against trade with countries outside the region (Garnaut & Drysdale 1994).

If, as argued, both theory and evidence point toward selective globalisation rather than deglobalisation, how should such ideas be translated into policy and operational terms? There is considerable disagreement among professional economists and policy-makers as well as international institutions. Some, such as the IMF, see considerable merit in fostering capital account liberalisation as a primary goal for all developing economies, but agree that it must be accompanied by the reform of international financial architecture (global capitalism) and a strengthening of domestic financial institutions.[9] Others note that it simply takes too long to build domestic financial institutions and prudential regulation in developing economies to the required international standards (Cole & Slade 1999). Hence, discouraging short-term capital flows through a combination of taxes and quantitative but prudential controls ought to be a medium-term policy goal for the crisis-affected economies of East Asia.[10] The

People's Republic of China (the PRC) has shown it can work. Malaysia is convinced it will work, and instituted capital controls in September 1998.

Of course, capital controls can generate allocative inefficiencies. They should not become a permanent feature of an economy and should not be used as a substitute for sound economic policies. Gradually, as financial systems approach international standards, a country can ease capital controls to reap the rewards of globalisation. The alternative approach—hasty and premature capital account liberalisation—that characterised pre-crisis Asia produces undue risks and uncertain gains.

Some critics argue for capital controls as a medium-term strategy on different grounds. Krugman (1998b, 1999a) notes that they prevent domestic policy-makers from falling hostage to the whims of global investors. Admittedly, such policy independence can be achieved by adopting a fully flexible exchange rate, but the Bretton Woods system allowed developed countries to pursue full-employment policies by combining fixed exchange rates with capital controls.[11] Is there a case for going back to Bretton Woods in order to renew the trust in the Keynesian compact in East Asia?

REVISITING THE KEYNESIAN COMPACT

The Keynesian compact relates to the notion that governments can, and ought to, use countercyclical policy instruments to curb recessions and inflationary episodes. It grew out, as Krugman (1999a: ch. 6) maintains, of the terrible experiences of the Great Depression. Governments in the industrialised world assimilated the quintessential Keynesian knowledge that it is possible to fight economic slumps rather than rely on the fatalistic idea that markets will eventually find a way to cure depressions. It was the Keynesian compact that restored faith in the free market economy in the West.

Breakdown of the Keynesian compact: Worldwide inflation and the external debt crisis

For a while after the onset of worldwide inflation in the 1970s and the external debt crisis that swept Latin America in the 1980s, the Keynesian compact became unfashionable. Monetarist ideas—and the more extreme variants such as supply-side-economics—gained ascendancy in the corridors of central banks and finance ministries and in the cloistered confines of academia. The control of inflation became the primary objective of macroeconomic policy. More generally, sound money and fiscal prudence became the pillars of macroeconomic management and sticking to them resolutely became the primary yardstick of economic performance. Not surprisingly, these intellectual trends became entrenched in the Washington consensus of the 1980s.

Breakdown of the Keynesian compact: Macroeconomic policy as hostage to the interests of global investors

There is another important way in which the Keynesian compact was adversely affected, particularly as it applied to developing economies. The composition of the external finance flowing into the developing world changed under the relentless pace of globalisation of finance. Foreign aid and external assistance through bilateral and multilateral donor agencies dwindled in significance, while private flows became ever more important. In the case of East Asia, a burst of financial liberalisation measures in the 1980s and early 1990s set the stage for a surge in short-term capital to the region. Thus, the purveyors of hot money—call it the interests of Wall Street—began to cast a major influence on the evolution of macroeconomic policy at the national level. As local financial institutions and domestic corporations piled up their liabilities in foreign currencies (although their revenues were primarily generated in local currencies), macroeconomic policy progressively became hostage to the interests of Wall Street.

This hostage phenomenon manifests in two ways. First, Wall Street and its constituencies display a distinct preference for macroeconomic conservatism. This is clearly brought out by the Asian Development Bank (ADB 1999: 19) in its articulation of the benefits of short-term capital movements:

> As the domestic capital market becomes integrated with the international capital market, domestic policy-makers become subject to scrutiny by global investors. The discipline that this scrutiny brings helps to discourage the pursuit of excessive monetary and fiscal expansion (which can quickly lead to reserve outflows and currency depreciation).

Prudent monetary and fiscal policies are virtuous objectives. It makes considerable sense to insist on them in cases of countries with a history of erratic and irresponsible macropolicies. There may even be a case for implementing institutional arrangements, for example central bank independence and deficit-limitation legislation, in such circumstances. However, an unwavering commitment to monetary restraint and fiscal prudence can lead to perverse and asymmetric responses. Although macroeconomic conservatism can embolden governments to fight inflation, it can also stifle their capacity to deal with recessions.[12]

Second, the need to win the confidence of international money markets may lead governments toward a resolute commitment to fixed exchange rates. This may be regarded as a means of assuring the domestic corporate and financial lobby that the servicing costs of foreign currency denominated liabilities will be protected. It is also a signal to international money markets that governments will not allow the domestic private sector to default on foreign debt, thus sustaining the capital flows. Unfortunately, such a 'deal' involves potentially great costs. It builds up contingent or unfunded government liabilities,[13] impairing its long-term fiscal position even though the need to win investor confidence pushes governments in the direction of macroeconomic conservatism in the short run.

More importantly, as elaborated in chapter 3, prioritising the maintenance of investor confidence exposes governments to the problem of the 'impossible trinity' in macroeconomic management. Policy-makers face the difficulty of managing a fixed exchange rate, an open capital account, and policy independence. Governments can at most retain two objectives. Events following the East Asian crisis have shown that governments gave up—or were forced to give up—policy independence to defend the fixed exchange rate regime and open capital accounts. This means that governments forfeited the ability to fight an incipient recession through expansionary demand management policies. In the initial stages of the crisis, the policy preoccupation became—with the support and exhortation of the Washington-led international community—the need to win the confidence game at all costs.[14] Thus, interest rates were raised and budgets were tightened. The Keynesian compact was broken, albeit temporarily, but its inexorable logic prevailed. A prospective recession became stark reality.

Prominent voices in the economics profession now display open disdain and profound sadness at the way in which breaching the Keynesian compact for the sake of soothing the frayed nerves of international money markets was urged on East Asia by the international community. 'Washington', as Krugman (1998b:1) remarks, 'worsened Asia's crash'. Macroeconomic policy became 'an exercise in amateur psychology, in which the IMF ... and the [US] Treasury Department try to convince countries to do things they hope will be perceived by the market as favourable ... The perceived need to play the confidence game supersedes the normal concerns of economic policy. It sounds pretty crazy—and it is' (Krugman 1998a: 5).

Sachs (1998: 3–4) concurs.

The IMF worked mightily, and wrongheadedly, to make the world safe for ... short-term money managers [and] bought into the investment bankers' mantra: exchange rate stability above all else ... The IMF encouraged central banks from Jakarta to Moscow to Brasilia to raise interest rates to stratospheric levels to protect their currencies, lest they lose the confidence of the money managers. Of course the money managers could see one step beyond the IMF: investors do not gain confidence when short-term rates are pushed to dozens of percent ... The more these economies tried to defend their currencies, the more they incited panic.

Stiglitz (1998b: 5–6) highlights the fallacy and futility of winning the confidence of external investors rather than harnessing the tools of monetary policy to pre-empt economic contractions.[15] 'High interest rates', he observes, 'were supposed to restore confidence in East Asia. Instead they weakened the economies, causing even more depreciated exchange rates and thus undermining confidence still further'. This follows from the logic that 'the interest rate is only the promised rate of return on domestic assets. If a higher interest rate leads to a greater probability of bankruptcy, then the expected rate of return on domestic assets may go down, leading to a weaker exchange rate'.

Corden (1999: 35) offers a strikingly similar analysis.[16] He notes:

One paradoxical possibility which is not at all unrealistic and which is possibly borne out by recent events, and which goes against the IMF approach, should be noted. Higher interest rates may actually lead to more, rather than less, depreciation. The higher the interest rate, the deeper the recession. The deeper the recession, the more domestic bankruptcies and the greater social unrest. And the more of these domestic troubles, the more adverse will be market expectations about the ability of the government to cope ... and the more adverse these expectations, the more the exchange rate will depreciate.

If, as it seems clear, playing the confidence game generates perverse macroeconomic policy responses and involves enormous social costs, developing economies in general, and East Asian economies in particular, must renew their trust in the Keynesian compact. This means dismantling the policy regime of fixed exchange rates and open capital accounts. One will have to be forfeited. Which?

Renewing trust in the Keynesian compact: Exchange rate systems and capital controls

For nearly three decades after World War II, the Bretton Woods system combined a fixed exchange rate system with capital controls. This gave developed countries the ability to pursue full employment policies. It meant forsaking open capital accounts in favour of protecting the Keynesian compact. After the mid 1970s, the Bretton Woods system gave way to flexible exhange rates, marking the beginning of the demise of the Keynesian compact. Is it possible to return to the Bretton Woods system, and the golden age of Keynesianism?

Many economists now believe that a fixed exchange system of the sort pursued in pre-crisis East Asia is thoroughly discredited (see Garnaut 1999a, 1999b for a comprehensive review).[17] Such a system becomes indefensible in the wake of a massive speculative attack. One alternative is a fully flexible exchange rate regime that restores policy independence to domestic constituencies while enabling them to run an open capital account. Radelet and Sachs (1999: 14) strongly favour such a regime for East Asia, noting that 'We are not aware of an example of a significant financial or currency crisis in an emerging market with flexible exchange rates'. In any case, the crisis-affected economies of East Asia (except Malaysia) have been forced into a de facto flexible exchange rate.

However, as mentioned earlier (and in chapter 3), although a flexible exchange rate regime gives the domestic monetary authority control over monetary policy, countries lose their sovereignty over macroeconomic policy intervention in an environment of capital flows. They become hostage to the international capital market and are forced to maintain a tight fiscal stance and an interest rate regime in line with the international money market. Thus, even when the fixed exchange rate system is abandoned, a fully open capital account may not be entirely desirable. This is especially true for developing countries with financial systems and institutional structures that are not resilient enough to deal with the pitfalls of short-term capital flows.

Many now breathe a sigh of relief that the PRC did not relinquish capital controls and weathered the East Asian crisis by observing the Keynesian compact.[18] They admit that Malaysia's bold decision to implement capital controls in September 1998 does not appear to have been a silly, self-destructive move. Capital controls do not seem to have discouraged FDI (Hiebert 1999): Malaysian-style FDI has even won guarded approval from the IMF.[19]

There are several ways of resolving the impossible trinity in macro-economic management. The paramount concern must be the renewal of trust in the Keynesian compact that is taken for granted in developed countries but compromised in the case of emerging markets simply because they have to play the confidence game. If allowed to persist, this double standard will ultimately prove counterproductive and fail to foster global capitalism with a human face.

Bretton Woods institutions and the reform of global capitalism

It is banal, but true, to make the point that the agenda of reform in Asia must proceed from a clear appreciation of the causes of the 1997 financial catastrophe. In the early stages of the crisis, many pundits, who had formerly heaped praise on East Asia for its miraculous economic and social achievements, rushed to explain its fall from grace from the perspective of inappropriate domestic policies and imperfect institutions. 'Crony capitalism' became an epitaph for the death of the East Asian tigers.

Gradually, professional opinion has shifted towards the view that imperfections in the international financial architecture also have a prominent role in explaining the tragedy of East Asia. This has led to the realisation that there are few effective mechanisms to prevent international financial panics in emerging economies. Industrialised countries have developed various mechanisms such as lender of last resort, tough banking supervision and regulation, deposit insurance, and bankruptcy laws, that have given them resilience against financial crises. There are no international counterparts to these national regulatory mechanisms. Not surprisingly, a core element of the reform of the international financial architecture involves the need to upgrade the financial system of developing countries to industrial country norms.[20] Harmonisation of financial systems will allow all countries— rich and poor—to reap the rewards of globalisation.

Harmonising financial systems across countries

The harmonisation of financial systems across countries at disparate levels of development can be pursued in two ways. First, reform of financial systems can be regarded as a purely national agenda, left to domestic policy-makers and the domestic political process. Experience suggests that this route will be painfully slow and will entrench the dichotomy of laggards and leaders in the domain of financial sector reform. Second, the reform process can be internationalised, as it is anyway through the conditionality instruments applied by the IMF to the crisis-affected economies in East Asia. Once the crisis-management phase is over, there may be a case for formalising the harmonisation agenda through the IMF as a long-term strategy. Under one such scheme, proposed by Calomiris (1998), countries will have to satisfy a set of strict conditions—robust financial systems aligned with international norms, macroeconomic prudence, low incidence of short-term foreign debt—in order to retain membership of the IMF.

A variation of this proposal entails two tiers of membership in the IMF: a top tier of members with special privileges and a standard tier without them. Those who satisfy the strict conditions will be entitled to a new facility that will activate financing in the event of a crisis without having to go through a protracted phase of negotiations (as currently happens in IMF interventions).[21] The alleged advantage of the two-tier system is that it may provide an incentive for all members to aspire to reach the top tier. In this way, the agenda of harmonisation that will collectively raise the resilience of all nations against financial crisis may be achieved.

There are a number of problems with these proposals. They try to persuade economies into a 'one size fits all' category and may be seen as an attempt to salvage the Washington consensus and adapt it to the circumstances of the twenty-first century. The view espoused by this chapter is that the principle of selective globalisation and the need to align the goals of macroeconomic policy to the interests of domestic constituencies, rather than the interests of global investors, should guide the reform agenda in post-crisis Asia. This suggests the persistence of disparate systems of macroeconomic governance, some with varying degrees of capital controls, others without. Financial sector reform should primarily be a national agenda. Such reforms generate benefits that are ends in themselves (greater diversity and efficiency of financial services delivered to domestic clients, reduced probability of banking crises) and need not be justified solely on the basis of their capacity for national economies to have fully open capital accounts. Indeed, the original architects of financial liberalisation in developing economies justified their case by arguing that it was necessary to drive domestic industrialisation, not to serve as a mechanism for nourishing short-term capital mobility.

Reforming Bretton Woods as part of the reform of global capitalism

Perhaps the fundamental political economy objection to an IMF-led reform of global capitalism is that the legitimacy of the Bretton Woods institutions has been seriously undermined by the experiences of the East Asian crisis. They have always been criticised by left-wing scholars and dissidents; the novelty lies in the chorus of dissent from eminent professional economists against the Bretton Woods institutions, in particular the IMF.[22] When Sachs (1998: 3) says that 'The IMF and World Bank have behaved with stunning arrogance in developing countries', he is presumably not doing so as a grand-standing exercise. To him—and others—the development policy agenda is in very serious danger of being derailed, because it is seen to lack legitimacy and ownership by emerging economies.

The thesis of the impaired legitimacy of Bretton Woods institutions is not really about the competence or motives of the professionals who form the core analytical capacity of the IMF and the World Bank, although one could argue that 'In reality, the IMF has been seeking a new permanent role ever since the demise of the Bretton Woods system it was designed to oversee' (Obstfeld 1998: 27). Nevertheless, it is necessary to point out that the institutions have highly professional, compassionate, and honest analysts and managers—to make malicious inferences about their analytical capacity or integrity is a travesty of the truth. The fundamental problem is that the Bretton Woods institutions lack organisational independence because its shareholders overrepresent the interests of creditor nations.[23] As Corden (1999: 52) notes: 'One has to remember that the IMF is governed by its Executive Board, not by its staff. The governments are the owners of the IMF, and the largest owner is the United States'. Now that the USA, whether by design or default, has become the guardian of the New World Order, it has unrestrained opportunities to push its national agenda through the IMF in particular. This view is widely shared, even among economists of impeccable credentials who are normally wary of peddling conspiracy theories.

Feldstein (1998), for example, is convinced that the IMF interventions in East Asia have been compromised because of the need to reflect the trade and investment agenda of creditor nations. This is reflected in a long and detailed list of fundamental changes in economic and institutional structures required as a condition for receiving IMF funds. He regards this as a major departure from the IMF's traditional practice, when it focused on short-term measures to rectify macroeconomic imbalances. Corden (1999: 51), reviewing the IMF intervention in Korea, remarks: 'Certain conditions in the Korean programme ... clearly reflect the interests of US exporters, investors and especially financial firms. These proposals have thus become suspect'.

Among mainstream economists, Bhagwati (1998: 5) has perhaps gone furthest in propounding the view that US interests have usurped the development policy agenda. This is reflected in his thesis of the Wall Street–Treasury complex. As he puts it:

> Wall Street has exceptional clout with Washington for the simple reason that ... there is a definite networking of like-minded luminaries among the powerful institutions—Wall Street, the Treasury Department, the State Department, the IMF and the World Bank ... This powerful network which may be aptly, if loosely called the Wall Street–Treasury complex, is unable to look much beyond the interests of Wall Street, which it equates with the good of the world.

The thesis of impaired legitimacy means that the vision of constructing a new East Asia after the crisis is unlikely to be enthusiastically embraced by domestic stakeholders. There will certainly be sullen acceptance of the vision by the crisis-affected economies under IMF pressure, but there will also be lingering resentment that the reform agenda is externally driven. As Chalmers Johnson (1999) observes:

> With the end of the Cold War, the United States decided it had to launch a rollback operation in East Asia if it was to maintain its global hegemony. The high-growth economies of East Asia had the main challengers to American power in the region, and it was time they were brought to heel.

Reinventing the World Bank

How have the Bretton Woods institutions responded to the growing allegations of impaired legitimacy? It seems plausible to speculate that Stiglitz has assumed the mantle of leading a post-Washington consensus largely because he wants to differentiate the World Bank from the much-maligned IMF and reposition the Bank as a warm, caring institution. The fruits of his endeavours are reflected in the adoption of the Comprehensive Development Framework (CDF) by the World Bank. The CDF, which is being field-tested in thirteen countries, is based on a number of principles:[24]

- *ownership by the country*, in the sense that the country, not external actors, determines the goals, phasing, timing, and sequencing of the country's development programs

- *partnership* between government, civil society, assistance agencies, and the private sector in defining development needs and implementing programs

- *a long-term vision of needs and solutions*, based on national consultations, which can engender nationwide support

- *structural and social concerns* which receive the same priority as macroeconomic and financial concerns.

It is widely seen as an attempt by the World Bank—a premier international financial institution (IFI)—to enhance its acceptability among client countries, particularly given that most development assistance by IFIs uses conditionality to initiate comprehensive, Washington consensus-based policy reform in developing countries.[25]

While the CDF is a laudable move, it may not be enough. Critics point out that the idea has existed in the development assistance agenda for some time (see OECD 1996a). More importantly, critics wonder whether:

> the IFIs can overcome their bias towards a particular, 'neo-liberal' socio-economic model—a model that is approximated, if not fully replicated, in the real world by the United States ... Even if the IFIs could shed their preference in favor of the neo-liberal model, there would remain an organisational bias towards providing similar, if not identical advice, to client governments. It would be difficult for institutions like the World Bank and IMF to adopt a 'let a hundred flowers bloom' strategy ... The result is likely to be at best unfriendly to institutional experimentation on the part of client governments (Rodrik 1999: 33–4).

Others view the reform of the World Bank from a somewhat different perspective. Sachs (1998: 4) points out that the World Bank should disengage from the banking business, where it is little needed, and move into the knowledge business where it could 'truly serve the world'. This would mean privatising a large part of its operations, since much infrastructure aid can be privately financed with long-term capital. This would give the World Bank the scope and incentive to emerge as the 'pre-eminent international institution to mobilise the knowledge to address the problems of the developing world'.

Reinventing the IMF

The thesis of the impaired legitimacy of the IMF has led some practitioners to suggest that IMF operations should be more transparent. Stanley Fischer (1998: 5), Deputy Managing Director of the IMF, has responded by maintaining that much progress has been achieved in recent years. He says that 'if more details of IMF operations were published, there would be more room for appraisal by outsiders—which would be to the good'.[26] But Fischer is unlikely, or unable, to respond to the suggestion that restructuring the powers and procedures of the IMF and its voting rights is necessary to lessen the inordinate influence of creditor nations on the development agenda. There is also a suggestion that the IMF's monopoly as an institution dealing with macroeconomic imbalances in emerging markets ought to be counterbalanced with a regional institution—a sort of Asian IMF. A US-led lobby argued that such an institution would cause confusion about the domain of IMF responsibility and cause debt-ridden economies to seek a soft option.[27] Thus the idea was promptly shot down. It is not clear why a regional equivalent of the IMF is so controversial, because there are quite a few regional equivalents of the World Bank.

A recent development in the proposals to reform the IMF appears in a report by experts to the New York-based Council for Foreign Affairs.[28] It appears to be a synthesis of the key ideas discussed earlier under the rubric of the reform of global capitalism. The authors argue that:

- the IMF should 'go back to basics' and focus on monetary and exchange rate policies rather than structural reforms—a point that Feldstein (1998) made forcefully

- the IMF should lend on more favourable terms to countries adopting sound policies that appear less likely to face financial crises. This resurrects the notion of a two-tiered membership discussed above. In addition, no lending should be available to countries that try to maintain unsustainable currency pegs

- the IMF should publish a standards report on each country, effectively joining the ratings game

- the IMF should stick to its normal lending limits and abandon the large rescue packages that characterised its response to the Asian crisis

- borrowing countries should include collective action clauses in new bond contracts which would make it harder for individual international investors to sue. This seems to be a revival of the notion that private borrowers should share the cost of resolving crises

- countries should impose transparent and non-discriminatory taxes on hot money in order to discourage short-term capital flows and encourage long-term investment.

Some of these proposals coincide with causes that are supported in this book, such as capital controls, but they leave untouched the issue of ownership of the IMF by ignoring the influence of creditor nations on its agenda. Will such radical issues—or even the more moderate reform proposals—have a chance of being tested? The prospects are not particularly good. There are signs that the recession in East Asia has bottomed out and some countries, such as Korea, show persuasive evidence of a recovery. Thus the pressure to dismantle the Washington consensus will abate. If growth indeed consolidates across the region and Japan recovers from its dire straits, the pain and trauma of the past few years will recede from collective memory. Washington and the Bretton Woods institutions will be seen as the saviours of East Asia. For example, Dornbusch (1999: 28) observes, 'So what are the lessons from the past two years? It's that the IMF ... has been right about the remedies for these crises ... So in the end, three cheers for the IMF'. In such an atmosphere, the mistakes and mismanagement by the IMF of the crisis will probably be forgotten. The need for circumspection on globalisation and the importance of upholding the Keynesian compact as the cornerstone of macroeconomic policy in developing countries may become less pressing. Instead, there may be a greater effort to improve governance in East Asia, justifying the view that the crisis was, after all, home-grown.

TOWARDS IMPROVED GOVERNANCE IN EAST ASIA

In some respects, the post-Washington consensus has truly arrived. The notion of inculcating democratic governance in East Asia in particular and in the developing world in general, the need to consider social equity a major policy goal, and the need to protect the environment are regarded as ideals to which both rich and poor nations should aspire.

Fostering and sustaining democracy in East Asia

For a while, robust and historically unprecedented growth in East Asia led to the view among regional elites that such outcomes were facilitated by Asian values.[29] These values, it was argued, involved a resolute commitment to the work ethic, an almost reverential attitude towards education, and respect for order and authority. As discussed in previous chapters, some pundits, in analysing the sources of hypergrowth in pre-crisis East Asia, also discovered quintessential Asian institutions. These were identified as close government–business relations, internal capital markets, and technocratic insulation by authoritarian governments that shielded policy-makers from the rapacious, rent-seeking proclivities of societal groups.

In the wake of the 1997 financial crisis these views have been dramatically reversed, often by the very same pundits who espoused them. Quintessential Asian virtues have become, almost overnight, conspicuous vices. Crony capitalism is now used as a metaphor for the region's fatal institutional weaknesses. Muted concerns about past problems, particularly in the domain of human rights, have come to the forefront of discussions on designing regional social policy to suit the mood and requirements of the twenty-first century.

A key goal is the inculcation and consolidation of democratic governance. Considerable progress certainly appears to have been made. Korea and Taiwan have continued their journey towards democratisation of their political systems since the mid 1980s. Thailand and the Philippines have also become important players in the pan-Asian trend towards democratisation. Indonesia is the latest example of a large East Asian economy engaged in the difficult transition toward political liberalisation. With the successful completion (in June 1999) of reasonably free and fair elections after forty-four years of authoritarian rule, Indonesia is poised for major political and social changes.

Enigmatic cases and conspicuous exceptions remain. Malaysia and Singapore may be described as semi-democracies: although they have parliamentary institutions, there is no free press and there are stringent constraints on political dissent.[30] The PRC is stuck in an authoritarian mould. Despite the very public tragedy of Tiananmen Square, the PRC shows no sign of political liberalisation. It professes unwavering faith in the separation of politics and economics, thus enabling it to combine communism in the political sphere with the progressive introduction of capitalism in the economic domain. Apparently, its political leadership has declared that such a system can last 'tens of generations'.[31]

Although some countries in the region are resisting the transition to democratic governance, the spotlight on these issues will not go away. As Sen (1997: 14–15) notes, 'the case for them stands, even without having to show that democracy actually encourages growth'. Democracy and human rights are intrinsic values and may be regarded as ends in themselves as well as a means to an end.

In more concrete terms, there are a number of areas in which policy-makers in East Asia can work harder to improve its poor record of human rights. In particular, the issue of labour rights needs a lot more attention (see chapter 5). A start could be made by ratifying the core International Labour Organization (ILO) conventions pertaining to labour standards and by incorporating social dialogue with relevant stakeholders—the government, employers, trade unions, and civil society—as a core principle of designing social policy. Korea has shown how this can be done. Indonesia agreed to ratify the core ILO conventions in the midst of considerable economic and political turmoil.

The issue of social dialogue need not be confined to the domain of social policy. It should become a general principle of policy formulation. Greater public discussion, openness, and accountability during policy formulation will expedite the consolidation of democratic governance in the region.[32]

BUILDING SUSTAINABLE SOCIAL PROTECTION POLICY

The crisis has demonstrated that countries cannot rely on rapid, employment-intensive growth to act as a de facto social safety-net or social protection policy. Certainly, in the pre-crisis period, rapid growth brought sustained reductions in poverty without marked deterioration in income inequality. That proud record is now tarnished. Even on the eve of the crisis, the PRC, Indonesia, and Thailand exhibited evidence of rising inequality. There have been significant reversals in poverty, particularly in Indonesia.

It is widely recognised that the burden of sharing the crisis has been iniquitous. Some of the most vulnerable segments of East Asian society—women, children, workers, farmers, day labourers, and small businessmen—bore its brunt although they had no role in bringing it about. This reflects a system that became hostage to the perceptions and interests of the international investor community and its domestic beneficiaries. Even worse, when the crisis struck, the vulnerable social groups were largely left to fend for themselves. They had to seek refuge in traditional support systems (burden-sharing with the help of extended family and friends, returning to their village to work the family farm, finding work in the informal sector). Donor agencies ploughed substantial resources into building an emergency social safety-net system, but to be sustainable such initiatives must be financed by national governments and become a core part of social policy.

Why have East Asian governments overlooked the need to build a sustainable social protection policy?[33] To some extent, the long boom prior to the crisis created a sense of complacency among policymakers that they were immune from protracted recessions and hence the need to invest in social safety-net initiatives. Perhaps there has been excessive faith in the capacity of the informal and agricultural sectors—particularly in countries such as Indonesia and Thailand where these sectors remain significant—to act as informal social safety-net schemes. It is also possible that elite opinion in East Asia has been culturally averse to the notion of the Western welfare state. Welfare statism could have been associated with such Western stereotypes as the breakdown of the family, the destruction of the work ethic, and a general lack of discipline and social cohesion. Finally, it is possible that policy-makers have genuinely felt that the opportunity and fiscal costs of running a comprehensive social safety-net system are unaffordable in a typical East Asian economy.

The crisis and its aftermath have shown that all the reasons against a social protection policy in East Asia are largely misguided. Recessions are a real and constant danger in East Asia, as elsewhere. Informal systems of social protection simply cannot cope with a regional and severe recession. The cultural aversion to welfare statism is as misguided as the rationale of invoking Asian values in order to justify a 'business as usual' syndrome. The issue of affordability also appears to have been exaggerated. Some calculations show that 'an average required contribution of between 0.3 to 0.4 per cent of payroll from 1991 to 2000 would have been sufficient to provide all insured job-losers over this period, including during the current crisis, with 12 months of benefits' in Korea, Thailand, and Indonesia (Lee 1998: 83).

Towards a sustainable development strategy in East Asia

One area where pre-crisis growth in East Asia was always vulnerable was the allegation that politicians and policy-makers failed to listen to those concerned about the adverse impact of a high-growth strategy on the environment. Under every available environmental impact indicator, East Asia was a distressed region.[34] A belated recognition of these problems, together with the 'greening' of civil society in the region, has led to growing attempts to reverse—and prevent—environmental degradation.

Sadly, the gains from these initiatives are being reversed as the need to restore stability and recovery in the region takes precedence over long-term policy issues. Furthermore, the crisis itself unleashed forces inimical to the environment. As the ADB (1999: 17) observes:

The environment is suffering ... because of the crisis. Household attempts to obtain additional income often lead to increased environmental destruction, such as deforestation, erosion and overfishing. In Thailand, the devaluation of the baht has provided a strong stimulus to agricultural exports resulting in expansion and intensification of shrimp farming and, hence, destruction of wetlands and increased salinity of ricelands. An increase in illegal logging has also occurred in Thailand and neighbouring [countries].

Paul Duavergne (1999: 27) has expressed similar sentiments:

The financial crisis has exacerbated old environmental problems as well as created new ones. It has undercut environmental budgets and conservation efforts. Even more important, it has weakened the capacity and resolve of government to enforce environmental regulations. At the same time, corporate and individual efforts to ride out the crisis have meant greater illegal activities. Some firms are dumping more untreated waste into nearby water systems ... Now that Asia appears to be emerging from the financial crisis, aggressive moves are essential to address environmental problems.

The agenda of improved governance in East Asia involves renewed efforts to tackle the long-term issues that represented weaknesses in the pre-crisis period. There is much unfinished business in the domains of democratic governance, social protection policy, and management of the environment. The fact that the region's economies are preoccupied with restoring stability and engineering a recovery must not be considered an excuse for neglecting pressing long-term issues, or the agenda of improved governance in East Asia—and the implementation of the post-Washington consensus in the region—will remain incomplete.

CONCLUSION

The East Asian crisis and its aftermath have set the stage for the forging of a post-Washington consensus in development policy. This chapter has argued that such a consensus should build on the principle of selective globalisation as a medium-term goal. It should build on the notion that macroeconomic policy should never become hostage to the interests of the international investor community. It should build on the idea that improved governance in East Asia ought to focus on the democratisation of institutions, the construction of a sustainable social protection policy, and a renewed emphasis on sustainable development.

How broad is the support for such a post-Washington consensus, within East Asia and outside? There are troubling trends. On the one hand, the ethos and language of the post-Washington consensus—democracy, social equity, sustainability of the environment—are powerful enough to elicit a wide following within the development policy community, the extant regimes, and the emerging political forces within East Asia. On the other hand, the idea that East Asia may not be ready to embrace the ideology of unfettered capital mobility for some time may not receive much sympathy from key players in the original coalition that formed the Washington consensus. This is largely because of the inordinate influence of international money markets on the US Treasury and the Bretton Woods institutions. The IMF in particular is widely seen as a thinly veiled agent of a Wall Street–Treasury complex that is expanding its domain of influence. The World Bank is seeking to differentiate itself from the IMF, but unless more profound reform of the Bretton Woods institutions occurs they will suffer from a perception of impaired legitimacy. This means that the vision of a post-Washington consensus led by the Bretton Woods institutions will not find ready acceptance among key stakeholders in East Asia. Both policy-makers and civil society in the region, humbled and hobbled by the crisis, are likely to interpret any systemic reform agenda directed at strengthening East Asian domestic institutions as an ill-intentioned ploy led by the creditor nations that dominate the global development policy community. As Stiglitz (1998a: 33) warns, 'whatever the new consensus is, it cannot be based on Washington'.

To make matters worse, the bottoming-out of the recession in the region, and evidence of pretty robust recovery in some cases, will breed a sense of vindication among key players of the Wall Street–Treasury complex. The pain and trauma of the 1997 financial crisis will fade from collective memory and the cheerleaders in the rest of the world will regard the Bretton Woods institutions as the saviours of East Asia. But a fundamental question will remain unresolved: will East Asia become safe from the scourge of short-term capital flows as a result of the painful reforms it is undergoing?

Notes

CHAPTER 1

1   The term 'developmental state' was coined by Johnson.

2   Biggs and Levy (1991) and the classic studies by Westphal (1978, 1990) on Korea are sympathetic to the notion of interventionist industry policy in explaining East Asian success. For a more critical account, see Smith (1995).

3   A reader of a preliminary draft of this book qualifies this argument by noting that, in the case of Southeast Asia, the 'crisis imperative has been overstated' as has been the 'weak bureaucracy argument'. In most cases, efforts towards export-oriented industrialisation preceded the crisis imperative. The reader makes the cogent point that only in Indonesia is there clear evidence that the fall in oil prices after 1979 was followed by significant reforms in the mid 1980s.

4   A reader of a preliminary draft of this book expresses reservations about using the energy sector as an appropriate example for highlighting the role of the state in Japanese development. He makes the point that understanding the role of the state in Japanese industrialisation requires an understanding of the 'dual nature of Japanese commerce'. On the one hand, Japanese industry is characterised by a super-efficient exporter that has been able to compete in world markets, despite the exchange rate realignments following the Plaza Accord. On the other hand, Japan has an antiquated high-cost economy that is nurtured by a subtle system of import restrictions. It is in that domain that state autonomy is compromised.

CHAPTER TWO

1   For example, Chenery and Strout (1966) suggested that the maximum achievable rate of growth was 6–8 per cent.

2   The World Economic Outlook has been revised upward with most Asian economies turning around earlier than expected, and again shows the importance of these economies for the world economy.

3   Other terms include 'open economy trilemma' and 'eternal triangle'. Chapter 3 examines this issue in greater detail.

4   However, ICOR may rise if output is decelerating relative to capital for other reasons, such as the economy's structural shift towards more capital-intensive production as part of the normal industrialisation process.

5   See 'Symposium on Poverty, Economic Growth, Poverty and Income Inequality in the Asia–Pacific Region', *Journal of the Asia Pacific Economy*, 5(1/2).

CHAPTER THREE

1   See Frankel (1995) for a simple exposition of the problem.

2   See Hossain and Chowdhury (1998) for a clear exposition of the Mundell-Fleming model in the developing-country context.

3   Matthews (1968) provides a detailed account of how industrialised countries were able to have a fiscal surplus (or a small deficit) despite high expenditure prior to financial liberalisation: high levels of investment by the private sector, encouraged by a public sector commitment to growth and employment, resulted in healthy fiscal balances and relatively small current account deficits.

4   This accord has been blocked by the USA, which insists on including labour and environmental standards in the document.

CHAPTER FOUR

1   As Patrick (1966) notes, economic growth creates demands for financial services ('demand-following' expansion of the financial system). Economic growth is also preceded by financial development ('supply-leading' evolution of the financial system). Disentangling this two-way causality is not easy, although Jung's (1986) analysis of fifty-six countries (including some of the Asia–Pacific economies) suggests that causality changes over the course of economic development. In the initial stages of development, supply-leading forces are dominant; in later stages demand-following forces are at work.

CHAPTER FIVE

1   This is analogous to the issue of harmonising environmental standards.

CHAPTER SIX

1   The food poverty line is the level of private consumption per person (or, if available, per adult equivalent) at which minimum calorie requirements, plus a small allowance for nonfood consumption, are met.

CHAPTER SEVEN

1   Stiglitz announced his resignation from the World Bank on 26 November 1999. His term was due to expire at the end of February 2000.

2   The clearest expression of this view can be found in Stiglitz (1998a). Other pertinent contributions include Stiglitz (1997a, 1998b, 1998c). Chapter 1 mentioned that the term 'Washington consensus' was coined by Williamson (1990). See also Williamson (1994). The issues discussed in this chapter have also been influenced by Sachs (1998), Radelet and Sachs (1998, 1999), Krugman (1998b, 1999a), and Bhagwati (1998).

3   Some authors, including Stiglitz, now argue that the dismal experience of the ex-Soviet Union and a large number of economies of the East European communist bloc in making the transition to a market economy has reinforced the critique against the Washington consensus (see Stiglitz 1999). See also Rodrik (1999: 2), where he refers to the 'dismal failure in Russia of price reform and privatisation in the absence of supportive legal, regulatory, and political apparatus'. For a review of the experience of Eastern Europe, see Nsouli (1999).

4   Stiglitz (1998a: 4) emphasises the key influence of the Latin American experience, but does not explicitly refer to East Asia in shaping the Washington consensus. One could argue that orthodoxy is strengthened if it can show that poor economic performance results when its basic tenets are not followed (as in Latin America), and stunning economic success occurs when its basic tenets are embraced (as in East Asia).

5   It must be emphasised that Stiglitz would not agree with all the propositions that are being subsumed under the post-Washington

consensus. The reform of the Bretton Woods institutions is the most controversial proposition. As will be argued later, prominent voices outside those institutions have put forward a fundamental reform agenda. Others do not make this point explicitly, but it is implied in their analyses.

6   Of course, governments sanction free movement of labour within designated zones. For example, the European Union provides for unrestricted labour mobility among members, but not from other sources. One could argue that a cross-border flow of services requires the free movement of people with specific skills, such as software programmers.

7   See Obstfeld (1994, 1998) for a fuller treatment of these issues. The ADB (1999: 199) draws attention to additional—and more contentious—benefits of an open capital account. It maintains that the free flow of financial capital can 'force the domestic financial sector to become more efficient and innovative in response to import competition from foreign capital'. It also maintains that the public scrutiny of global investors can impose macroeconomic discipline. Cole and Slade (1999) dismiss the notion that a free flow of financial capital can upgrade the quality of the domestic financial sector, arguing, on the basis of Indonesia's experience, that foreign financial institutions adapt to local conditions rather than the other way around. The fear of public scrutiny of domestic macropolicies by global investors can make national policy-makers hostage to the expectations and perceptions of such investors, with devastating results (see Krugman 1999a).

8   It is worth remembering that, in one year, five East Asian economies experienced short-term capital reversals (from an inflow of $US97 billion in 1996 to an outflow of $US12 billion in 1997) that amounted to 10 per cent of their pre-crisis GDP (see Radelet & Sachs 1999: 2).

9   In its annual meeting in Hong Kong in September 1997, the IMF issued a statement that endorsed an eventual move to capital account convertibility among IMF members. This was a fundamental departure from the 1944 Article of Agreement that included current account liberalisation only as an obligation and a goal; it did not embrace capital account convertibility as an obligation and eventual goal.

10 Perhaps the most widely cited case of imaginatively designed capital controls is that of Chile, that combined market-based instruments with non-remunerative reserve requirements on short-term flows for a year. There is also a resurgence of interest in the Tobin tax, advocated by James Tobin in 1972, which proposed an international uniform, but moderate, tax on spot transactions in foreign exchange (see Kaul et al. 1996).

11 Capital account liberalisation did not gain strength among OECD nations until the late 1980s. In some European countries, such as Ireland and Portugal, capital account liberalisation was not implemented until the 1990s (see Bhagwati 1998: 12).

12 Research indicates that the social costs of inflation have been exaggerated and the growth-enhancing effects of mild inflation have been neglected (see Akerlof, Dickens & Perry 1996).

13 The concept of unfunded government liabilities—created by implicit and explicit government guarantees to finance possible defaults of private-sector indebtedness—has become a major issue in the wake of the East Asian crisis. In 1997, contingent government liabilities for the crisis-affected East Asian economies were in the top decile among a sample of forty-six developing and developed economies (see Polackova 1999: 4).

14 This was, of course, the much-criticised IMF strategy launched initially in Indonesia, Korea, and Thailand. The strategy was significantly modified after some time. Critics contend that the initial strategy worsened the recession in all the countries. The IMF contends that the initial policy called for a temporary increase in the interest rate to stabilise the currencies of the affected countries. The alternative of a low interest rate policy would have made matters worse by causing a free-fall in the currencies of the affected economies and worsening the dollar-denominated debt of the corporate sector. The IMF also says that an initial fiscal tightening would not have been recommended had it anticipated the severity of the economic downturn in the region (see Fischer 1998).

15 Furnham and Stiglitz (1998) have explored these ideas in greater depth and substantiate the arguments noted here.

16 Corden (1999) interprets the East Asian crisis as a straightforward Keynesian-style recession and argues that Keynesian-style countercyclical policies are an appropriate remedy.

17   A fixed exchange rate system can be applied in various ways: pegging to a single currency (such as the $US), pegging to a basket of currencies, or a currency board. The logical extreme of a fixed exchange rate system is the adoption of a common currency, as in the euro.

18   In an interview with Reuters, Stiglitz commended the PRC as a 'brilliant case' that maintained aggregate demand and output through countercyclical policies during the regional crisis (*Jakarta Post*, 4 June 1999, 'WB Heretic Wins Mainstream Backing').

19   In an interview with CNBC Asia, the managing director of the IMF said: 'I praise the way in which Malaysia has been able to adopt a soft system of controls' (*Development News*, World Bank website (www.worldbank.org), 20 May 1999). Krugman (1999b: 4) emphasises that 'Malaysia has proved a point—namely, controlling capital in a crisis is at least feasible. Until the Malaysian experiment, the prevailing view among pundits was that even if financial crises were driven by self-justifying panic, there was nothing that governments could do'. Critics of Malaysia continue to maintain that capital controls cannot be held responsible for the economic recovery because other crisis-affected economies have recovered without resorting to capital controls.

20   For an exhaustive review of proposed reforms of the international financial architecture, see Griffith-Jones (1998). One popular proposal pertains to the need to formalise orderly debt workouts that involves the private sector, under IMF supervision, from the earliest stages of an externaly driven financial crisis.

21   This proposal, and the one by Calomiris (1998), is discussed in Radelet and Sachs (1999: 18). *The Economist* (24 April 1999: 80) reports that the IMF 'is about to introduce a new "Credit Contingency Line" ... designed to help healthy emerging economies to ward off financial collapse, by giving them access to substantial amounts of cash when they are threatened by "contagion" from other markets'.

22   Some of the international media have taken up the anti-IMF cause with considerable vigour. *The Asian Wall Street Journal* editorial laments: 'Why there should be conditions for IMF aid

to other countries but virtually none for bailouts for the IMF itself when it makes mistakes is one of the great mysteries of our time' ('IMF 1, Democracy 0', 21 June 1999).

23   This is analogous to theories of corporate governance. Research indicates that a fundamental problem of corporate governance is that majority shareholders often block the diverse interests of minority shareholders. Among Bretton Woods institutions, creditor nations may be considered the majority shareholders that dominate the organisational agenda of such multilateral agencies as the IMF.

24   The World Bank released an update on the CDF on 13 September 1999 (see www.worldbank.org/cdf). Pertinent discussion papers include Wolfensohn (1999) and a paper released by the Bank on 20 May 1998.

25   The most recent critique of the ineffectiveness of conditionality in engendering policy reform in developing countries is Stiglitz. Others include Paul Collier and Jan Willem Gunning. The observations of Stiglitz and Collier/Gunning are covered in the *Financial Times* ('World Bank Aid Strategy Flawed', 29 November 1999), based on the November 1999 issue of the *Economic Journal*. The World Bank, in a 1998 report written by Lant Pritchett and David Dollar, also emphasises that 'conditionality is unlikely to bring about lasting reform if there is no strong domestic movement for change' (Pritchett & Dollar 1998: 18).

26   The proceedings of IMF consultations with its member countries are now posted on the IMF website (www.imf.org) as PINs (public information notices).

27   Johnson notes that 'these issues came to a head in Kuala Lumpur in November 1998. The US Trade Representative accused the Japanese of offering $30 billion in aid to the stricken countries of East Asia as a way of buying their votes against further market opening measures' (*Indonesian Observer*, 30 June 1999).

28   As compiled by Reuters in *Jakarta Post*, 'IMF Must Go Back to Basics, say Expert Group', 20 September 1999.

29   See Islam and Chowdhury (1997: ch. 8) and Box 2.3 in this book. The most prominent advocates of Asian values are Lee Kuan Yew, ex-Prime Minister of Singapore, and Mahathir Mohammad, Prime Minister of Malaysia. For a critique, see Lee (1998: ch. 4).

30 The sad case in Malaysia of the imprisonment of Anwar Ibrahim, at one time heir-apparent to the prime ministership, by a Mahathir-led faction in government highlights the problems of a semi-democratic regime.

31 See interview with Cao Siyuan, a leading Chinese dissident, in *Newsweek*, 21 June 1999: 66.

32 Stiglitz (1998a), in his advocacy of the post-Washington consensus, makes a strong plea for these ideas.

33 Answers to this question are discussed in Lee (1998: ch. 4).

34 A comprehensive review of these issues can be found in ADB (1997).

Bibliography

Abel, A., Gregory, M., Summers, L. & Zeckhauser, R. (1989), 'Assessing Dynamic Efficiency: Theory and Evidence', *Review of Economic Studies*, 56(10): 1–20.

ADB (1971), *Southeast Asia's Economy in the 1970s*, London, Longman.

ADB (1984), *Asian Development Outlook*, Hong Kong, Oxford University Press.

ADB (1994), *Asian Development Outlook 1994*, Manila, Asian Development Bank.

ADB (1997), *Emerging Asia: Changes and Challenges*, Manila, Asian Development Bank.

ADB (1998), 'The Financial Crisis in Asia' in *Asian Development Outlook 1998*, Hong Kong, Oxford University Press.

ADB (1999), *Asian Development Outlook*, special chapter on 'Economic Openness: Growth and Recovery in Asia', New York, Oxford University Press.

Addison, T. & Demery, L. (1987), *Wages and Labour Conditions in the Newly Industrialising Countries of Asia*, London, Overseas Development Institute.

Adelman, I. & Morris, C.T. (1973), *Economic Growth and Social Equity in Developing Countries*, Stanford, Stanford University Press.

Agarwala, R. (1983), 'Price Distortions and Developing Countries', *World Bank Staff Working Papers*, No. 575, Washington DC, World Bank.

Ahmad, E. & Wang, Y. (1991), 'Inequality and Poverty in China', *World Bank Economic Review*, 5(2): 231–58.

Akerlof, G., Dickens, W. & Perry, G. (1996), 'The Macroeconomics of Low Inflation', *Brookings Papers on Economic Activity*, 1: 1–76.

Akyuz, Y. (1998), 'The East Asian Financial Crisis: Back to the Future' in K.S. Jomo (ed.), *Tigers in Trouble: Financial Governance, Liberalisation and Crises in East Asia*, London, Zed Books.

Alagappa, M. (1995), 'Democracy's Future: The Asian Spectrum', *Journal of Democracy*, 6(1): 28–36.

Alavi, H. (1972), 'The State in Post-Colonial Societies', *New Left Review*, 74.

Alba, P. et al. (1998), 'Volatility and Contagion in a Financially-Integrated World: Lessons from East Asia's Recent Experience', paper presented to the PAFTAD conference, *Asia–Pacific Financial Liberalization and Reform*, Chiangmai, Thailand, 20–22 May.

Alesina, A. & Rodrik, D. (1994), 'Distributive Politics and Economic Growth', *Quarterly Journal of Economics*, May: 464–90.

Alesina, A. & Roubini, N. (1992), 'Political Cycles in OECD Economies', *Review of Economic Studies*, 59(4): 663–8.

Alt, J. (1985), 'Political Parties, World Demand, and Unemployment: Domestic and International Sources of Economic Activity', *American Political Science Review*, 79(4): 1016–40.

Amin, S. (1974), *Accumulation on a World Scale*, New York, Monthly Review Press.

Amin, S. (1976), *Unequal Development*, New York, Monthly Review Press.

Amsden, A. (1979), 'Taiwan's Economic History: A Case of *Etatisme* and a Challenge to Dependency Theory', *Modern China*, 5(3): 341–80.

Amsden, A. (1989), *Asia's Next Giant: South Korea and Late Industrialization*, New York, Oxford University Press.

Amsden, A. (1991), 'Diffusion of Development: The Late Industrializing Model and Greater Asia', *American Economic Review, Papers and Proceedings*, 81(2): 282–6.

Amsden, A. & Euh, Y-D. (1993), 'South Korea's 1980s Financial Reforms: Goodbye Financial Repression (Maybe), Hello New Institutional Restraints', *World Development*, March: 379–90.

Anand & Kanbur (1984), 'Poverty under the Kuznets Process', *Economic Journal*, supplement, 95: 42–9.

Arndt, H.W. (1987), Economic Development: *The History of an Idea*, Chicago, University of Chicago Press.

Atchana, Wattananukit & Teerana, Bhongmakapit (1989), 'The Impact of the External Sector on the Thai Economy and its

Determinants', *TDRI Annual Conference*, Bangkok, 17–18 December.

Athukorala, P. (1993), 'International Migration in the Asia–Pacific Region: Patterns, Policies, and Economic Implications', *Asian–Pacific Economic Literature*, 7(2): 28–57.

Awanohara (1993), 'The Magnificent Eight', *Far Eastern Economic Review*, 22 July: 79–80.

Axelrod, R. (1984), *The Evolution of Cooperation*, New York, Oxford University Press.

Balassa, B. (1981), *The Newly Industrializing Countries in the World Economy*, New York, Pergamon Press.

Ban, S.H., Moon, P.Y. & Perkins, D.H. (1980), *Studies in the Modernization of the Republic of Korea*, 1945–1975, Harvard, Council on East Asian Studies, Harvard University.

Bandiera, O., Capiro, G., Honohan, P. & Schiantarelli, F. (1998), 'Does Financial Reform Raise or Reduce Savings?' mimeo, Washington DC, World Bank.

Bank for International Settlements (1996), *Central Bank Survey of Foreign Exchange and Derivative Market Activity 1995*, Basle, Bank for International Settlements.

Bardhan, P (1990), 'Symposium on the State and Economic Development', *Journal of Economic Perspectives*, 4(3): 3–8.

Barro, R. (1997), *Determinants of Economic Growth: A Cross-Country Empirical Study*, Cambridge, Mass., MIT Press.

Barth, J., Capiro, G. & Levine, R. (1998), 'Financial Regulation and Performance: Cross-country Evidence', mimeo, Washington DC, World Bank.

Beckerman, W. (1977), 'Some Reflections on Redistribution with Growth', *World Development*, 5(8): 665–76.

Bello, W. (1999), 'Rethinking Asia. The Answer: De-globalize', *Far Eastern Economic Review*, 29 April: 61.

Bello, W. & Rosenfeld, S. (1992), *Dragons in Distress: Asian Miracle Economies in Crisis*, London, Penguin.

Bennet, D.C. & Sharpe, K.E. (1983), *Transnational Corporations vs the State: The Political Economy of the Mexican Auto Industry*, Princeton, Princeton University Press.

Benziger, V. (1998), 'Can China's Gradualist Reform be Applied to Eastern Europe'?, *Journal of the Asia Pacific Economy*, 3(1): 38–61.

Bhagwati, J. (1966), *The Economics of Underdeveloped Countries*, London, Weidenfeld & Nicolson.

Bhagwati, J. (1978), *Foreign Trade Regimes and Economic Development: Anatomy and Consequences of Exchange Rate Controls*, Cambridge, Ballinger.

Bhagwati, J. (1984), 'Development Economics: What Have We Learned?' *Asian Development Review*, 2(1): 23–38.

Bhagwati, J. (1986), 'Rethinking Trade Strategy' in J.P. Lewis & V. Kallab (eds), *Development Strategies Reconsidered*, New York, Transaction Books.

Bhagwati, J. (1994), 'Policy Perspectives and Future Directions; A View from Academia' in US Department of Labor, *International Labour Standards and Global Economic Integration*, Washington DC, July.

Bhagwati, J. (1995), 'The New Thinking on Development', *Journal of Democracy*, 6(4).

Bhagwati, J. (1997), 'Interview', *Times of India*, 31 December.

Bhagwati, J. (1998), 'The Capital Myth: The Difference between Trade in Widgets and Dollars', *Foreign Affairs*, 77(3): 7–12.

Bhagwati, J. & Hudec, R.E. (eds) (1996), *Fair Trade and Harmonisation: Prerequisites for Free Trade?*, Cambridge, Mass., MIT Press.

Biggs, T. & Levy, B.D. (1991), 'Strategic Interventions and the Political Economy of Industrial Policy in Developing Countries' in D.H. Perkins & P. Roemer (eds), *Reforming Economic Systems in Developing Countries*, Harvard, Harvard University Press.

Bigsten, A. (1989), 'Poverty, Inequality and Development' in N. Gemmel (ed.), *Surveys in Development Economics*, Oxford, Basil Blackwell.

Birdsall, N. (1995), 'Roundtable Discussion: Employment and Development', *Proceedings of the World Bank Annual Conference on Development Economics, 1994*, Washington DC, World Bank.

Birdsall, N. & Sabot, R. (1994), 'Virtuous Circles: Human Capital, Equity and Growth in East Asia', mimeo, quoted in Birdsall, N. (1995), 'Roundtable Discussion: Employment and Development', *Proceedings of the World Bank Annual Conference on Development Economics 1994*, Washington DC, World Bank.

Bloom, D.E. & Williamson, J.G. (1998), 'Demographic Transitions and Economic Miracles in Emerging Asia', *World Bank Economic Review*, 12(3): 419–56.

Bollen, K. (1983), 'World System Position, Dependency and Democracy', *American Sociological Review*, 48: 468–79.

Booth, A. (1999), 'The Social Impact of the Asian Crisis: What Do We Know Two Years On?', *Asian–Pacific Economic Literature*, 13(2): 16–29.

Bosworth, B. & Collins, S. (1996), 'Economic Growth in East Asia; Accumulation versus Assimilation', *Brookings Papers on Economic Activity*, 2: 135–205.

Brandon, C. (1994), 'Reversing Pollution Trends in Asia', *Finance and Development*, June: 21–3.

Brownbridge, M. & Kirkpatrick, C. (1998), 'Financial Sector Regulation: The Lessons of the Asian Crisis', mimeo, Institute for Development Policy and Management, University of Manchester.

Byrd, W.A. (1991), *The Market Mechanism and Economic Reform in China*, New York, M.E.Sharpe.

Calomiris, C. (1998), 'Blueprints for a New Global Financial Architecture', mimeo, September.

Capiro, G. & Klingebiel, D. (1996), 'Bank Insolvencies: Cross Country Experience', *Policy Research Working Papers*, No. 1620, Washington DC, World Bank.

Cardoso, F.H. & Falleto, E. (1979), *Dependency and Development in Latin America*, Berkeley, University of California Press.

Carruth, A. & Oswald, A.J. (1987), 'On Union Preferences and Labour Market Models: Insiders and Outsiders', *Economic Journal*, 97(386): 431–45.

Chang, H.J. (1998), 'The Hazard of Moral Hazard', *Financial Times*, 7 October.

Chen, E.K.Y. (1997), 'Factor Inputs, Total Factor Productivity and Economic Growth: The Asian Case', *Developing Economies*, 15(2): 121–43.

Chen, E.Y.K. (1979), *Hyper-Growth in Asian Economies: A Comparative Study of Hong Kong, Japan, Korea, Singapore and Taiwan*, London, Macmillan.

Chenery, H. & Strout, A. (1966), 'Foreign Assistance and Economic Development', *American Economic Review*, 56(3): 679–733.

Choo, H. (1975), 'Some Sources of Relative Equity in Korean Income Distribution: A Historical Perspective' in *Income Distribution, Employment and Economic Development in Southeast Asia*, Tokyo and Manila, Japan Research Centre/Asian Council of Manpower Studies.

Chowdhury A. (1994), 'Centralised Vs. Decentralised Wage Setting Systems and Capital Accumulation: Evidence from OECD Countries, 1960–90', *Economic Labour Relations Review*, 5(2): 84–101.

Chowdhury, A. (1996), 'Macroeconomic Management in East Asian Newly Industrialising Economies' in B. Kapur et al. (eds), *Trade, Development and the Asia–Pacific*, Singapore, Prentice Hall.

Chowdhury, A. & Islam, I. (1993), *The Newly Industrialising Economies of East Asia*, London, Routledge.

Chowdhury, A. & Islam, I. (1996), 'The Institutional and Political Framework of Growth in an Ethnically Diverse Society: The Case of Malaysia', *Canadian Journal of Development Studies*, XVIII(3): 487–511.

Cole, D. & Park, Y.C. (1983), *Financial Development in Korea, 1945–78*, Cambridge, Mass., Harvard University Press.

Cole, D. & Patrick, H. (1986), 'Financial Development in the Pacific Basin Market Economies' in A. Tan & B. Kapur (eds), *Pacific Growth and Financial Interdependence*, Sydney, Allen & Unwin.

Cole, D. & Slade, B. (1992), 'Indonesian Financial Development: A Different Sequencing?' in D. Vittas (ed.), *Financial Regulation: Changing the Rule of the Game*, Washington DC, EDI, Development Studies, World Bank.

Cole, D. & Slade, B. (1999), 'The Crisis and Financial Sector Reform' in H.W. Arndt & H. Hill (eds), *Southeast Asia's Economic Crisis: Origins, Lessons and the Way Forward*, Singapore, Institute of Southeast Asian Studies.

Corbett, J. & Vines, D. (1998), 'The Asian Crisis: Competing Explanations', paper presented to the Ford Foundation Project: International Capital Markets and the Future of Economic Policy, Cambridge, 16–17 April.

Corbo, V., Krueger, A. & Ossa, F. (1985), *Export-oriented Development Strategies*, Boulder, Colo., Westview Press.

Corden, M. (1999), *The Asian Crisis: Is There a Way Out?*, Singapore, Institute of Southeast Asian Studies.

Cornia, G.A., Jolly, R. & Stewart, F. (1988), *Adjustment with a Human Face*, Oxford, Clarendon Press.

Corsetti, G., Pesenti, P. & Roubini, R. (1998), 'What Caused the Asian Currency and Financial Crisis?', paper presented to the CEPR/World Bank Conference, *Financial Crises: Contagion and Market Volatility*, London, 8–9 May.

Crafts, N. (1998), 'East Asian Growth Before and After the Crisis', *IMF Working Paper*, WP98/137, Geneva, International Monetary Fund.

Crouch, H. & Morley, J. (1993), 'The Dynamics of Political Change' in J. Morley (ed.), *Driven by Growth*, New York, M.E. Sharpe.

Cutright, P. (1963), 'National Political Development: Measurement and Analysis', *American Sociological Review*, 28 (April).

Dalla, I. & Khatkhate, D. (1995), 'Regulated Deregulation of the Financial System in Korea', *World Bank Discussion Paper*, No. 292, Washington, DC, World Bank.

de Walle, D.V. (1995), *Public Spending and the Poor: What We Know, What We Need to Know, World Bank Policy Research Working Paper*, No. 1476, Washington DC, World Bank.

Dean, J. (1996), 'Recent Capital Flows to Asia–Pacific Countries: Trade-offs and Dilemmas', *Journal of the Asia Pacific Economy*, 1(3): 287–318.

Deaton, A. (1995), 'Inequality in Aging and Growing Economies' in M. Quibria (ed.), *Critical Issues in Asian Development*, Hong Kong, Oxford University Press.

Demery, L. & Demery, D. (1991), 'Poverty and Macroeconomic Policy in Malaysia 1979–87', *World Development*, 19(11), 1620–30.

Demirguc-Kunt, A. & Detragiache, E. (1998), 'Financial Liberalization and Financial Fragility', mimeo, Washington DC, World Bank.

Deyo, F. (1987), 'State and Labour: Modes of Exclusion in East Asian Development' in F. Deyo (ed.), *The Political Economy of the New Asian Industrialism*, Ithaca, Cornell University Press.

Deyo, F. (1989), *Beneath the Economic Miracle: Labour Subordination in the New Asian Industrialism*, Berkeley, University of California Press.

Deyo, F. (1998), 'Labour and Industrial Restructuring in South–East Asia' in G. Rodan, K. Hewison & R. Robison (eds), *The Political Economy of South–East Asia: An Introduction*, Melbourne, Oxford University Press.

Diamond, P. (1965), 'National Debt in a Neoclassical Growth Model', *American Economic Review*, 55: 1126–50.

Documents on Democracy (1995), 'The Asia–Pacific Region', *Journal of Democracy*, 6 (July): 186.

Dodsworth, J. & Mihaljek, D. (1997), 'Hong Kong China: Growth, Structural Change and Economic Stability during the Transition',

Occasional Paper, No. 152, Washington DC, International Monetary Fund.

Doner, R.F. (1991a), 'Approaches to the Politics of Economic Growth in Southeast Asia', *Journal of Asian Studies*, 50(4): 818–49.

Doner, R.F. (1991b), *Driving a Bargain: Automobile Industrialization and Japanese Firms in Southeast Asia*, Berkeley, University of California Press.

Doner, R.F. (1992), 'Limits of State Strength: Toward an Institutionalist View of Economic Development', *World Politics*, 44(4): 398–431.

Dooley, M., Fernandez-Arias, E. & Kletzer, K. (1996), 'Is Debt Crisis History? Recent Private Capital Inflows to Developing Countries', *World Bank Economic Review*, 10(1): 27–50.

Dornbusch, R. (1999), 'The IMF Didn't Fail', *Far Eastern Economic Review*, 2 December: 28.

Dornbusch, R. & Edwards, S. (1990), 'The Macroeconomic Populism in Latin America', *Journal of Development Economics*, 32: 247–77.

Dowling, M. & Summers, P. (1998), 'Total Factor Productivity and Economic Growth: Issues for Asia', *Economic Record*, 74(225): 170–85.

Dreze, J. & Sen, A.K. (1990), *Hunger and Public Action*, Oxford, Clarendon Press.

Duavergne, P. (1999), 'Environmental Crisis', *Far Eastern Economic Review*, 15 July: 27.

Eatwell, J. (1996), 'The Performance of Liberalized Capital Markets', *Working Paper*, No. 8, New York, Center for Economic Policy Analysis, New School for Social Research.

Eatwell, J. & Taylor, L. (1998), 'International Capital Markets and the Future of Economic Policy', *Working Paper*, No. 9, New York, Center for Economic Policy Analysis, New School for Social Research.

Economist (1994), 'Democracy and Growth: Why Voting is Good for You', 27 August: 15–17.

Economist (1997), 'Is it Over?', obtained from http://www.stern.nyu.edu/~nroubini/asia/sf0839.html.

Economist (1998), 'Asian Values Revisited: What Would Confucius Say Now?', 25 July: 23–5.

Edwards, S. (1984), 'The Order of Liberalization of the External Sector in Developing Countries', *Princeton Essays in International Finance*, No. 156.

Eichengreen, B. (1999), *Towards a New International Financial Architecture: A Practical Post-Asia Agenda*, Washington DC, Institute for International Economics.

Elek, A. & Wilson, D. (1999), 'The East Asian Crisis and International Capital Markets', *Asian–Pacific Economic Literature*, 13(1): 1–22.

ESCAP (1999), *Social Impact of the Economic Crisis*, mimeo, obtained from Povertynet website of the World Bank (www.worldbank.org).

Evans, P. (1979), *Dependent Development: The Alliance of Multinational, State, and Local Capital in Brazil*, Princeton, Princeton University Press.

Evans, P. (1989), 'Predatory, Developmental and other Apparatuses: A Comparative Political Economy Perspective on the Third World', *Sociological Forum*, 4(4).

Evans, P. (1992), 'The State as Problem and Solution: Predation, Embedded Autonomy and Structural Change' in S. Haggard & Kaufman (eds), *The Politics of Economic Adjustment*, Princeton, Princeton University Press.

'Experience of Korea in Transition', *Economic Development and Cultural Change*, 46(2): 305–27.

Fane, G. (1998), 'Prudential Regulation of Financial Institutions in 1997–98 Crisis in Southeast Asia' in R. McLeod & R. Garnaut (eds), *The East Asian Crisis: From Being a Miracle to Needing one?*, London, Routledge.

Far Eastern Economic Review (1998), 'Cover Story: Going for Gold', 2 April: 10–16.

Far Eastern Economic Review (1999), 'Is Democracy China's Goal?', 9 December: 33.

Feldstein, M. (1998), 'Refocusing the IMF', *Foreign Affairs*, March/April (website version).

Fields, G. (1995), 'Income Distribution in Developing Economies: Conceptual, Data and Policy Issues in Broad-based Growth' in M. Quibria (ed.), *Critical Issues in Asian Development*, Hong Kong, Oxford University Press.

Fields, G. (1997), 'Data for Measuring Poverty and Inequality in Developing Countries', *Journal of Developing Economies*.

Fields, G.S. (1984), 'Employment, Income Distribution and Growth in Seven, Small Open Economies', *Cambridge Journal of Economics*, 24: 74–83.

Fields, G. & Wan, H. Jr (1989), 'Wage Setting Institutions and Economic Growth', *World Development*, 17(9): 1471–83.

Findlay, C. & Watson, A. (1992), 'Surrounding the Cities from the Countryside' in R. Garnaut & G. Liu (eds), *Economic Reform and Internationalisation: China and the Pacific Region*, Sydney, Allen & Unwin.

Fischer, S. (1994), 'Discussion of Sachs and Woo', *Economic Policy: A European Forum*, 9(18): 131–5.

Fischer, S. (1997), 'Capital Account Liberalisation and the Role of the IMF', IMF Seminar, *Asia and the IMF*, 19 September (website version, IMF homepage: www.imf.org).

Fischer, S. (1998a), 'Reforming World Finance: Lessons from a Crisis', *Economist*, 3–9 October (website version: www.imf.org).

Fischer, S. (1998b), 'The Asian Crisis: A View from the IMF', Address by the First Deputy Managing Director of the IMF to the Midwinter Conference of the Bankers Association for Foreign Trade, Washington DC, 22 January.

Folkerts-Landau, D. et al. (1995), 'Effects of Capital Flows on the Domestic Financial Sectors in APEC Developing Countries' in M. Khan & C. Reinhart (eds), *Capital Flows in the APEC Region*, Occasional Paper, No. 122, Washington DC, International Monetary Fund.

Frank, A.G. (1967), *Capitalism and Underdevelopment in Latin America*, New York, Monthly Press Review.

Frankel, J. (1995), 'Sterilization of Money Inflows: Difficult (Calvo), or Easy (Reisin)?', *International Monetary Fund Working Paper*, No. WP/94/159.

Frankel, J. & Wei, S.J. (1993), 'Yen Bloc or Dollar Bloc: Exchange Rate Policies of the East Asian Economies' in T. Ito & A. Krueger (eds), *Macroeconomic Linkage: Savings, Exchange Rates and Capital Flows*, Chicago, Chicago University Press.

Freeman, R. (1994), 'A Hard-headed look at Labour Standards' in W. Senberger & D. Campbell (eds), *International Labour Standards and Economic Interdependence*, Geneva, International Institute for Labour Studies.

Freeman, R.B. (1993a), 'Labour Market Institutions: Help or Hindrance to Economic Development?', *Proceedings of the World Bank Annual Conference on Development Economics 1992*, Washington DC, World Bank.

Freeman, R.B. (1993b), 'Labour Markets and Institutions in Economic Development', *American Economic Association, Papers and Proceedings*, May: 403–8.

Freeman, R.B. & Medoff, J.L. (1984), *What Do Unions Do?*, New York, Basic Books.

Frenkel,S. (ed.) (1993), *Organised Labour in the Asia–Pacific Region: A Comparative Study of Unionism in Nine Countries*, Cornell International and Labour Relations Report No. 24, Ithaca, ILR Press.

Friedman, D. (1988), *The Misunderstood Miracle: Industrial Development and Political Change in Japan*, Ithaca, Cornell University Press.

Friedman, M. (1971), 'Government Revenue from Inflation', *Journal of Political Economy*, 79: 323–37.

Frobel, F., Heinrich, J. & Kreyo, O. (1980), *The New International Division of Labour: Structural Unemployment in Industrialised Countries and Industrialisation in Developing Countries*, Cambridge, Cambridge University Press.

Fry, M. (1990), 'Nine Financial Sector Issues in Eleven Asian Developing Countries', *International Finance Group Working Paper*, No. IFGWP–90–09, University of Birmingham.

Fukuyama, F. (1992), 'Capitalism and Democracy: The Missing Link', *Journal of Democracy*, 3(2): 106–7.

Fukuyama, F. (1995a), 'Democracy's Future: The Primacy of Culture', *Journal of Democracy*, 6(1): 7–14.

Fukuyama, F. (1995b), 'Confucianism and Democracy', *Journal of Democracy*, 6(2): 20–33.

Furnham, J. & Stiglitz, J. (1998), 'Economic Crises: Evidence and Insights from East Asia', *Brookings Papers on Economic Activity*, 2.

Furtado, C. (1973), 'The Concept of External Dependence in the Study of Underdevelopment' in C.K. Widler (ed.), *The Political Economy of Development and Underdevelopment*, New York, Random House.

Galenson, W. (ed.) (1985), *Foreign Trade and Investment: Economic Growth in the Newly Industrializing Asian Countries*, Madison, University of Wisconsin Press.

Galenson, W. (1992), *Labour and Economic Growth in Five Asian Countries: South Korea, Malaysia, Taiwan, Thailand and Philippines*, New York, Praeger.

Gang, F., Perkins, D. & Sabin, L. (1996), 'China's Economic Performance and Prospects', *Background Paper*, Manila, Asian Development Bank.

Garnaut, R. (1999a), 'Exchange Rates in the East Asian Crisis' in *Southeast Asia's Economic Crisis: Origins, Lessons and the Way Forward*, Singapore, Institute of Southeast Asian Studies.

Garnaut, R. (1999b), 'Economic Lessons' in R. McLeod & R. Garnaut (eds), *East Asia in Crisis: From Being a Miracle to Needing One?*, London, Routledge.

Garnaut, R. & Drysdale, P. (eds) (1994), *Asia–Pacific Regionalism: Readings in International Economic Relations*, Sydney, HarperCollins.

Garrett, G. & Lange, P. (1996), 'Internationalization, Institutions, and Political Change' in R. Keohane & H. Milner (eds), *Internationalization and Domestic Politics*, Cambridge, Cambridge University Press.

Gereffie, G. (1982), *The Pharmaceutical Industry and Dependency in the Third World*, Princeton, Princeton University Press.

Geroski, P., Gregg, P. & Van Reenen, J. (1996), 'Market Imperfections and Employment', *OECD Economic Studies*, 26: 117–56.

Gerschenkron, A. (1962), *Economic Backwardness in Historical Perspective*, Cambridge, Mass., Harvard University Press.

Glick, R. (1998), 'Overview' in R. Glick (ed.), *Managing Capital Flows and Exchange Rates*, Cambridge, Cambridge University Press.

Glick, R. & Moreno, R. (1995), 'Capital Flows and Monetary Policy in East Asia' in *Monetary and Exchange Rate Management with International Capital Mobility: Experiences of Countries and Regions along the Pacific Rim*, Hong Kong, Hong Kong Monetary Authority.

Glick, R. & Rose, A. (1998), 'Contagion and Trade: Why Are Currency Crises Regional?', *Pacific Basin Working Paper*, No. PB98–03, Federal Reserve Bank of San Francisco.

Goldstein, M. (1998), 'The Asian Financial Crisis', *Asian Financial Crisis: Policy Brief*, No. 98-1, Washington DC, International Monetary Fund.

Golub, S. (1995), 'Comparative and Absolute Advantage in the Asia–Pacific Region', *Pacific Basin Working Paper*, No. PB95–06, Federal Reserve Bank of San Francisco.

Golub, S. (1996), 'Manufacturing Labour Costs, Productivity and International Trade in APEC' in R. Braddock (ed.), *Collaborative Labour Market Studies*, Asia–Pacific Research Institute.

Golub, S. (1997), 'International Labour Standards and International Trade', *IMF Working Paper*, No. WP 97/37, Washington DC, International Monetary Fund.

Grenville, S. (1999), 'Capital Flows and Crises', *Asian–Pacific Economic Literature*, 13(2): 1–15.

Griffith-Jones, S. (1998), 'How to Protect Developing Countries from Volatility of Capital Flows', Institute of Development Studies, Sussex University, paper prepared for the Commonwealth Secretariat for the Expert Group Meeting, London, 15–17 June.

Gurley, J.G. (1967), 'Financial Structure in Developing Countries' in D. Krivine (ed.), *Fiscal and Monetary Problems in Developing States*, New York, Praeger.

Haggard, S. (1988), 'The Politics of Industrialization in the Republic of Korea and Taiwan' in H. Hughes (ed.), *Achieving Industrialization in East Asia*, Cambridge, Cambridge University Press.

Haggard, S. (1990), *Pathways from the Periphery: Politics of Growth in the Newly Industrializing Countries*, Ithaca, Cornell University Press.

Haggard, S. (1994), 'Business, Politics and Policy in Northeast and Southeast Asia' in A. MacIntyre (ed.), *Business and Government in Industrialising Asia*, Ithaca, Cornell University Press.

Haggard, S. (1999), 'Governance and Growth: Lessons from the Asian Crisis', *Asian Pacific Economic Literature*, 13(2): 30–42.

Hammer, J.S. & Shetty, S. (1995), 'East Asia's Environment: Principles and Priorities for Action', *World Bank Discussion Paper*, No. 287, Washington DC, World Bank.

Hanna, D.P. (1994), 'Indonesian Experience with Financial Sector Reform', *World Bank Discussion Paper*, No. 237, Washington DC, World Bank.

Harris, N. (1988), 'New Bourgeoisies?', *Journal of Development Studies*, 24(2).

Hawes, G. & Liu, H. (1993), 'Explaining the Dynamics of the Southeast Asian Political Economy: State, Society and the Search for Economic Growth', *World Politics*, 45(4): 629–61.

Heleniak, T. (1995), 'Dramatic Population Trends in the Countries of the FSU', *Transition*, 6(9–10): 1–4.

Helleiner, E. (1994), *States and the Re-emergence of Global Finance: From Bretton Woods to the 1990s*, Ithaca, Cornell University Press.

Heller, P. (1998), 'Ageing in the Asian Tiger Economies', *Finance and Development*, June: 1–7.

Hewison, K., Robison, R. & Rodan, G. (eds) (1993), *Southeast Asia in the 1990s: Authoritarianism, Democracy and Capitalism*, Sydney, Allen & Unwin.

Hicks, G. (1989), 'The Four Little Dragons: An Enthusiast's Reading Guide', *Asian–Pacific Economic Literature*, 3(2): 35–49.

Hiebert, M. (1999), 'Eyes Wide Open', *Far Eastern Economic Review*, 13 May: 50.

Hill, H. (1997), 'Towards a Political Economy Explanation of Rapid Growth in Southeast Asia' in H. Soesastro (ed.), *One Southeast Asia in a New Regional and International Setting*, Jakarta, Centre for Strategic and International Studies.

Hofheinz, R & Calder, K.E. (1982), *The Eastasia Edge*, New York, Basic Books.

Horton, S., Kanbur, R. & Mazumdar, D. (1994), *Labour Markets in an Era of Adjustment*, vol.1, Economic Development Institute, Washington DC, World Bank.

Hossain, A. & Chowdhury, A. (1996), *Monetary and Financial Policies in Developing Countries: Growth and Stabilisation*, London, Routledge.

Hossain, A. & Chowdhury, A. (1998), *Open-economy Macroeconomics for Developing Countries*, London, Edward Elgar.

Hsieh, C.T. (1999), 'Productivity Growth and Factor Prices in East Asia', *American Economic Review* (Papers and Proceedings), May: 133–8.

Hughes, H. (1989), 'Catching-up: The Asian Newly Industrializing Economies in the 1990s', *Asian Development Review*, 7(2): 128–44.

Human Rights Watch (1998), 'Bearing the Brunt of the Asian Crisis: The Impact on Labour Rights and Migrant Workers in Asia', 10, 02, March (website version).

Huntington, S. (1996), 'Democracy for the Long Haul', *Journal of Democracy*, 7(2).

Huntington, S.P. (1991), *The Third Wave: Democratization in the Late Twentieth Century*, Norman, University of Oklahoma Press.

ILO (1991a), 'Employment Policies in the Economic Restructuring of Latin America and the Caribbean', World Employment Program (WEP), 1–07–07 (Doc 2), August, Geneva, International Labour Organization.

ILO (1991b), 'Social Protection, Safety Nets and Structural Adjustment', Governing Body Committee on Employment, GB.25111/CE/4/5, November, Geneva, International Labour Organization.

ILO (1995), *World Labour Report*, Geneva, International Labour Organization.

ILO (1998a), *Report of the High-level Meeting on Social Responses to the Financial Crisis in East and South-east Asian Countries*, Bangkok, 22–24 April (website version).

ILO (1998b), 'Human Rights: Human Rights in the Working World' (website version).

ILO (1998c), 'Freedom of Association remains Elusive in much of East and Southeast Asia', ILO Press Release, 24 November (website version: www.ilo.org).

ILO (1999), *Demystifying the Core Conventions of the ILO through Social Dialogue: The Indonesian Experience*, Jakarta and Geneva, International Labour Organization.

IMF (1998), *World Economic Outlook 1998*, September, Washington DC, International Monetary Fund.

IMF (1995), *International Capital Markets*, Washington DC, International Monetary Fund.

Islam, I. (1992), 'Political Economy and East Asian Economic Development', *Asian–Pacific Economic Literature*, 6(2): 69–101.

Islam, I. (1994), 'Between the State and the Market: The Case for Eclectic Neoclassical Political Economy' in A. MacIntyre (ed.), *Business and Government in Industrialising Asia*, Ithaca, Cornell University Press.

Islam, I. & Chowdhury, A. (1997), *The Asia–Pacific Economies: A Survey*, London, Routledge.

Ito, T. (1997), 'Japan and the Asian Economies: A "Miracle" in Transition', *Brookings Papers on Economic Activity*, 2: 205–72.

Jacoby (1966), *US Aid to Taiwan: A Study of Foreign Aid, Self-help and Development*, New York, Praeger.

Johansen, F. (1993), 'Poverty Reduction in East Asia: The Silent Revolution', *World Bank Discussion Paper*, No. 203, Washington DC, World Bank.

Johnson, C. (1982), *MITI and the Japanese Economic Miracle*, Stanford, Stanford University Press.

Johnson, C. (1985), 'Political Institutions and Economic Performance: The Government–Business Relations in Japan, South Korea and Taiwan' in R. Scalapino et al. (eds), *Asian Economic Development: Present and Future*, Berkeley: Institute of East Asian Studies. Reprinted in Deyo, F. (ed.) (1987), *The Political Economy of the New Asian Industrialism*, Ithaca, Cornell University Press.

Johnson, C. (1999), 'Revisiting Asia's Crony Capitalism', *Indonesian Observer*, 30 June (originally published in *Los Angeles Times*).

Jomo, K.S. (ed.) (1997), *Southeast Asia's Misunderstood Miracle: Industrial Policy and Economic Development in Thailand, Malaysia and Indonesia*, Boulder, Colo., Westview Press.

Jones, D.M. (1997), *Political Development in Pacific Asia*, Cambridge, Polity Press.

Joshi, V. & Little, I.M.D. (1994), *India: Macroeconomic and Political Economy 1964–1991*, Washington DC, Oxford University Press.

Jung, W. (1986), 'Financial Development and Economic Growth: International Evidence', *Economic Development and Cultural Change*, 34(2): 333–46.

Kaldor, N. (1955–56), 'Alternative Theories of Distribution', *Review of Economic Studies*, 23: 83–100.

Kalecki, M. (1976), *Essays on Development Economics*, Brighton, Sussex, Harvester Press.

Kang, D.C. (1995), 'South Korea and Taiwanese Development and the New Institutional Economics', *Industrial Organization*, 49(3): 555–87.

Kasa, K. (1997), 'Does Singapore Invest too Much?', *Federal Reserve Bank of San Francisco Economic Letter*, No. 97-15, May.

Kaul, I., Grunberg, I. & Ul Haq et al. (eds) (1996), *The Tobin Tax: Coping with Financial Volatility*, New York, Oxford University Press.

Kay, J. & Vickers, J. (1988), 'Regulatory Reform in Britain', *Economic Policy*, October.

Keynes, J.M. (1933) [1982], '*National Self-sufficiency*', *The Collected Writings of J.M. Keynes*, Vol. XXI, London, Macmillan.

Killick, T. (1984), *The Quest for Economic Stabilisation: The IMF and the Third World*, London, Heinemann.

Killick, T. (1989), *A Reaction Too Far: Economic Theory and the Role of the State in Developing Countries*, London, Overseas Development Institute.

Kim, J. (1986), *Wages, Employment and Income Distribution in South Korea: 1960–83*, Bangkok and Geneva, International Labour Organisation/ARTEP.

Kim, J. & Lau, L. (1994), 'The Sources of Economic Growth of the East Asian Newly Industrialized Countries', *Journal of Japanese and International Economics*, 8: 235–71.

Kindleberger, C. (1989), *Manias, Panics and Crashes: A History of Financial Crises*, New York, Basic Books.

Kolodko, G.W. (1999), 'Ten Years of Post-socialist Transition: Lessons for Policy Reform', *World Bank Policy Research Working Paper*, No. 2095, April, Washington DC, World Bank.

Krueger, A. (1983), *Alternative Trade Strategies and Employment, vol. 3: Synthesis and Conclusions*, Chicago, University of Chicago Press.

Krueger, A. (1993), 'Virtuous and Vicious Circles in Economic Development', *American Economic Association, Papers and Proceedings*, May: 351–5.

Krugman, P. (1994), 'The Myth of Asia's Miracle', *Foreign Affairs*, 73(6): 62–78.

Krugman, P. (1998a), 'Will Asia Bounce Back?', mimeo, March (website version).

Krugman, P. (1998b), 'The Confidence Game', *New Republic*, 5 October.

Krugman, P. (1998c), 'Firesale FDI', mimeo (website version).

Krugman, P. (1998d), 'The Eternal Triangle', mimeo (website version http://web.mit.edu/krugman/www/triangle.html).

Krugman, P. (1999a), *The Return of Depression Economics*, New York, W.W. Norton.

Krugman, P. (1999b), 'Capital Control Freaks: How Malaysia Got Away with Economic Heresy', *Slate*, 27 September (website version).

Krugman, P. (1999c), 'Balance Sheets, the Transfer Problem and Financial Crisis' (website version: http://web.mit.edu/krugman).

Kuo, S. (1975), 'Income Distribution by Size in Taiwan: Changes and Causes' in *Income Distribution, Employment and Economic Development in Southeast Asia*, Tokyo, Japan Research Centre/Asian Council of Manpower Studies.

Kuznets, S. (1955), 'Economic Growth and Income Inequality', *American Economic Review*, 45(1): 1–28.

Lal, D. (1976), 'Distribution and Development: A Review Article', *World Development*, 5(9): 725–38.

Lal, D. (1995), 'India and China: Contrasts in Economic Liberalization?', *World Development*, 23(9): 1475–94.

Lamb, D. (1998), 'From Cheap Labor to Economic Burden', *Los Angeles Times*, 3 February.

Laothamas, A. (1988), 'Business and Politics in Thailand: New Patterns of Influence', *Asian Survey*, 28 (April): 451–70.

Laothamas, A. (1992), *Business Associations and the New Political Economy of Thailand: From Bureaucratic Polity to Liberal Corporatism*, Boulder, Colo., Westview Press.

Laothamas, A. (ed.) (1997), *Democratization in Southeast and East Asia*, Singapore, Institute for Southeast Asian Studies.

Lau, L. (1990), 'The Economy of Taiwan 1981–1988: A Time of Passages' in L. Lau (ed.), *Models of Development: A Comparative Study of Economic Growth in South Korea and Taiwan*, San Francisco, ICS Press.

Lee, C.H. (1992), 'The Government, Financial System and Large Enterprises in the Economic Development of South Korea', *World Development*, 20(2): 187–97.

Lee, C.H. & Naya, S. (1988), 'Trade in East Asian Development with Comparative Reference to Southeast Asian Experience', *Economic Development and Cultural Change*, 38(3):123–52.

Lee, E. (1984), 'Introduction' in E. Lee (ed.), *Export Processing Zones and Industrial Employment in Asia*, Bangkok and Geneva, International Labour Organisation/ARTEP.

Lee, E. (1997), 'Globalization and Labour Standards: A Review of Issues', *International Labour Review*, 136(2): 17 (website version).

Lee, E. (1999), *The Asian Financial Crisis: The Challenge for Social Policy*, Geneva, International Labour Organisation.

Leipziger, D. et al.(1992), *The Distribution of Income and Wealth in Korea*, Washington DC, World Bank, EDI Development Studies.

Liew, L. (1995), 'Gradualism in China's Economic Reform and the Role for a Strong Central State', *Journal of Economic Issues*, XXIX: 883–95.

Liew, L. (1998), 'Introduction: Some Issues of Chinese Economic Reform', *Journal of the Asia Pacific Economy*, 3(1): 35–7.

Lim, C.Y., Chowdhury, A., Islam, I. et al. (1988), *Policy Options for Singapore*, Singapore, McGraw Hill.

Lim, L.Y.C. (1990), 'Singapore' in *Labour Standards and Development in a Global Economy*, Washington DC, US Department of Labor.

Lin, T.B. (1985), 'Growth Equity and Income Distribution Policies in Hong Kong', *Developing Economies*, 23(4): 397–411.

Lin, T.B. (1994), 'De-industrialization, Integration and the Great U-Turn in Hong Kong', mimeo, New Asia College, Chinese University of Hong Kong.

Lin, T.B. & Ho, (1984), *Industrial Restructuring in Hong Kong*, Bangkok and Geneva, International Labour Organisation/ARTEP.

Lindgren, C., Garcia, G. & Saal, M. (1996), *Bank Soundness and Macroeconomic Policy*, Washington DC, International Monetary Fund.

Lingle, C. (1998), *The Rise and Decline of the Asian Century: False Starts on the Path to the Global Millenium*, Barcelona, Sirocco.

Lipset, S.M. (1959), 'Some Social Requisites of Democracy: Economic Development and Political Legitimacy', *American Political Science Review*, 53: 69–105.

Lipsey, R.G. & Lancaster, K.J. (1956–57), 'The General Theory of the Second Best', *Review of Economic Studies*, 24: 11–32.

Little, I.M.D. (1979), 'An Economic Reconnaissance' in W. Galenson (ed.), *Economic Growth and Structural Change in Taiwan: The Post-War Experience of the Republic of China*, Ithaca, Cornell University Press.

Little, I.M.D. (1981), 'The Experiences and Causes of Rapid, Labour-Intensive Development in Korea, Taiwan Province, Hong Kong and Singapore and the Possibilities of Emulation' in E. Lee (ed.), *Export Processing Zones and Industrial Employment in Asia*, Bangkok and Geneva, International Labour Organisation/ARTEP.

Little, I.M.D. (1982), *Economic Development: Theory, Policy and International Relations*, New York, Basic Books.

Little, I.M.D., Scitovksy, T. & Scott, M. (1970), *Industry and Trade in Some Developing Countries: A Comparative Perspective*, Oxford, Oxford University Press.

Lucas, R. (1988), 'On the Mechanics of Economic Development', *Journal of Monetary Economics*, 22(1): 3–42.

MacIntyre, A.J.(1990), *Business and Politics in Indonesia*, Sydney, Allen & Unwin.

MacIntyre, A.J. (1992), 'Indonesia, Thailand and the Northeast Asia Connection' in R. Higgot, R. Leaver & J. Ravenhill (eds), *Economic Relations in the Pacific in the 1990s: Conflict or Cooperation?*, Sydney, Allen & Unwin.

MacIntyre, A.J. (1993), 'The Politics of Finance in Indonesia: Command, Confusion and Competition' in S. Haggard, C.H. Lee & S.Maxfield (eds), *The Politics of Finance in Developing Countries*, Ithaca, Cornell University Press.

MacIntyre, A.J. (1994), 'Business, Government and Development: Northeast and Southeast Asian Comparisons' in A. MacIntyre (ed.), *Business and Government in Industrialising Asia*, Ithaca, Cornell University Press.

MacIntyre, A.J. & Jayasuriya, K. (eds) (1992), *The Dynamics of Economic Policy Reform in Southeast Asia and Southwest Pacific*, Singapore, Oxford University Press.

Mackie, J. (1988), 'Economic Growth in the ASEAN Region: The Political Underpinnings' in H. Hughes (ed.), *Achieving Industrialization in East Asia*, Cambridge, Cambridge University Press.

Malhotra, A. (1997), 'Private Participation in Infrastructure: Lessons from Asia's Power Sector', *Finance and Development*, 33: 33–5.

Mallampally, P. & Sauvant, K.P. (1999), 'Foreign Direct Investment in Developing Countries,' *Finance and Development*, 36(1): 7 (website version).

Mammer, J. & Shetty, S. (1995), 'East Asia's Environment: Principles and Priorities for Action', *World Bank Discussion Paper*, No. 287, Washington DC, World Bank.

Mankiw, G. (1995), 'The Growth of Nations', *Brookings Papers on Economic Activity*, 1: 275–376.

Manning, C. (1998), *Indonesian Labour in Transition: An East Asian Success Story?*, Cambridge, Cambridge University Press.

Manning, C. & Pang, E.F. (1990), 'Labour Market Structures in ASEAN and the East Asian NIEs', *Asian–Pacific Economic Literature*, 4(2): 59–81.

Matthews, R. (1968), 'Why Has Britain Had Full Employment since the War?', *Economic Journal*, 78: 555–69.

Matthews, T. & Ravenhill, J. (1994), 'Strategic Trade Policy: The Northeast Asian Experience' in A. MacIntyre (ed.), *Business and*

Government in Industrialising Asia, Ithaca, Cornell University Press.

Mayer, C. (1996), 'Corporate Governance: Competition and Performance', *OECD Economic Studies*, II(27): 8–32.

McKinnon, R. (1973), *Money and Capital in Economic Development*, Washington DC, Brookings Institution.

McKinnon, R.I. (1982), 'The Order of Liberalization: Lessons from Chile and Argentina' in K. Brunner & A. Metzler (eds), *Economic Policy in a World of Change*, Amsterdam, North Holland.

McKinnon, R.I. (1984), 'Pacific Growth and Financial Interdependence: An Overview of Bank Regulation and Monetary Control', *Pacific Economic Papers*, No. 117, Research School of Pacific Studies, Australian National University.

McKinnon, R.I. (1988), 'Financial Liberalization in Retrospect: Interest Rate Policies in LDCs' in G. Ranis & P. Schultz (eds), *The State of Development Economics*, Oxford, Basil Blackwell.

McKinnon, R.I. & Pill, H. (1996), 'Credible Liberalizations and International Capital Flows: The Overborrowing Syndrome' in I. Takahisho & A. Krueger (eds), *Financial Deregulation and Integration in East Asia*, National Bureau of Economic Research East Asia Seminar on Economics, vol. 5, Chicago, University of Chicago Press.

McKinnon, R. & Pill, H. (1998), 'The Overborrowing Syndrome: Are East Asian Economies Different?' in R. Glick (ed.), *Managing Capital Flows and Exchange Rates*, Cambridge, Cambridge University Press.

McMillan, J. & Noughton, B. (1992), 'How to Reform a Planned Economy: Lessons from China', *Oxford Review of Economic Policy*, 8(1): 130–43.

Medhi, Krongkiew (1994), 'Income Distribution in East Asian Developing Countries', *Asian–Pacific Economic Literature*, 8(2): 58–74.

Moreno, T. & Spiegel, M. (1997), 'Are Asian Economies Exempt from the "Impossible Trinity"? Evidence from Singapore', *Pacific Basin Working Paper*, No. PB97–01, Federal Reserve Bank of San Francisco.

Mosley, P., Harrigan, J. & Toye, J. (1991), *Aid and Power: The World Bank and Policy-based Lending*, London, Routledge.

Myint, H. (1972), *Southeast Asia's Economy: Development Policies in the 1970s*, Middlesex, Penguin.

Nelson, J. (1991), 'Organised Labour, Politics, and Labour Market Flexibility in Developing Countries', *World Bank Research Observer*, 6(1): 37–56.

Newfarmer, R. (ed.) (1985), *Profits, Progress and Poverty: Case Studies of International Industries in Latin America*, Notre Dame, University of Notre Dame Press.

Nolan, P. (1996–97), 'China's Rise, Russia's Fall', *Journal of Peasant Studies*, 24(1–2): 226–50.

Noughton, B. (1995), *Growing Out of the Plan: Chinese Economic Reform, 1978–1993*, Cambridge, Cambridge University Press.

Nsouli, S. (1999), 'A Decade of Transition: An Overview of the Achievements and Challenges', *Finance and Development*, June: 2–5 (website version).

Obstfeld, M. (1994), 'Risk-taking, Global Diversification and Growth', *American Economic Review*, 84(5): 1310–29.

Obstfeld, M (1998), 'The Global Capital Market: Benefactor or Menace?', *Journal of Economic Perspectives*, 12(4): 9–31.

OECD (1992), *Trends in International Migration*, Paris, Organization for Economic Cooperation and Development.

OECD (1996a), *Shaping the 21st Century: The Role of Development Cooperation*, Paris, Organization for Economic Cooperation and Development.

OECD (1996b), *Trade, Employment and Labour Standards*, Paris, Organization for Economic Cooperation and Development.

Okimoto, (1989), *Between MITI and the Market: Japanese Industrial Policy for High Technology*, Stanford, Stanford University Press.

Olson, M. (1982), *The Rise and Decline of Nations: Economic Growth, Stagflation and Social Rigidities*, New Haven, Yale University Press.

Olson, M. (1986), 'A Theory of Incentives facing Political Organization: Neo-corporatism and the Hegemonic State', *International Political Science Review*, 7(2): 165–89.

Onis, Z. (1991), 'The Logic of the Developmental State', *Comparative Politics*, October: 109–26.

Pang, E.F. (1998), 'Review of C. Manning (1998), *Indonesian Labour in Transition: An East Asian Success Story?*', *Asian–Pacific Economic Literature*, 12(2): 69.

Park, M.K. (1997), 'Economic Hardships, Political Opportunity Structure, and Challenging Actions: A Time-series Analysis of South Korean Industrial Disputes, 1979–1991', *Asian Perspective*, 21(2): 147–77.

Park, Y.C. (1994), 'Comment on the Role of the State in Financial Markets' in Proceedings of the World Bank Annual Conference on Development Economics, 1993: Supplement to *World Bank Economic Review* and *World Bank Research Observer*, 1: 57–8.

Patrick, H. (1966), 'Financial Development and Economic Growth in Underdeveloped Countries', *Economic Development and Cultural Change*, 14(2): 174–89.

Pei, M. (1994), *From Reform to Revolution: The Demise of Communism in China*, Cambridge, Mass., Harvard University Press.

Pencavel, J.(1995), 'The Role of Unions in Fostering Economic Development', *World Bank Policy Research Working Paper*, No. 1469, Washington DC, World Bank.

Perkins, D.H. (1994), 'There are at least Three Models of East Asian Development', *World Development*, 22(4): 655–61.

Piore, M.J. (1990), 'Labor Standards and Business Strategies' in S. Herzenberg & P.L. Jorge (eds), *Labor Standards and Development in a Global Economy*, Washington DC, US Department of Labor.

Polackova, H. (1999), 'Contingent Government Liabilities: A Hidden Fiscal Risk', *Finance and Development*, 36(1): 7 (website version).

Porter, M. (1992), 'Capital Choices: Changing the Way America Invests in Industry', *Journal of Applied Corporate Finance*, 5(2): 4–16.

Pranee, T. (1997), 'Industrialization and Welfare: How Poverty and Income Distribution are Affected' in K. Medhi (ed.), *Thailand's Industrialization and its Consequences*, London, Macmillan.

Pritchett, L. & Dollar, D. (1998), *Assessing Aid: What Works, What Doesn't and Why, A World Bank Policy Research Report*, New York, Oxford University Press.

Prybala, J. (1995), 'Books in Review: Departures from Communism', *Journal of Democracy*, 6(4): 164–8.

Pye, L. (1990), 'Political Science and the Crisis of Authoritarianism', *American Political Science Review*, March.

Quinn, D. (1997), 'The Correlates of Change in International Financial Regulation', *American Political Science Review*, 91(3): 531–42.

Radelet, S. & Sachs, J. (1997), 'Asia's Re-emergence', *Foreign Affairs*, 76(6): 44–59.

Radelet, S. & Sachs, J. (1998), 'The East Asian Financial Crisis: Diagnosis, Remedies, Prospect', mimeo, Harvard Institute for International Development, 20 April.

Radelet, S. & Sachs, J. (1999), 'What Have We Learned, So Far, from the Asian Financial Crisis?', Harvard Institute for International Development, January.

Radelet, S., Sachs, J. & Lee, J.W. (1996), 'Economic Growth in Asia', *Asian Development Bank Background Paper*, Manila, Asian Development Bank.

Rahman, M.Z. (1998), 'The Role of Accounting and Disclosure Standards in the East Asian Financial Crisis: Lessons Learned', mimeo, Geneva, UNCTAD.

Rajan, R. & Zingales, L. (1998), 'Which Capitalism? Lessons from the East Asian Crisis', mimeo, Graduate School of Business, University of Chicago.

Ranis, G. (1981), 'Challenges and Opportunities Posed Asia's Superexporters: Implications for Manufactured Exports from Latin America' in W. Bower & M. Collins (eds), *Export Diversification and the New Protectionism: The Experiences of Latin America*, Urbana, University of Illinois Press.

Rauch, J. (1994), Demosclerosis: *The Silent Killer of American Government*, New York, Times Books.

Ravllion, M. & Sen, B. (1994), 'When Method Matters :Towards a Resolution of the Debate over Bangladesh's Poverty Measures', *World Bank Policy Research Working Paper*, No. 1359, Washington DC, World Bank.

Razin, A. & Rose, A. (1994), 'Business Cycle Volatility and Openness' in L. Leiderman & A. Razin (eds), *Capital Mobility: The Impact of Consumption, Investment and Growth*, Cambridge, Cambridge University Press.

Reisen, H. (1993a), 'Southeast Asia and the "Impossible Trinity"', *International Economic Insights*.

Reisen, H. (1993b), 'Macroeconomic Policies towards Capital Account Convertibility' in H. Reisen & S. Fischer (eds), *Financial Opening: Policy Issues and Experiences in Developing Countries*, Paris, Organisation for Economic Cooperation and Development.

Reisen, H. (1998), 'Domestic Causes of Currency Crisis: Policy

Lessons for Crisis Avoidance', *Technical Paper*, No. 136, Paris, Organisation for Economic Cooperation and Development.

Robinson, D. et al. (1991), *Thailand: Adjusting to Success—Current Policy Issues*, Washington DC, International Monetary Fund.

Robinson, S. (1976), 'A Note on the U-hypothesis Relating Income Inequality and Economic Development', *American Economic Review*, 66(3): 437–40.

Rodan, G., Hewison, K. & Robison, R. (eds) (1998), *The Political Economy of South–East Asia: An Introduction*, Melbourne, Oxford University Press.

Rodrik, D. (1992), 'The Limits of Trade Policy Reform in Developing Countries', *Journal of Economic Perspectives*, 6(1): 87–105.

Rodrik, D. (1996a), 'Coordination Failures and Government Policy: A Model with Applications to East Asia and Eastern Europe', *Journal of International Economics*, 40: 1–22.

Rodrik, D. (1996b), 'Understanding the Economics of Policy Reform', *Journal of Economic Literature*, 34 (March): 1–41.

Rodrik, D. (1997), *Has Globalization Gone Too Far?*, Washington DC, Institute for International Economics.

Rodrik, D. (1998), 'Who Needs Capital Account Convertibility?', Symposium Paper, *Princeton Essays in International Finance*, February (website version).

Rodrik, D. (1999), 'Institutions for High Quality Growth; What They Are and How to Acquire Them', Harvard University, Paper for the International Monetary Fund Conference on Second-generation Reforms, Washington DC, 8–9 November.

Romer, P. (1990), 'Endogenous Technical Change', *Journal of Political Economy*, 98: S71–S102.

Romer, P. (1993), 'Two Strategies for Economic Development: Using Ideas and Producing Ideas', *Proceedings of the World Bank Annual Conference on Development Economics 1992*, Washington DC, World Bank.

Rosenstein-Rodan, P. (1943), 'Problems of Industrialisation of Eastern and South-eastern Europe', *Economic Journal*, June–September. Reprinted in A.N. Agarwala & S.P. Singh (eds) (1963), The *Economics of Underdevelopment*, New York, Oxford University Press.

Sachs, J. (1997a), 'IMF is a Power unto Itself', *Financial Times*, 11 December (website version).

Sachs, J. (1997b), 'The Wrong Medicine for Asia', *New York Times*, 3 November.

Sachs, J. (1998), 'Global Capitalism: Making it Work', *Economist*, 23 September (website version).

Sachs, J. & Woo, W.T. (1994), 'Reform in China and Russia', *Economic Policy: A European Forum*, 9(18): 101–31.

Sachs, J. & Woo, W.T. (1995), 'Reforms in Eastern Europe and the Former Soviet Union in Light of the East Asian Experiences', *Journal of Japanese and International Economies*, 9(4): 454–85.

Sachs, J. & Woo, W.T. (1996), 'China's Transition Experience Re-examined', *Transition*, 7(3–4): 1–5.

Sah, R.K. (1991), 'Fallibility in Human Organizations and Political Systems', *Journal of Economic Perspectives*, 5(2): 67–88.

Salt, J. (1992), 'The Future of International Labour Migration' *International Migration Review*, 26(4): 1077–111.

Samuels, R. (1987), *The Business of the Japanese State: Energy Markets in Comparative and Historical Perspective*, Ithaca, Cornell University Press.

Sarel, M. (1997), 'Growth in East Asia: What We Can and What We Cannot Infer', *Economic Issues*, ·1: 1–14 (http://www.imf.org/external/pubs/ft/issues/index.html).

Scarpetta, S. (1996), 'Assessing the Role of Labour Market Policies and Institutional Settings on Unemployment: A Cross-country Study', *OECD Economic Studies*, 26: 43–98.

Seers, D. (1984) [1962], 'The Limitations of the Special Case' in G.M. Meier, *Leading Issues in Economic Development*, New York, Oxford University Press.

Seguino, S. (1998), 'Gender Wage Inequality and Export-led Growth in South Korea', *Journal of Development Studies*, 34(2): 102–32.

Sen, A.K. (1976), 'Poverty: An Optimal Approach', *Econometrica*, 44(2): 219–31.

Sen, A.K. (1981), 'Public Action and the Quality of Life in Developing Countries', *Oxford Bulletin of Economics and Statistics*, 43(4): 287–317.

Sen, A.K. (1985), *Commodities and Capabilities*, Amsterdam, North Holland.

Sen, A.K. (1997), 'Development Thinking at the Beginning of the 21st Century', London School of Economics, STICERD Development Economics Research Programme, *Working Paper*, No. 2, March.

Sengenberger, W. (1991), 'The Role of the Labour Market in Industrial Restructuring' in G. Standing & V. Tokman (eds), *Towards Social Adjustment*, Geneva, International Labour Organisation.

Shari, I. (1998), 'Economic Growth and Income Inequality in Malaysia, 1971–95', Paper presented to International Conference on Economic Growth, Poverty and Income Inequality in the Asia–Pacific Region, University of New South Wales, Sydney, 19–20 March.

Shaw, E. (1973), *Financial Deepening in Economic Development*, New York, Oxford University Press.

Sheng, A. (1992), 'Bank Restructuring in Malaysia' in D. Vittas (ed.) (1992), *Financial Regulation: Changing the Rules of the Game*, Washington DC, EDI Development Studies, World Bank.

Shirk, S.L. (1992), 'The Chinese Political System and the Political Strategy of Economic Reform' in K. Leiberthal & D. Lampton (eds), *Bureaucracy, Politics and Decision-making in post-Mao China*, Berkeley, University of California Press.

Smil, V. (1984), *The Bad Earth: Environmental Degradation in China*, New York, M.E. Sharpe.

Smith, H. (1995), 'Industrial Policy in East Asia', *Asian–Pacific Economic Literature*, 9(1): 17–39.

Spiegel, M. (1995), 'Sterilization of Capital Inflows through the Banking Sector: Evidence from Asia', *Economic Review, Federal Reserve Bank of San Francisco*, 3(1): 17–34.

Squire, L. (1993), 'Fighting Poverty', *American Economic Review, Papers and Proceedings*, 83(2): 377–83.

Srinivasan, T.N. (1990), 'Comments on Fields and Piore' in *Labor Standards and Development in a Global Economy*, Washington DC, US Department of Labor.

Standing, G. (1992), 'Do Unions Impede or Accelarate Structural Adjustment? Industrial vs company Unions in an Industrialising Labour Market', *Cambridge Journal of Economics*, 16 (September): 327–54.

Stern, J., Kim, J.H., Perkins, D.H. & Yoo, J.H. (1995), 'Industrialization and the State: The Korean Heavy and Chemical Industry Drive' in *Harvard Studies in International Development*, Cambridge, Mass., Harvard Institute for International Development.

Stiglitz, J. (1989), 'Financial Markets and Development', *Oxford Review of Economic Policy*, 5(4): 55–68.

Stiglitz, J. (1994), 'The Role of the State in Financial Markets', Proceedings of the World Bank Annual Conference on Development Economics 1993: Supplement to *World Bank Economic Review* and *World Bank Research Observer*, 1: 19–62.

Stiglitz, J. (1997a), 'An Agenda for Development in the 21st Century', Keynote Address to the 9th Annual World Bank Conference on Development Economics, Washington DC, 30 April.

Stiglitz, J. (1997b), 'The Payoff for Taming Asia's Wild Ride to Integration', *New York Times*, 31 October (website version).

Stiglitz, J. (1997c), 'How to Fix the Asian Economies', *New York Times*, 31 October.

Stiglitz, J. (1998a), 'More Instruments and Broader Goals: Moving Towards the Post-Washington Consensus', 1998 WIDER Annual Lecture, Helsinki.

Stiglitz, J. (1998b), 'Responding to Economic Crises: Policy Alternatives for Equitable Recovery and Development', North–South Institute Seminar, Ottawa, 29 September.

Stiglitz, J. (1998c), 'Redefining the Role of the State: What Should it Do? How Should it Do it? And How Should these Decisions be Made?', Address at the 10th Anniversary of MITI Research Institute, Tokyo, 17 March.

Stiglitz, J. (1998d), 'Participation and Development: Perspectives from the Comprehensive Development Paradigm', 27 February, Seoul.

Stiglitz, J. (1998e), 'Road to Recovery: Restoring Growth in the Region could be a Long and Difficult Process', *Asiaweek*, 24(28): 66–7.

Stiglitz, J. (1998f), 'Knowledge for Development: Economic Science, Economic Policy and Economic Advice', Address to the World Bank's 10th Annual Bank Conference on Development Economics.

Stiglitz, J. (1999), 'Whither Reform? Ten Years of the Transition', mimeo, Washington DC, World Bank.

Stiglitz, J. & Weiss, A. (1981), 'Credit Rationing in Markets with Imperfect Information', *American Economic Review*, 71(3): 393–410.

Streeten, P. et al. (1981), *First Things First: Meeting Basic Needs in Developing Countries*, New York, Oxford University Press.

Summers, L.H. & Pritchett, L.H. (1993), 'The Structural-adjustment Debate', *American Economic Review, Papers and Proceedings*, 83(2): 393–9.

Sundrum, R.M. (1990), *Income Distribution in Less Developed Countries*, London, Routledge.

Sunkel, O. (1969), 'National Development and External Dependence in Latin America', *Journal of Development Studies*, October.

Taylor, L. (1998), 'Lax Public Sector, Destabilizing Private Sector: Origins of Capital Market Crises', *Working Paper*, No. 6, New York, Center for Economic Policy Analysis, New School for Social Research.

Tcha, M.J. (1998), 'Labour Disputes and Direct Foreign Investment: The

Thorbecke, E. (1991), 'Adjustment, Growth and Income Distribution in Indonesia', *World Development*, 19(11): 1595–641.

Tobin, J. (1965), 'Money and Economic Growth', *Econometrica*, 33: 671–84.

Turner, M. & Hulme, D. (1997), *Governance, Administration and Development: Making the State Work*, London, Macmillan.

UNCTAD (1998), *Trade and Development Report*, New York, United Nations.

United Nations (1991), *Global Estimates and Projections of Populations by Age and Sex*, New York, United Nations.

Vittas, D. (1992), 'Introduction and Overview' in D. Vittas (ed.), *Financial Regulation: Changing the Rules of the Game*, Washington DC, EDI Development Studies, World Bank.

Wade, R. (1988), 'The Role of Government in Overcoming Market Failure: Taiwan, Republic of Korea and Japan' in H. Hughes (ed.), *Achieving Industrialization in Asia*, Cambridge, Cambridge University Press.

Wade, R. (1990), *Governing the Market: Economic Theory and the Role of Government in East Asian Industrialization*, Princeton, Princeton University Press.

Wade, R. & Veneroso, F. (1998), 'The Asian Crisis: The High Debt Model vs the Wall Street–Treasury–IMF Complex', *New Left Review*, March–April.

Walton, M. (1997), 'The Maturation of the East Asian Miracle', *Finance and Development*, 37(3): 1–6.

Warr, P. (1992), 'Exchange Rate Policy, Petroleum Prices, and the Balance of Payments' in A. Booth (ed.), *The Oil Boom in Asia: Indonesian Economic Policy and Performance in the Soeharto Era*, Singapore, Oxford University Press.

Watson, A. (1994), 'China's Economic Reforms: Growth and Cycles', *Asian–Pacific Economic Literature*, 8(1): 48–65.

Watson, L. (1998), 'Labour Relations and the Law in South Korea', *Pacific Rim Law and Policy Journal*, 7(1):229–47.

Wei, S.J. (1995), 'Attracting Direct Foreign Investment: Has China Reached its Potential?', *China Economic Review*, 6(2): 187–99.

Weiss, L. (1996), 'Sources of the East Asian Advantage: An Institutional Analysis' in R. Robison (ed.) (1996), *Pathways to Asia: The Politics of Engagement*, Sydney, Allen & Unwin.

Westphal, L.E. (1978), 'The Republic of Korea's Experience with Export-led Industrial Development', *World Development*, 6 (March): 347–82.

Westphal, L.E. (1990), 'Industrial Policy in an Export-propelled Economy: Lessons from South Korea's Experience', *Journal of Economic Perspectives*, 4(3): 41–59.

Westphal, L.E., Kim, L. & Kim, K.K. (1985), 'Reflections on Korea's Acquisition of Technological Capability' in I. Rosenberg & C. Frischtak (eds), *International Technology Transfer: Concepts, Measures and Comparisons*, New York, Praeger.

Williamson, J. (1990), 'What Washington Means by Policy Reform' in J. Williamson (ed.), *Latin American Adjustment: How Much Has Happened?*, Washington DC, Institute for International Economics.

Williamson, J. (ed.) (1994), *The Political Economy of Policy Reform*, Washington DC, Institute for International Economics.

Williamson, O. (1975), *Markets and Hierarchies: Analysis and Antitrust Implications*, New York, Free Press.

Williamson, O. (1985), *The Economic Institutions of Capitalism*, New York, Free Press.

Wolfensohn, J.D. (1999), 'A Proposal for a Comprehensive Development Framework', *World Bank Discussion Draft*, 21 January, Washington DC, World Bank.

Wood, A. (1997), 'Openness and Wage Inequality in Developing Countries: The Latin American Challenge to East Asian Conventional Wisdom', *World Bank Economic Review*, 11(1): 33–58.

World Bank (1987), *World Development Report 1987*, New York, Oxford University Press.

World Bank (1989), *World Development Report 1989: Financial Systems and Development*, New York, Oxford University Press.

World Bank (1990), *World Development Report 1990*, New York, Oxford University Press.

World Bank (1992), *World Development Report 1992: Development and the Environment*, New York, Oxford University Press.

World Bank (1993a), *The East Asian Miracle: Economic Growth and Public Policy*, New York, Oxford University Press.

World Bank (1993b), *Sustaining Rapid Development in East Asia and the Pacific*, Washington DC, World Bank.

World Bank (1993c), *World Bank Policy Research Bulletin*, January–February, 4(1).

World Bank (1995), *Trends in Developing Economies*, Washington DC, World Bank.

World Bank (1997), *Everyone's Miracle? Revisiting Inequality and Poverty in East Asia*, Washington DC, World Bank (website version, News Release No. 98/1450: www.worldbank.org).

World Bank (1998a), 'Partnership for Development: Proposed Actions for the World Bank', *World Bank Discussion Paper*, 20 May, Washington DC, World Bank.

World Bank (1998b), *East Asia: The Road to Recovery*, Washington DC, World Bank.

World Bank (1998c), *Social Consequences of the Asian Financial Crisis*, September, Washington DC, World Bank.

World Bank (1999), *Gender Dimensions of the East Asian Crisis*, mimeo, obtained from the Povertynet website of the World Bank (www.worldbank.org).

Woronoff, J. (1986), *Asia's Miracle Economies: Korea, Japan, Taiwan, Singapore and Hong Kong*, New York, M.E. Sharpe.

Xio, G. (1991), 'A Comparative Study of Chinese State and Collective Enterprises' *China Economic Review*, 2(1): 47–73.

Yoshihara, K. (1988), *The Rise of Ersatz Capitalism in South–East Asia*, Singapore, Oxford University Press.

Young, A. (1994), 'Lessons from the East Asian NICs: A Contrarian View', *European Economic Review, Papers and Proceedings*, May.

Young, A. (1995), 'The Tyranny of Numbers: Confronting the Statistical Realities of the East Asian Growth Experience', *Quarterly Journal of Economics*, 110(3): 641–80.

Young, S. (1998), 'The Chinese Private Sector in Two Decades of Reform', *Journal of the Asia–Pacific Economy*, 3(1): 80–103.

Zakaria, F. (1994), 'Interview with Lee Kuan Yew', *Foreign Affairs*, 73 (March–April): 109–26.

Zysman, J. (1983), *Government, Markets and Growth: Financial Systems and the Politics of Industrial Change*, Ithaca, Cornell University Press.

Index